PRICING, HEDGING, AND TRADING EXOTIC OPTIONS

Other Titles in the Irwin Library of Investment and Finance

Convertible Securities
by John P. Calamos (1-55738-921-7)

Pricing and Managing Exotic and Hybrid Options
by Vineer Bhansali (0-07-006669-8)

Risk Management and Financial Derivatives
by Satyajit Das (0-07-015378-7)

Valuing Intangible Assets
by Robert F. Reilly and Robert P. Schweihs (0-7863-1065-0)

Managing Financial Risk
by Charles W. Smithson (0-7863-0440-5)

High-Yield Bonds
by Theodore Barnhill, William Maxwell, and Mark Shenkman
(0-07-006786-4)

Valuing Small Business and Professional Practices, Third Edition
by Shannon Pratt, Robert F. Reilly, and Robert P. Schweihs
(0-7863-1168-X)

Implementing Credit Derivatives
by Israel Nelken (0-07-047237-8)

Option Embedded Bonds
edited by Israel Nelken (0-7863-0818-4)

The Handbook of Exotic Options
edited by Israel Nelken (1-55738-904-7)

The Handbook of Credit Derivatives
by Jack Clark Francis, Joyce Frost, and J. Gregg Whittaker
(0-07-022588-5)

PRICING, HEDGING, AND TRADING EXOTIC OPTIONS

UNDERSTAND THE INTRICACIES OF EXOTIC OPTIONS AND HOW TO USE THEM TO MAXIMIZE ADVANTAGE

DR. ISRAEL "IZZY" NELKEN

Super Computer Consulting, Inc.
www.supercc.com

McGraw-Hill

New York   San Francisco   Washington, D.C.   Auckland   Bogotá
Caracas   Lisbon   London   Madrid   Mexico City   Milan
Montreal   New Delhi   San Juan   Singapore
Sydney   Tokyo   Toronto

Library of Congress Cataloging-in-Publication Data

Nelken, Izzy.
   Pricing, hedging, and trading exotic options : understand the
intricacies of exotic options and how to use them to maximum
advantage / by Izzy Nelken.
     p. cm.
    ISBN 0-07-047236-X
    1. Exotic options (Finance)   I. Title.
HG6024.A3N455   1999
332.64'5—dc21   99-34153
                                     CIP

McGraw-Hill

A Division of The McGraw·Hill Companies

1 2 3 4 5 6 7 8 9 0 DOC/DOC 9 0 9 8 7 6 5 4 3 2 1 0 9

ISBN 0-07-047236-X

*The sponsoring editor for this book was Stephen Isaacs, the editing supervisor was Paul R.
Sobel, and the production supervisor was Modestine Cameron. It was set in New Century
Schoolbook by North Market Street Graphics.*

Printed and bound by R.R. Donnelley & Sons Company.

This publication is designed to provide accurate and authoritative information in regard to
the subject matter covered. It is sold with the understanding that neither the author nor
the publisher is engaged in rendering legal, accounting, or other professional service. If
legal advice or other expert assistance is required, the services of a competent professional
person should be sought.
—*From a declaration of Principles jointly adopted by a Committee of the
American Bar Association and a Committee of Publishers.*

McGraw-Hill books are available at special quantity discounts to use as premiums and
sales promotions, or for use in corporate training programs. For more information, please
write to the Director of Spcial Sales, McGraw-Hill, 11 West 19th Street, New York, NY
10011. Or contact your local bookstore.

This books is printed on recycled, acid-free paper containing
a minimum of 50% recycled de-inked fiber.

In memory of Marvin Merrick. Your light has not dimmed for it is carried on by those who loved you and miss you.

CONTENTS

CHAPTER 1

Motivation for Using Exotic Options

WHY DEAL WITH EXOTICS?

Before beginning our study of exotic options which are complicated derivatives with bizarre names such as: Lookback, Choosen, Compound, Asian, etc., we need to ask ourselves a question. After all, there have been so many cases of catastrophes and near catastrophes. So why deal with these instruments at all?

Several foreign exchange options desks report that 15 percent of the volume of their foreign exchange options business is done in exotics. Furthermore, that 15 percent generates 50 percent of the profit. Thus, the profit margins on exotic options tend to be much higher than the profit margins on vanilla products.

Consider the following example: If you sell a regular interest rate cap in the U.S., the price competition is 0.1 basis point. Every bank can sell a cap. Even if you sell it, how much profit is in it for you at 0.1 basis point? (In London the profit margins are somewhat better at 0.25 basis point.) Even if you managed to sell the cap you haven't made much money.

However, with exotic options the margins are much larger. Typically, the margins are quite large at the inception of the exotic options market in a particular country. When only one bank can provide a specific type of option, it can charge wide bid-ask spreads. Then, as other banks come in, the spreads gradually diminish. This happens as other banks learn about these products and begin to offer them. There is a price competition that intensifies as other banks join in.

If you take the barrier options in New York in 1992–1993, the bid-ask spreads were 10 times those of European options. Currently, they are about 1½ to 2 times those of European. The saying is now that "barriers have become vanilla."

Today banks that do not offer exotics find it difficult to succeed. If a company is offered barrier options by five out of the six banks in its banking group, it will also ask the sixth bank to provide them. The sixth bank is almost forced into this market. However, rather than being followers and being forced into the markets, many banks are entering new and untapped markets to become leaders in those markets.

GLOBALIZATION AND DEMOCRATIZATION OF FINANCE

One very important trend in finance is globalization. It means people can do business anywhere in the world. This is markedly different from how it used to be. Fifteen years ago an investor from, say, Iowa would invest in either U.S. stocks or U.S. bonds. That was basically his choice. He didn't even know that Japanese stock existed. Or perhaps our investor was very savvy. He knew of a particular Japanese company, and he wanted to buy some shares. So he wrote the company and requested a copy of its annual report. It took a month before he received the information he asked for. And when he did get it, it was printed in Japanese, so he couldn't comprehend any of it anyway without a translator.

Look at what happens to the same investor today. As long as he has a computer, he can live anywhere. All he has to do is look on the Internet, type the name of the Japanese company, and out comes the latest annual report. And if it comes up in Japanese, he can select the English version and, presto, it is now in English.

The moral of the story—today you have a wide array of investment choices that you didn't have before. You have a lot more opportunities to invest and a lot fewer barriers to investments than ever before. In terms of exotic options, there are special types of structures designed to allow investors in one country to take advantage of the economy of another—for example, the increased usage of quanto options. These allow you to play a foreign stock market without exposing yourself to currency risks.

The second type of major trend in finance is what has been called democratization. Fifteen years ago, the dealers had major information advantages as compared with their clients. Now, the information advantage has almost disappeared. So, for example, fifteen years ago, a foreign exchange salesperson might have called up a company to tell them what the U.S. dollar–German mark rate had done yesterday. But nowadays the company has the same information on its own screens. Even a retail investor can get access to exactly the same information on a dedicated Internet site.

Think of the following paradigm. Fifteen years ago the client was like a person walking in the desert—superthirsty for information, begging for a drop or two of water. Now, the same client sits beside an on-time screen with live quotes, very much the same screen as the trader watches. In addition, there are thirty-seven e-mail messages, fifty-five voice-mail messages, and a host of faxes and newsletters to read. The client is now like a person drowning in information. He needs a life jacket or, in other words, some way to interpret and make use of all this raw information. As a result of the availability of the raw information, the dealers have started supplying their clients with various tools to interpret the information. For example, the risk management tools such as: RiskMetrics and CorporateMetrics are supplied free (or almost free) to the clients. The dealer makes the client aware of the various risks he is facing and hopes that then the client will then hedge those by purchasing derivatives, which include exotic options, from the same dealer.

SOME DANGERS

The example in Figure 1.1 shows us the difference between a vanilla option mentality and an exotic option mentality. Banks often do deals back-to-back. They sell a structure to a client, and they buy exactly the same type of deal from another bank.

At the beginning of 1997 J. P. Morgan sold an option to the Bank of China. J. P. Morgan bought the exact same option from a counterparty back-to-back. It had been doing back-to-back deals

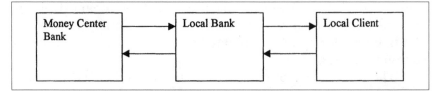

Figure 1.1   A typical back-to-back deal: A local bank puts on a trade with a client and, at the same time, places a mirror trade with another counterparty.

for many years; it had never had a problem doing options before. This option was to mature on May 1, 1997. In this case, it was a barrier option on the U.S. dollar–Japanese yen, with a strike of 123 and a barrier of 127.30. The notional amount was 800 million U.S. dollars. J. P. Morgan then bought exactly the same option with exactly the same underlying, exactly the same strike, exactly the same barrier. Everything was the same. On May 1 when the option expired, the U.S. dollar–Japanese yen was at 127.10. The option owned by the Bank of China was deep in the money. So J. P. Morgan had to pay the bank an amount close to $20 million.

Then J. P. Morgan came to cash its offsetting option. Here comes the hitch. The one it sold to the Bank of China was set to expire at Tokyo time. It was the Tokyo market, and so the "cut" was to be determined using Tokyo standards. However, the offset option was purchased in New York, and so the cut for the offset was to be determined using New York standards.

There is a six-hour difference between the "cut" time of Tokyo and New York. What can happen in a six-hour time period if you had a back-to-back trade in European options? Not very much. A six-hour time difference on a five-month option is a pretty good cover. You have to pay somebody $20 million and you receive $19.9 million.

But now look what happened in our case. At the Tokyo cut time, the rate was 127.10. Then, within the next six hours the dollar climbed just a little bit, past 127.30 (see Figure 1.2). By the time J. P. Morgan came to exercise its offsetting option in New York, it was totally knocked out. J. P. Morgan received nothing, and there was a big loss. This story illustrates the differences between exotic options and European (vanilla) options. The back-

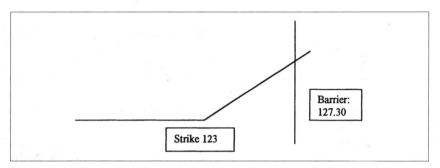

Figure 1.2   The J.P. Morgan–Bank of China barrier option.

to-back strategy has been working for a long time; many banks have done hundreds of such deals. Since the back-to-back strategy works so well, why not do it with barrier options? In fact, many a time back-to-back deals are also done with barrier options. This works fine also. Most of the time, the underlying is not very close to the barrier at expiration.

The very nature of exotic options, and the nonlinear characteristics of them, makes them difficult to deal with. However, difficult is not impossible. Many market makers are earning a very good living with exotics.

CHARACTERISTICS OF THE MARKET

- First of all, we see complicated risk profiles—the nonlinear nature of these options makes them difficult to understand, monitor, price, and hedge. For example, in a European call option the delta is between zero and 1 and goes up nicely. But in an exotic it can go up and then go sharply down. You can get these huge gamma swings. The delta can be very positive at one moment and very negative at the next moment. We will see examples where the delta might reach 1,000 percent. An option that was sold with a notional of $10 million might require a delta hedge of $100 million in the spot market, as compared with about $5 million for a European. Obviously, a hedge of $100 million is not reasonable, but a hedge of $5 million is.

- Then we have difficulties in pricing, hedging, and replication. Take the J. P. Morgan back-to-back deal, for example. Everyone thought it was perfectly replicated, and everybody approved it. Just the same, the loss totaled about $20 million.

- The exotic option, because it is a structured type of deal, usually has low volumes of trading. It is not an exchange-traded product that has huge amounts of volume on it. That means that if you are a client and you bought such a structure, it can be very difficult for you to sell it in the secondary market. You can't always readily get out. Typically, the market maker who sold you the product will stand behind it. So the market maker may buy it back from you, but at what price?

- Exotic options are over-the-counter products and are a special design, not generic. They are not something that you go to the exchange and buy at the money call for a month. For an exotic option, you have to specify where you will put the strike and where you will put the barrier. You have to know how long the maturity is, what the average is, when the averaging period begins, etc. All these extra parameters make this into a very specially designed product for a limited range of customers. So, for example, a sales team can go and argue that every company needs an 8 percent cap, and it will sell as many of them as it can. But not every company needs an Asian option with a knockout. Because the exotic option is designed specifically to target the customer, there is a lack of liquidity.

- In the exotic options market, most investors are long on the option. This is different from an exchange-traded market. For example, suppose you are standing in Chicago in the pit. Some people are buying, and some people are selling. At more or less every moment of the day you have a balanced book. It is not perfectly balanced because people trade all the time. But about half are long and half are short. In an exotic options market you are just selling options to clients. No companies want to sell you a chooser option. They are only interested in purchasing chooser options. So your book becomes naturally short. Running a one-sided book poses special challenges that we will have to address later.

USER GROUPS

Who are the users of exotic options?

- Investors and asset managers
- Derivatives dealers
- Nondealer financial institutions
- Nonfinancial institutions (e.g., corporations)

Each of these groups uses exotic options in special ways.

Investors and Asset Managers

These people are on the buy side. We can further divide the buy side into asset managers, or investment managers, who are close to the market, and retail investors, who are somewhat removed from the market. The investment managers sit by their Reuters screen all day, and they are connected to the market. They know what is going on every day. Retail clients have a much more passive interest in the market. They may read the evening paper and glance at quotes of stocks that they own. In terms of products, we can differentiate between *active* products and *passive* products. Active products demand participation by the client. Passive products (after they are sold) do not require active participation. Active products are more suited to asset managers and cannot be sold to retail investors.

Derivatives Dealers

Derivatives dealers are interested in option premiums. The premiums for exotic options are much larger than those for vanilla options. Many banks find that they do 15 percent of their volume in the foreign exchange options business in exotics, and yet the exotics generate 50 percent of the profits. Of course, the premiums tend to diminish as the products become more common.

Consider the dealers. They have big problems contending with the democratization of finance. It is not enough for them to give the client some raw information. The client needs advice on how to use that information. The dealers have developed insight into and understanding of risk measurement and management, proprietary trading, etc. They can pass on the knowledge to the client and thus build the relationship. The dealers also understand volatility and correlation better than others, and this is another place where they can assist the client.

The dealers are interested in the option premiums and the large bid-ask spreads. In order to earn these, the dealer establishes an exotic options desk. It is the desk's responsibility to price the options correctly and also to adequately hedge the resulting exposures. Bear in mind that this process is very complicated, and sometimes, even the most sophisticated dealers can get hurt. Even a highly regarded company such as J. P. Morgan lost $20 million on a barrier option trade. Hence, dealers who are selling exotic options must do so very carefully and pay special attention to issues of pricing, hedging, and overall risk management. However, getting things right, while difficult, is not impossible.

Example: Limited-Payout Cap

As noted above, the premiums tend to diminish as the products become more commonplace. Here is an example from a corporate treasurer's point of view. Let's suppose that the treasurer wants to buy an interest rate cap. Of course, the treasurer can consider buying a standard interest rate cap. Since this is a five-year cap with quarterly resets, the cap is composed of twenty caplets. The corporate treasurer then calls up the six or so banks in his banking group and obtains quotes that are within 0.1 basis point of each other. So he is assured that these prices represent fair value.

An exotic options dealer approaches the same corporate treasurer and offers him a chance to buy a *limited-payout cap*. This is also a five-year structure, and it is still reset quarterly, but there are only ten caplets (rather than twenty in the original cap). At the beginning of each quarter, the client will call the dealer and choose whether to activate the cap or not. However, the client may only activate the cap for ten out of the twenty quarters. This is similar to a rifle with half the cartridges, although you get to choose when you want to shoot.

To compensate for the smaller number of caplets, the dealer offers to sell the option to the corporate treasurer at a 15 to 20 percent discount compared with the cost of the standard cap. The client considers the past five years when he purchased a standard interest rate cap. A lot of times the cap expired out of the money. During many periods, protection wasn't required at all. Further, during some quarters, interest rates were so low that the client was almost certain at the beginning of the periods that he wouldn't need the protection for that period. For example, during the life of the five-year cap there were three years that interest rates were so low that there was no way that this cap would be in the money any time soon. The point is that the client didn't really need all of the twenty caplets. He only needed seven or eight of them. Here is a chance to buy one with ten.

The corporate treasurer has to make a decision:

- If he buys the standard cap, he knows the price is correct up to a 0.1 basis points. Everyone gave him the same pricing.
- If he buys the limited-payout cap, his company gets a 15 percent discount on the price. But he can only get a quote on this product from this one bank that offered it because no other bank knows how to do the price or hedge it yet.

The limited-payout cap looks very interesting from the corporate treasurer's point of view. But he doesn't know how to judge whether the price is fair, and he certainly doesn't have a computational model that can price such a structure. Is this a fair value? Is a 15 percent discount enough? How should the treasurer determine whether he is giving away the farm by accepting the 15 percent discount? The treasurer cannot know. And, of course, the premiums tend to diminish as the products become more common. For example, assume that the real value is a 25 percent discount. Well, if there is a lot more competition, the price is going to drop very close to its fair value.

Note that there are several different types of limited-payout-cap structures. In one type you can choose at the beginning of the five years the specific quarters at which you want the caps placed. In the other type (the one we've just described), you get to choose every three months if you want to activate the cap. Other caps automatically exercise the first ten caplets that are in the money.

Nondealer Financial Institutions

Commercial banks or insurance companies frequently have needs that have to do with asset liability mismatches. These can be handled quite well with exotics.

The nondealer financial institutions typically have yield curve risks. A commercial bank takes money from clients and places the funds in demand accounts. It credits its depositors with the interest on short-term deposits. Meanwhile the bank invests the same funds in long-term products. The bank receives proceeds based on the long end of the yield curve. This strategy is called "riding the yield curve." The bank borrows short and invests long. As long as the yield curve is upward sloping, things are going OK. What if it flattens a little or even inverts? Then the bank will suffer losses. Exotic options may be used to hedge these risks. For example, an insurance company has assets and liability gaps. Money from premiums comes in, and the company has these potential liabilities later on. For instance, it has to pay out when someone passes away. The insurance company has to perform asset and liability management. Can it generate potentially high-yielding assets?

The differences between insurance products and derivatives are eroding. What is the difference between default insurance offered by a monoline insurer and a credit derivative offered by a dealer? What is the difference between hurricane insurance and a catastrophe-linked bond? In essence, the answer is none. So the distinctions are rapidly blurring.

Corporations

Corporations use exotic options for two primary purposes:

- To generate cost-effective funding
- To create complex hedge structures to match underlying exposures

Cost-Effective Funding

The bond originator sells structured notes to the public. When an investor buys the security, the investor is selling an option to the originator. The price of the option is usually very much reduced. The bond originator then strips the embedded options (usually in collaboration with the underwriter). The options will be sold at fair value in the secondary market. The difference between what was paid for the options and what was received for them represents extra cash inflow to the issuer. This in turn equates with sub-Libor funding. Many times these structures are done as medium-term notes.

Imagine you sell someone a bond. Within that bond you paid $5 for an option, but you immediately turn around and sell that option for $20. That is cash in your hand, and that translates into sub-Libor funding or very low-cost funding. We'll examine a few examples of those. In 1996 several U.S. federal agencies such as the Federal Home Loan Bank (FHLB) issued one-year step-up callable bonds (see Figure 1.3). These were bought by investors. They liked the short maturity of these bonds and their excellent credit rating. However, it turns out that the investors were not able to evaluate these bonds properly. Very short-term bonds need to be modeled with the entire Libor curve taken into account. However, there is no popular bond portfolio management system that adequately handles very short-term bonds as well as long-term

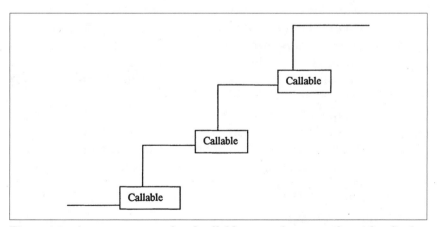

Figure 1.3   A step-up coupon bond callable every three months with a final maturity of one year.

bonds within the same portfolio. It seems that if a portfolio model handles regular corporate bonds, then it does not handle short bonds very well. The FHLB bonds sold for par, but their real price was closer to $99.50, so that generated cost-effective funding.

Hedging of Corporate Risks

The science of risk management has become much more sophisticated and a lot more fine-tuned. This is where the banks or dealers can help the corporations. This is where their value-added lies.

The banks have already been managing their own risks for quite some time. Their clients are usually companies that sell various products. For example, suppose a company arranges to export products to foreign clients. It takes time for the company to make the deal, and even more time until someone pays the company. Meanwhile, fluctuations in the foreign exchange rate may hurt the company. It is the job of the banks to help the client companies cope with foreign exchange rate risks.

Suppose a company sells in many different countries and now it is expanding into new markets in several Eastern European countries and some former Communist countries that it couldn't sell to before. The company must face all kinds of different risks that it was not used to handling before. As it enters new markets, it acquires foreign currency exposures, interest rate exposures, etc. There are also political and other risks to consider.

Exotic options are products that can precisely offset the cash flows being hedged—Asian options and basket options are good examples. There are also correlation-based hedges that have to do with the correlation between fixed income and equity or between currency and equity. Corporations are especially interested in low-cost hedging strategies.

An example of a customized hedging tool is the crack spread option. Consider an oil refinery, a plant that converts raw oil into heating oil. The refinery is not concerned with the price of crude oil or the price of heating oil. The refinery wants to know that it can sell the difference for $2 a barrel. So if crude oil costs $18 per barrel and heating oil costs $20, then the refinery makes $2 per barrel and it is happy. Even if crude is at $25 and heating is at $27, the refinery is still happy. But it is not going to be happy if crude is at $18 and heating is at $19. The NYMEX (New York Mercantile Exchange) offers the crack spread options, which are options on the difference.

The use of customized hedging tools has to do with increasingly precise dissection and management of corporate risk. Thus a company might use a basket option to hedge its exposure to many different currencies using a single trade. In addition, from a taxation standpoint, companies like to utilize zero-cost or low-cost strategies.

KEY APPLICATIONS

The key applications of exotic options are:

- Yield enhancement
- Proprietary trading/positioning
- Structured protection
- Premium reduction strategies

We now review these applications in detail.

Yield Enhancement

Interest rates are at an all-time low almost everywhere in the world. This spells trouble for investors who want to achieve reasonable rates of return on their capital. For many years, investors have gotten used to earning respectable yields on highly rated fixed income securities. These high yields have all but disappeared. In addition, many funds have promised their investors a minimal return on their investments. For example, some Japanese funds have promised their investors yields of 5 percent or better. The yields on highly rated Japanese bonds are about 80 basis points. One way to obtain higher yields is to invest in various structured notes and hope for the best. Such structured notes are bonds with an increased coupon but their principal might be subject to increased market risk. Thus at the maturity of the structured note, the investor may lose a part of their principal. For taking on that risk, the investor receives a high coupon during the life of the note.

Consider an institutional investor who manages a fixed income portfolio. These portfolio managers must report their returns at the end of each quarter. All portfolio managers are struggling to report returns which are as high as possible. They would like their funds to come out ahead in the relative rankings. Here is the difficulty: returns on fixed-income securities are very low. The coupons paid by the U.S. Treasury bonds are very low compared to historical standards. Even corporate bonds pay low interest rates as spreads have become razor thin.

Why have spreads become so narrow in the corporate sector? Because there are fewer bankruptcies; everybody is doing well. Companies don't need to borrow as much. So unless you go into the junk bond markets (so-called high-growth or emerging markets), you get very thin spreads. Even in the growth or emerging markets, you get much lower spreads than you used to. So the question is, how do you get some more juice? To add to the problem, fixed-income funds have to compete with equity funds and commingled funds. The fixed-income fund managers have started to focus on second-order effects. How can they take advantage of the steepness of the yield curve? What does the volatility in a certain area of the curve mean? Can they do some correlation plays between two different interest rate curves? Exotic options can be used to very efficiently focus on these views.

In equities there is an increased demand for global funds that have the mandate to invest in many different countries. Some "Tactical Asset Allocation" (TAA) funds may shift their assets from country to country. Each month they determine the best market to be invested in, and then they shift their portfolio to be heavily invested in that market. For example, one month the fund may choose to invest in the U.S. index, the next month in Norway, the third month in Thailand, and so on. Such funds rarely shift their portfolios in the cash market. This is due to the high bid-ask spreads and the large transaction costs. Such funds will typically replicate the shift in the allocation of their portfolio between the different indices by using equity swaps. Equity swaps have allowed such funds to rapidly shift their portfolios to be heavily weighted in the markets they think will outperform. However, even if a portfolio manager chooses to invest in a particular country, they may not want to be exposed to the currency of that country. In such situations, the Quanto and Flexo options may be used. These options allow investors to reap the returns from an equity investment while being isolated from the foreign exchange movements. Another situation arises in which the portfolio manager is unable to choose between two market indices. In such cases, the portfolio manager may decide to purchase a "best of" option whose payout will be tied to the performance of the better index. In this fashion, the portfolio manager has captured the return of that index which will have the better performance at the end of the month.

With the current emphasis on emerging markets and international trading, clients are very interested in index swaps, Quanto, "best of" options, and much more.

Proprietary Trading/Positioning

Exotic options can also be applied to proprietary trading. Assume that a client wants to take a position on the European currencies converging. The client wants to ensure that their risk-reward profile is going to be reasonable. If they are correct, they want to make a lot. If they are wrong, they wish to lose little. Here is an example. Assume that the client wants to be short volatility because they think currencies are converging, or interest rates are converging, or equity indexes are converging. If the currencies are converging toward each other, the volatility of the exchange rate declines.

Traditionally a dealer would advise a client to be short a straddle or short a strangle (see Figure 1.4). The client can sell a call and simultaneously sell a put to be short a straddle. The client has a short position. If the client is correct and the underlying does not move, then they earn both of the premiums. That is great. If the client is wrong, they can lose their entire company. If prices do move up or down, then the client will be in really big trouble because they are short options.

In our example, the underlying is at $100 and the one-year straddle costs $11.58 (see Figure 1.5). If, at the end of the year, the underlying will stay at $100, the client will have earned the entire premium of $11.58. Even if the underlying moves a bit to $105, say, the client will still come out ahead. The client receives $11.58 and pays $5. But what if the underlying ends up at $150? In that case, the client will be obliged to pay $50—a big loss.

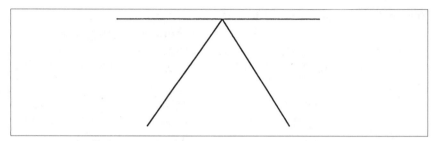

Figure 1.4   A short straddle.

Now assume that the client wants to be short volatility but they want a different risk-reward profile. Wall Street came up with the idea of the double barrier option. In our case, the client pays $4.30 and receives two double barrier options. The double barrier "box" will pay the client $112 − $88 = $24 if, throughout

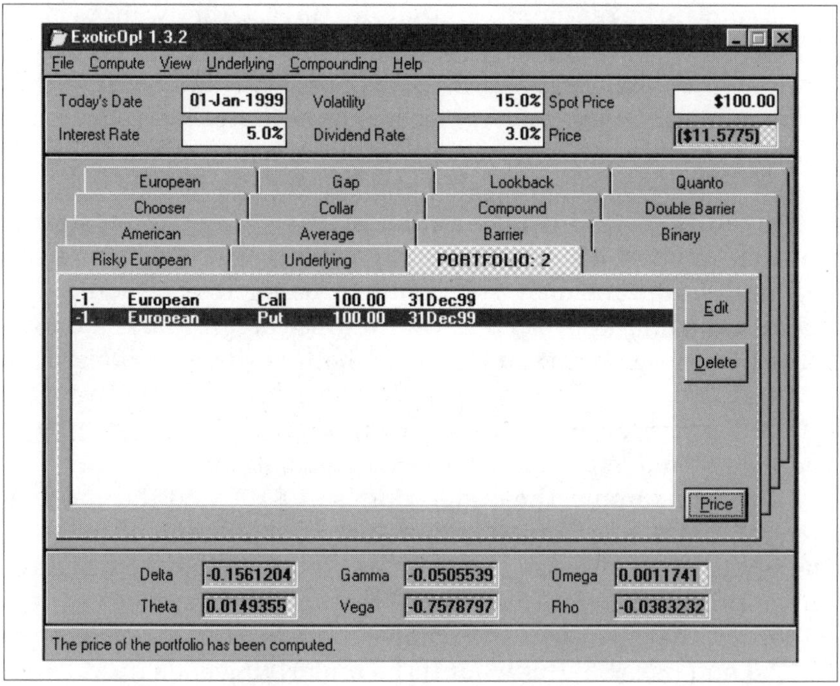

Figure 1.5   A short straddle.

the entire year, the underlying has not touched either $88 or $112 (see Figure 1.6). If the underlying touches either of these values, the double barrier pays nothing.

In our example of a short straddle position, a client earns $11.58 to potentially lose an unlimited amount. In a double barrier box trade, the same client spends $4.30 to potentially earn $24. This has a more "interesting" risk-reward profile. If a client wants to have a specific trading strategy, then some of these exotics really make sense.

Another example concerns Canadians before the Quebec referendum. Consider a Canadian client who thinks the Canadian dollar will go up or down depending on the results of a new referendum. If Quebec stays within Canada, the Canadian dollar will go up, but if it separates, the Canadian dollar will go down. The investor is convinced that she will know which way the currency

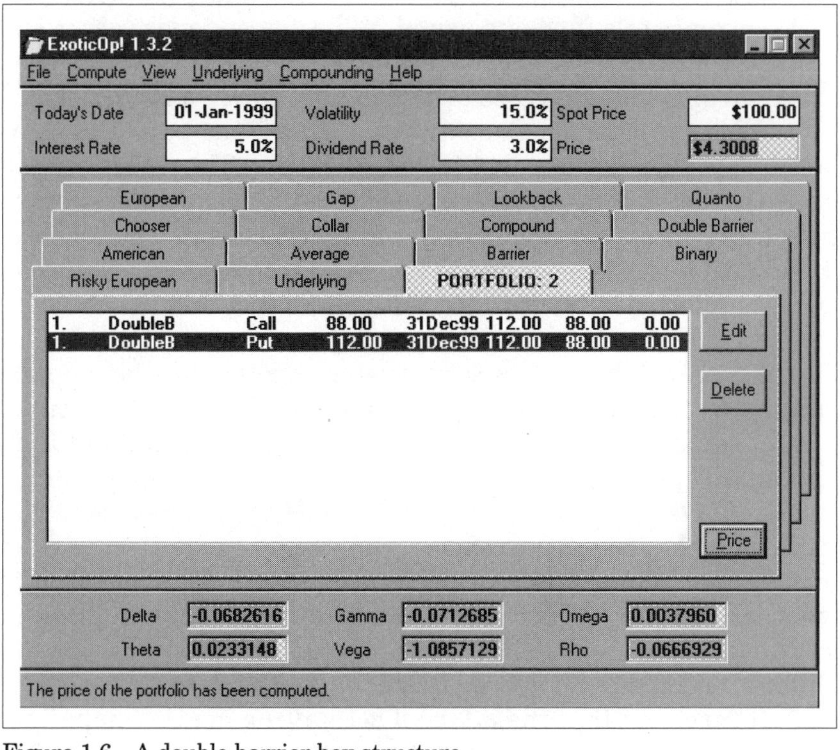

Figure 1.6   A double barrier box structure.

is headed as soon as the referendum is over. In this situation, the client may choose to buy a straddle, but as we will see in a later chapter, the chooser option is cheaper. A chooser option is an option that is not labelled. It doesn't say "put" or "call," but after a certain date the client has to choose whether she wants the put or call. As soon as the client knows whether Quebec separates or not, she has an idea of where the Canadian dollar is going to go and then she can choose a call or a put.

Structured Protection

A third key application of exotic options is structured protection. This would be useful for a company like Gillette. Gillette makes shavers in different countries and sells them in other countries. Now, because it is a big company, it has foreign currency exposures in some thirteen different currencies. How can we give it an umbrella protection that will protect it against its exposure, not in each currency at a time but over all? A basket option is very useful in this regard—and, in fact, is one Gillette used. To generate even more savings, Gillette chose to do an Asian option on the basket.

Another example: Consider an airline that buys the same amount of oil every day just to run its planes. The airline has already sold its tickets for the next summer in advance. If oil prices rise, the airline is not going to make as much as it previously hoped. How can it hedge its exposure to oil? It can buy a string of European options. Alternatively, it can buy a payout that is linked to the average price of oil, like an Asian option over the next three or four months. As will be discussed in a later chapter the Asian option alternative is much cheaper than the string of European options.

Structured protection is much harder to sell to a client than "standard" protection. For example, consider two types of businesses. On the one hand is Gillette. It does an Asian average rate option on the basket currencies. Gillette was able to save a lot money with this scheme. A dealer suggested the same idea to another company, which also has operations in many different countries. And, like Gillette, it has foreign currency exposures in different countries. However, this company said no.

It turns out that the internal accounting in this company is a bit different. Gillette takes all cash flows, nets them out, and reports their profits in U.S. dollars. For accounting purposes, this company separates its units. For example, it has a European unit and a Japanese unit. Suppose the European unit made money and the Japanese unit lost money because of exchange rate movements. The European unit doesn't want to give up its profits in order to compensate the unit in Japan. On the other hand, the European unit still wants foreign currency protection.

The challenge is up to the dealer. When he offers an exotic option product to a client, he has to tailor it very carefully to the type of company he is dealing with. He has to be exceedingly familiar with his clients. Suppose the dealer understood everything about his client except the internal accounting rules used in computing bonuses for each country's manager. Even something as subtle as that can cause a structure that fits one company not to be applicable to another. So the job of the exotic options salesperson has become highly complicated. The client only cares about risk management, low-cost tailor-made products that fit the client's needs. The salesperson has to design an exactly tuned product for each client, which is a difficult task. It is not one-size-fits-all. It is custom-tailored.

Consider a situation in which an institution doesn't care if a currency moves within a small range but worries about a large movement in the currency. Many Israeli real estate developers are facing this situation. The interest in Israel is about 13 percent per annum. Such builders typically borrow funds denominated in U.S. dollars, Euros, or Japanese yen. The builders use the borrowed funds to develop property in Israel. That property will eventually be sold in the Israeli market for Israeli shekels.

Assume a builder has borrowed U.S. dollars and developed real estate in Israel. The builder is happy so long as the relationship between the dollar and the shekel is stable. The dealer will start losing if the shekel depreciates as compared to the dollar. The developer is not too concerned even if the shekel depreciates slightly in comparison with the dollar. A slight depreciation may slightly hurt the profit margins but will not be catastrophic. What the developer is worried about however, is a major shift in the exchange rate. Consider what will happen to the builder if inflation in Israel were to soar and the government was to devaluate the shekel drastically. In this scenario, the shekels received for the property will not be enough to pay for the U.S. dollar loan. The builder cannot economically hedge this risk by buying an at-the-money option as these options are quite expensive. The builder would instead like to buy an option that will pay out only if the currency has moved significantly. But, in this case, the builder would like to be paid a lot. This type of payoff profile is simple to construct with digital options.

Premium Reduction Strategies

The last application we will deal with here is premium reduction strategies. Many corporations use a continous hedging process. They are not just buying an option and wanting to double their money. They are constantly hedging and rehedging. The hedging department in a corporation is typically construed as a cost center that doesn't bring in any money but just spends money on option premiums and other hedging costs.

The profit center is manned by factory workers working, most likely, for low salaries or minimum wage. Then there are the guys who manage the foreign exchange exposure. These guys come in suits, and they have trading hours and work in their nice air-conditioned offices. It is obvious to the factory workers that they are the ones who are producing, who are making money, who are a profit center. What are the guys in suits doing? They are buying options. They are a cost center. What have they done for the company? They bought some options, but even these options expired out of the money, so they produced nothing. The hedging department is a cost center that spends money on options premiums. How can the company reduce that cost?

In many jurisdictions, when a company buys an option, the option premium gets deducted from one account. But when the option pays out, it just gets credited in the general account. So there are tax and accounting issues on paying a premium and receiving the payout. There are tax and regulatory incentives for companies to use options with zero cost.

Be aware that many clients do not wish to pay very much for options. This becomes obvious when you examine which of the exotic options have been successful: the barrier, the Asian, and the basket. Note that the lookback doesn't make this list. A lookback option has a very nice return, but the lookback is very expensive. You have to pay such a high premium for it that it scares clients off. What really works for them is something that has a lower premium than a European option. It turns out that premium reduction is a very important theme.

From the point of view of financial mathematics, there are no advantages to a cheap option over an expensive option. In the case of the Asian as well as the lookback, the price is the present value of the expected value of the cash flows. The investor is expected to make (or lose) the same in both cases. However, investors prefer cheaper options. This is a matter for investor psychology, not financial mathematics.

ACTIVE AND PASSIVE STRUCTURES

As noted earlier, we divide structures into passive and active.

Passive Structures

Small retail investors are people who tend to buy structures themselves. They like the low premiums. They tend to buy barrier options, Asian options, some kind of zero cost, or something that looks like a bond but has an increased return. Some of these structures are not really options because retail investors don't have to do something to have to trigger a payout. It happens automatically. This is what we call a mandatory exercise or mandatory trigger. So these structures are passive rather than active.

Active Structures

However, we expect investment managers and asset managers to be much more in touch with the market. These professionals sit in front of screens that display live market quotes during the day. Therefore, these types of clients may be sold structures that demand active participation. For example, the "shout option" is a structure in which the investor must call the dealer and cause the structure to be activated. The level of the market at the exact time of the activation is taken into consideration at expiration time when the payout is determined. The shout option is clearly not applicable to a retail client who only looks at the closing prices of the market day by day and will have very little opportunity to activate it in real time.

As well, there is another type of option where the investor has to actively participate in every three months (this is especially characteristic of interest rate options)—for example, the "investors choice range floater." Every three months you have to call the dealer and tell him your guess for Libor three months from now. If your guess proves to be correct, you receive a fantastic coupon for these three months. If your guess is wrong, you receive zero coupon. These are active structures because they demand active participation by the person who buys them.

Here is another example. For this structure you are given an insured simulated trading account. You have three months to trade on a simulated trading basis. You do so many trades, and if you are successful, you get back your principal plus however much you made in the simulation. On the other hand, if you lose, you get back your principal. This way you gain from your successes but are covered against your losses. This structure is suitable for someone who is actively trading, someone who can call the dealer on a regular basis. It is not for someone who goes away for three months and does not trade.

STRUCTURED NOTES

Many times exotic options are placed within bonds to form structured notes. Assume an institutional investor manages money for a risk-averse client such as a hospital. The hospital will require that their portfolio will be invested very conservatively. The hospital may specify, for example, that no more than 10 percent of the portfolio be invested in bonds rated BBB or lower. By doing so, the hospital is making sure that the credit risk in the portfolio is minimized. The hospital may also specify that no options or derivatives are allowed in the portfolio. Technically speaking however, the portfolio may still contain various structured notes. These are bonds whose credit rating is quite high. For example, a structured note may have a credit rating of AAA and be admitted into the portfolio. It is important to understand that the credit rating relates to the "issuer's ability to pay but not to their necessity to do so." Normally, we expect a bond, which is rated AAA, to pay its coupons and principal with a high probability. A structured note may have a AAA rating but may be exposed to huge market risks. Under the terms of such a note, if the market moves in a certain direction, the investor may forfeit his or her right to receive coupons or principal. The investor losses not because the issuer went into default but because the market moved. In this case, the issuer is quite solvent but they do not have to pay out on the bond. Hence the investor is exposed to "market risk" rather than "credit risk." This is of little consequence to the investor who may have lost their principal due to a market move.

The structured note has embedded derivatives that are not, by themselves, admissible into the portfolio. There have been many situations where portfolios, that are required to be risk averse, contained structured notes with some very risky payout patterns. Thus structured notes may be used to circumvent regulations or investment guidelines.

As a case in point, consider the "reverse convertible." This structure is very popular in Europe. In the United States, it is sometimes called PERCS (Preference Equity Redemption Cumulative Stock). For example, in March 1999, the price of a share of Compaq Computers (CPQ) was around $50. One bank offered a bond to wealthy investors that had the following terms:

Maturity: three years
Coupon: 10%
Credit Rating: AAA

At the maturity of the bond, the issuer may give the investor: a) $100 (the par amount) plus any unpaid coupons or b) three shares of CPQ.

It is obvious that the investor has effectively sold three put options on CPQ at a strike of $33.33. Since the CPQ stock was trading at $50, these put options are currently out of the money. Typical investors may be somewhat reluctant to sell put options, as selling options is considered a dangerous strategy. The same investors, curiously, are happy to purchase reverse convertible bonds.

The issuer is also very happy to sell reverse convertibles. Such an issuer may turn around and sell out of the money put options on the CPQ shares at the Chicago Board of Options Exchange (CBOE). As these are out of the money put options, the market is willing to pay a lot for them. The market will typically pay more for the options than the issuer will pay the investor. The difference in most cases is about 2 percent.

In our example, assume that AAA interest rates are at 5 percent. The reverse convertible pays a coupon of 10 percent. Thus the issuer is paying a coupon that is enhanced by 5 percent. The extra 5 percent per annum is the price paid for the put options. At the CBOE, these put options actually cost about 21 percent of the notional. Amortized over three years, this translates to about 7 percent per annum. So the issuer pays 5 percent and receives about 7 percent.

It is true that there is a matter of convenience, It would be difficult for a retail investor to sell put options on the CBOE. Such an investor would have to open a brokerage account, deposit margins, etc. On the other hand, purchasing a reverse convertible is quite simple administratively.

Now, consider our hospital once again. That hospital would probably be quite reluctant if their investment manager was to offer them to sell put options on CPQ shares. On the other hand, the investment manager may purchase the reverse convertibles and place them within the portfolio without a breach of any client guidelines. The hospital would receive a summary statement of their portfolio. Within the summary statement may be a line item which looks like this:

GGG Bank reverse convertible on CPQ, coupon 10 percent, credit rating AAA, price $100

The hospital may not even be aware that they have effectively sold put options.

As a matter of historical record, several weeks after the above bond was issued, Compaq announced weak earnings and the CPQ stock tumbled to a level of about $23. Any investor with such a reverse convertible would have a bond which is priced below par.

Cross-Category Structures

A relatively recent trend is the increased use of structures that combine several market segments. Traditionally, banks have had separate departments to deal in fixed income securities as opposed to say equity options. These two departments would have very little to communicate about. This is rapidly changing with the proliferation of structures that combine elements of fixed income with elements of equity options. A bank that structures and issues many reverse convertibles must have constant daily communication between the fixed-income desk and the equity options desk. Similarly, the issuance of a Quanto option requires the cooperation of the foreign exchange and equity option departments. In general, exotic options typically require efforts which span across departmental boundaries. Successful banks promote team work and less-than-rigid departmental boundaries.

HOW EXOTIC OPTIONS AFFECT THE SPOT MARKETS

We know that the spot market affects the exotic options market. Of course, when the spot moves, the options move, and the exotic options might move even more. We note that exotic options may also affect the spot. This happens because delta is not between zero and 1 but it can go to 1,000 percent. This may happen in the case of double barrier options. Delta becomes huge, reaching 1,000%. The trader delta-hedges and builds a position with a notional of 100 million in the spot market on a 10 million notional option that he has sold. All of a sudden the option gets knocked out, and the trader is left with a huge naked position of 100 million. He has to sell it really fast. The exotic book is not meant to deal with a 1,000-percent delta naked exposure. So the trader must sell it very quickly, but that is a big amount to move so fast. The spot dealers are going to see it.

Even spot traders have to understand where these flows are coming from. These flows are almost like stop losses. If you were a spot dealer, you would have to know where people put their stop losses. Now you have to know where people put their barriers. The spot dealer sees someone buying, buying, buying, and then selling the whole thing. George Soros made this observation very famous. He complained in *The Wall Street Journal* and other publications that digital and barrier options cause undue manipulation in the spot markets.

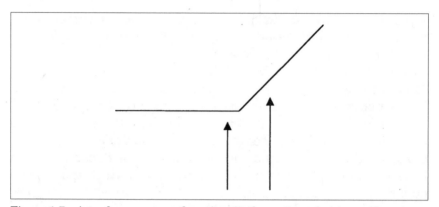

Figure 1.7   A trader can move the prices in the spot market to avoid paying on a European option. Savings: minimal.

Another source of manipulation is illustrated in Figures 1.7 and 1.8.

Suppose a trader has a short position in a European option, and the trader can manipulate the underlying price in the spot market. The option expires tomorrow, and the trader can manage to move the price from somewhat in the money to out of the money (see Figure 1.7). Now suppose the same trader has a short position in a digital option, as illustrated in Figure 1.8. There is much more incentive for the trader to start manipulat-

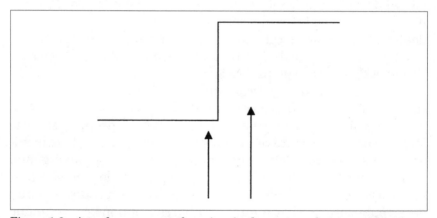

Figure 1.8   A trader can move the prices in the spot market to avoid paying on a digital option. Savings: huge.

ing the market. Most derivative dealers have a rule: "No trader shall manipulate the market." Were they really manipulating, or were they hedging? It is very hard to prove.

OTHER APPLICATIONS

Executive Pay Packages

Assume you get executive pay packages. A lot of your compensation is tied up in stock options. The rationale behind giving executives stock options is to give them incentive to raise the price of the company's stock. This may be quite difficult for the executives to manage. However, the executives know that if they manage to increase the volatility of the stock, their options will also become more expensive. To prevent executives from doing that, several companies now pay with barrier option warrants. They still give the executive a call option but with the proviso that if the underlying stock price ever falls below 90 percent, the executives will lose their entire bonus. This is a "down and out" option; if the stock price drops too much, the executives are going to lose the entire bonus. This assures that the executives will concentrate on increasing the stock price.

Swiss Life Insurance Products

Winterthur Insurance was a very large insurance company which has been acquired by the Credit Suisse First Boston (CSFB) group. Winterthur has marketed a life insurance policy whose payout was tied to the value of the Swiss Market Index (SMI). Traditionally, such insurance contracts are tied to the value of the index at the date of the maturity of the insurance contract. The insurance contract may mature after a certain number of years or may terminate early due to the death of the insured policy holder.

The idea was to cause the payout to be tied not to the value of the SMI on the maturity date. Rather, the payout of these contracts was to be tied to the average value of the SMI index. From the point of view of the client, this was a strong selling point. Even if the policy holder was to die at the moment of a stock market crash, the surviving relatives would still get a good payout. This is due to the fact that the payout is based on the average price rather than the price on a specific day. From the point of view of the insurance company, the averaging feature allowed them to hedge their exposure with Asian options. As will be discussed later, these options are much cheaper than normal options. This in turn enabled the insurance company to sell life insurance at reduced rates.

Insurance companies have become very active in marketing insurance policies and savings programs whose value is tied to the performance of equity indices. Traditionally, insurance companies and banks were thought of as "separate pillars of the financial markets." Nowadays, these distinctions have started to blur.

Conditional Premium Options

These options are created by combining European with exotic options. Such structures may require no up-front premium. They will be covered in detail in later chapters.

DERIVATIVES ARE BECOMING MAINSTREAM

Many banks now employ ex-derivatives personnel as top managers. Consider someone who specialized in complex derivative instruments derived by complicated mathematical formulas, who has developed these sophisticated computer models, etc. How does a person like that become a chief of a big institution or a manager of a large department?

"Derivatives have the image of being extraordinarily arcane, but I think they are the most general thing you can do. Derivatives touch all areas of the banking business, even those that other sides of the business don't touch, like operations," says Michael Rulle of the Canadian Imperial Bank of Commerce (CIBC).

So by specializing in derivatives, a trader becomes exposed to all the different areas within a bank. The trader will develop working relationships and know how to work with people from accounting, legal, front and back office, marketing, computer support desks, the compliance officer, the market risk manager, the credit risk manager, etc.

Derivatives people tend to have a broad understanding of the financial markets since derivatives are not an independent asset class. It is not that traders just trade fixed-income securities and all they need to know about is the U.S. short-term curve. But in order to specialize in derivatives, traders have to know more. Derivatives people also tend to bring an analytical and disciplined approach to solving even nonmathematical problems, which is a huge competitive advantage. Derivatives people are schooled in looking at customer needs and finding creative ways to solve customer problems. All successful derivative structures have been developed with the idea that someone is going to buy the product at the end and so it has to make sense to the client.

SUMMARY

Exotic options present some interesting alternatives to the corporate hedger, the issuer, and the intermediary dealer. While there are a lot more profits to be made with exotics, they must be approached with caution. Risk management is complicated, and so is the sales and structuring of a product to fit the client's needs.

CHAPTER 2

Bermudan Options

INTRODUCTION

A Bermudan option is somewhat like its European cousin and somewhat like its American cousin. A European option is an option that can be exercised only on its expiration—or, alternatively, one second before it expires. The American option can be exercised from the day it was purchased until its expiration date. The Bermudan option has characteristics that are somewhere between the two. It can be exercised on specific dates during its life.

Graphically, the situation can be drawn as in Figure 2.1. In this figure, X represents a day when the option can be exercised, and "the dashed rules" represents a day when the option cannot be used.

AMERICAN AND EUROPEAN OPTIONS

From Figure 2.1 it is evident that the price of the Bermudan option is between a European and an American. Clearly, the holder of the option gets more rights with the Bermudan than with the European, but fewer rights than with the American. So it stands to reason that the price of the Bermudan option has to be between them.

In equation form:

$$E <= B <= A$$

--------------------------------X European Option

XXXXXXXXXXXXXXXXXXXXXXXXXXXXXX American Option

------X------X------X-------X-----X Bermudan Option

Figure 2.1   Exercise dates for European, American, and Bermudan options.

where are the prices of the American, Bermudan, and European options respectively (A, B, and E)?

The difference between an American and an identical European option is called the *early exercise premium*. Consider the portfolio in Figure 2.2. The portfolio is long an American and short an identical European option. The price of the portfolio is the difference between them, the early exercise premium, which in Figure 2.2 is about 0.21. Now let's repeat the same calculation

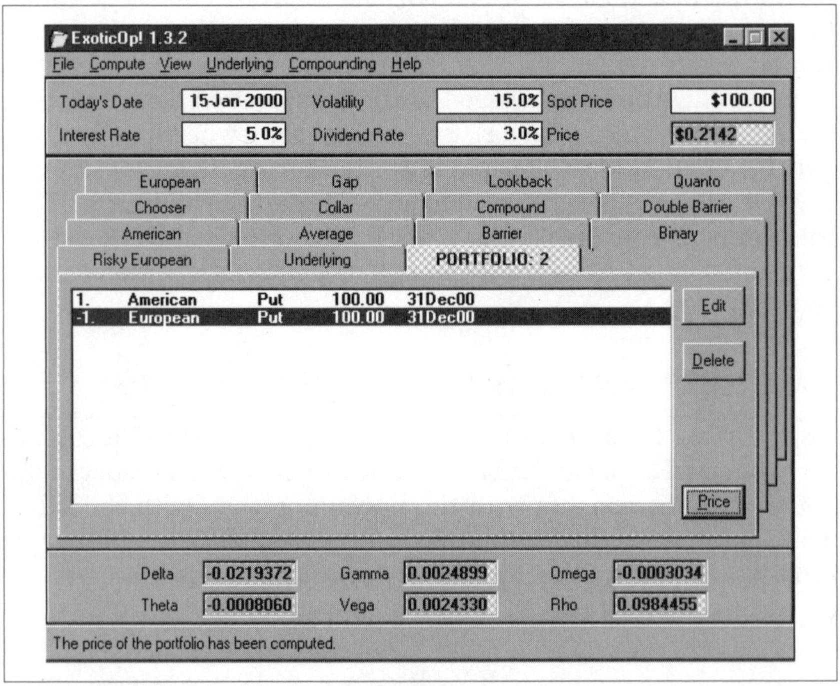

ExoticOp! 1.3.2				

File Compute View Underlying Compounding Help

| Today's Date | 15-Jan-2000 | Volatility | 15.0% | Spot Price | $100.00 |
| Interest Rate | 5.0% | Dividend Rate | 3.0% | Price | $0.2142 |

European	Gap	Lookback	Quanto
Chooser	Collar	Compound	Double Barrier
American	Average	Barrier	Binary
Risky European	Underlying	**PORTFOLIO: 2**	

1.	American	Put	100.00	31Dec00	Edit
-1.	European	Put	100.00	31Dec00	
					Delete
					Price

| Delta | -0.0219372 | Gamma | 0.0024899 | Omega | -0.0003034 |
| Theta | -0.0008060 | Vega | 0.0024330 | Rho | 0.0984455 |

The price of the portfolio has been computed.

Figure 2.2   The early exercise premium for a put option.

for call options. In this case, the difference is less than 1/100 of what it was before.

It is a fact that if the dividend rate is zero, then there should be no early exercise premium. The American call and the European call are priced the same. Even if someone owns an American call and it is deeply in the money, rather than exercising it, it makes more sense to either sell the option or hold it. Why isn't the same true for puts? Consider the following drastic example. Suppose the stock price is zero. Then the American put is worth $100 if it is exercised today, with a strike of $100. That's the most that it can ever be worth. So if the stock price goes to zero, the owner of the put will want to exercise early. If the holder waits for three months, say, and even if the stock stays at zero, he will get $100 three months later. From a time-value-of-money point of view, that's worse than getting it today. Furthermore, the stock price can start going up. That's why the holder wants to exercise right now. So this is one clear example where the owner of the put should exercise early.

Of course, if you consider the time value of money, the present value of the strike, the dividend rate (if it is not zero), and the risk-free rate, you can make this argument more precise and more formal. In our example, the early exercise premium of the put is greater than the early exercise premium of the call since the risk-free rate is greater than the dividend rate. The holder of the call option will have to borrow the strike price from somebody at the risk-free rate. The holder pays the strike price to receive a stock that pays a dividend rate. Only when the stock pays a high enough dividend rate is there a valid reason to exercise early.

Most people think about put-call parity and consider put and call as symmetric. That's almost the case, but it's not entirely true because the stock price can rise. And it can fall only so far. Once it hits zero, it cannot fall any more.

APPLICATIONS

The main applications of the Bermudan option are options on bonds, for example, callable bonds and puttable bonds. A bond may be callable by the issuer on several call dates. These dates constitute a *call schedule*. Once the issuer calls that bond, that's it; the option disappears. The issuer cannot call the bond again.

coupon	4.75%		final price	$99.921	
call schedule					call price
	1000	100	100		$0.986
now	one year	two year	three year		
			13.66%	$104.75	
			92.1614		
			92.1614		
		8.56%			
		91.7050			
		91.7050			
	5.208%		7.50%	$104.75	
	95.0664		97.4451		
	95.0664		97.4451		
3.00%		4.70%			
99.921		98.8306			
		98.8306			
	2.858%		4.11%	$104.75	
	101.2706		100.6108		
	101.2706		100.0000		
		2.58%			
		102.1177			
		100.0000			
			2.26%	$104.75	
			102.4371		
			100.0000		

Figure 2.3   Pricing a callable bond.

Figure 2.3 illustrates the pricing of a four-year bond paying an annual coupon of 4.75 percent which is callable two years from today and again three years from today. The par bond curve is as follows:

Term	1	2	3	4
Yield	3.00%	3.50%	4.00%	4.50%
Volatility		30%		

We typically price a callable bond with a tree. We build a tree going forward in time, and we price the bond going backward.

In Figure 2.3, we built a binomial interest rate tree going forward. On each node of the tree, the interest rate is on the top. The interest rate tree is made a little more complex since we have to make sure that it's calibrated to the forward curve of interest rates so as to price the regular noncallable bonds correctly.

Three years from now, the four-year bond is going to mature in one year. Consider the top right-hand node. There is a cash flow of $104.75 in one year. That cash flow is composed of $100 principal plus the $4.75 coupon. How much is that cash flow worth three years from now? If the interest rate is 13.66 percent (in the top right-hand node), then it's worth $104.75 discounted by 13.66 percent, or $92.1614. In other words, $92.1614 is the discounted value of $104.75 by 13.66 percent for one year.

In this fashion, we can fill all the nodes of the final level. For example, the next node has an interest rate of 7.50 percent. The same $104.75 is now worth $97.4451.

Once we fill the final level, we are ready to go backward in time. Consider the node on the second-to-last level where the interest rate is 8.56 percent. There is a probability that the bond will be worth $92.1614. There is also a probability that it will be worth $97.4451. Add the coupon, $4.75. Discount by the interest rate, which is 8.56 percent, to obtain $91.7050.

We keep on filling the second-to-last time level. At the point where the interest rate is 4.11 percent, the bond is worth $100.6108. On the other hand, the issuer can call this bond for $100.00. This is what happens. In the tree, we override the price of $100.6108 and replace it with $100.00. We do the very same thing on the last node. In that node, the interest rate is 2.26 percent. We obtain a price of $102.4371. In the tree, we override this price with $100.00.

It's quite clear that if interest rates are at 2.26 percent and the company can raise money at that rate, the company would rather do so than pay a coupon of 4.75 percent. We continue going backwards in time until we reach the very first level.

The value of the call option is computed as $0.986. This is the difference in prices between the callable bond (priced at

$99.921) and a similar bond that is not callable (which is priced at $100.907).

We repeat the computation for a bond that is callable only after two years, and again for a bond that is callable only after three years. We obtain:

Call Feature	Option Price
Only on year 2	$0.850
Only on year 3	$0.487
On year 2 and on year 3	$0.968

The Bermudan option, which can be exercised at year 2 and at year 3 has to be worth at least $0.85. It has to be worth at least as much as the two-year option and also at least as much as the three-year option. Suppose, for example, that the Bermudan option was worth less, say $0.60. Then nobody in his right mind would buy the European option for $0.85. It would be cheaper to buy the Bermudan option and just exercise it in year 2.

The Bermudan option cannot be worth more than the sum of the two options. Consider someone who owns both a two-year European option and a three-year European option. The holder of both options can exercise at year 2 and again at year 3. The holder of the Bermudan option has fewer rights. Once the Bermudan option is exercised on year 2, it cannot be exercised on year 3. If the Bermudan option was worth more, then a rational investor would buy the two options separately.

We have a general rule:

$$\text{Max}\ [E(t1), E(t2), \ldots, E(tn)] <=$$
$$B(t1, t2, \ldots, tn) <=$$
$$E(t1) + E(t2) + \ldots + E(tn)$$

Here, $t1, \ldots, tn$ are the exercise dates.

The Bermudan option is bounded below by the maximal value of the Europeans and above by the sum of the individual European options. In practice this rule is very useful. In many cases, a speedy calculation of the range of possible values of an option is just as important as an exact computation, which takes more time because it involves building a model, calibrating it, testing it, etc. Often a portfolio manager has to make a decision

coupon	4.75%		final price	$100.611			
call schedule						call price	
	1000	100	100			$0.296	
now	one year	two year	three year				
			9.42%	$104.75			
			95.7324				
			95.7324				
		6.71%					
		95.1835					
		95.1835					
	4.623%		6.98%	$104.75			
	97.1528		97.9172				
	97.1528		97.9172				
3.00%		4.97%					
100.611		98.6041					
		98.6041					
	3.424%		5.17%	$104.75			
	100.6068		99.6011				
	100.6068		99.6011				
		3.69%					
		100.8346					
		100.0000					
			3.83%	$104.75			
			100.8864				
			100.0000				

Figure 2.4 Pricing a callable bond, second example.

within a few minutes. Perhaps a broker offers the portfolio manager a Bermudan option for $1.50. In this case, the portfolio manager would be quite happy knowing that the option should be priced between $0.85 and $1.32.

We can repeat the computation for a case where the volatility is 15 percent. The tree is reproduced in Figure 2.4.

Again, summarize the option prices:

Call Feature	Option Price
Only on year 2	$0.296
Only on year 3	$0.100
On year 2 and on year 3	$0.296

We are not surprised that the option prices are cheaper than they were in the previous example since the volatility has been reduced. However, in this example, there is no extra premium for adding on the call at year 3. The price of the Bermudan is exactly the same as the call at year 2. Let's relate these numbers to the geometry of the tree. Consider the tree with a volatility of 15 percent, as in Figure 2.4. There is no way to get to the node at which the bond is called in year 3 without passing through the node in which the bond is called at year 2. In other words, there is no scenario in which the issuer would call the bond at year 3 if he or she hadn't already called it at year 2.

On the other hand, consider the situation where the volatility is 30 percent. There are a few possibilities that interest rates will move up and down and somehow will get to a place where the issuer would want to call it at year 3 without first calling it at year 2. This example is interesting since it relates the numbers to the geometry of the tree.

SWAPTION

Consider a five-year interest rate swap like the one shown in Figure 2.5. The company swaps payments based on the floating interest rate for a fixed rate. It is an interest rate swap that is settled semiannually. In addition, after at least two years have passed, the swap may be canceled by the buyer of the swap on any fixing date. The buyer of the swap is the party that pays a fixed rate and receives Libor. The buyer will cancel the swap when interest rates drop. Since the swap is cancelable at every fixing date, it includes a Bermudan option, in this case, a *Bermudan Swaption.*

In return for allowing the swap buyer to cancel the swap, the swap seller will demand a higher fixed rate. The premium of

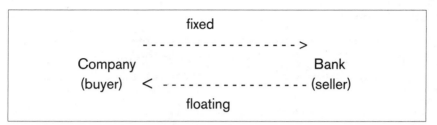

Figure 2.5   An interest rate swap.

the option will be amortized for two years and be converted to a higher fixed interest rate.

In addition to a normal swap, the company also purchased a receiver's swaption. A receiver's swaption gives the company the right to be a floating-rate payer. The swaption is Bermudan in style because it can be exercised on any fixing date after two years. The interest rate on the swaption exactly matches the interest rate on the swap. In other words, the company may elect to begin a swap whose cash flows will exactly cancel the cash flows on the original swap.

If interest rates decline, the company exercises the swaption and cancels the entire deal. On the other hand, should interest rates increase, the company elects to keep the swap active and the bank pays the company a high floating rate, as opposed to the company paying the bank the same fixed rate. The net cash flow is favorable to the company. At the same time, the bank is also very happy. Remember that the bank had amortized the cost of the swaption for two years and charged the company a higher fixed rate. So long as the company does not exercise its swaption, the company keeps paying the bank a fixed rate that is higher than the rate the bank would have received under a normal swap.

CALLABLE BONDS

Callable bonds are very similar to receiver's swaptions. They are exercised when interest rates decline. On the other hand, puttable bonds are very similar to payer's swaptions. They are exercised when interest rates increase.

MOTIVATION

Let's concentrate on the motivation of the buyer and the seller for a moment. Why should the company issue a callable bond in the first place? The price of the callable is less than the price of a regular bond. The whole purpose of the bond issue was to raise capital. By issuing a callable bond, the company is raising less capital than if it would have issued a noncallable bond.

The company can issue a noncallable bond paying a coupon of 4.75 percent at $100.907. On the other hand, should the company wish to issue a callable bond, it will only receive $99.921. Assume that the company issues $100 million face value of bonds. It will have to pay almost $1 million for the right to call the bond later on.

Consider this example. A company issued some bonds several years ago. The bonds have a coupon of about 13 percent since they were issued when interest rates were very high. The bonds are just sitting there, and at every coupon payment date the treasurer of the company has had to pay 13 percent annually. It's a big debt cost. The same company has just sold a subsidiary in Australia and now has the cash that was received as proceeds from the sale. Wouldn't it be nice for the company if it were able to cancel this debt? It wouldn't have to pay the high interest rate costs. In addition, credit rating agencies would probably consider the company to have smaller debt-to-equity ratios and thus upgrade its credit rating.

It is clear that had the company sold a callable bond, nothing would have been simpler. It would have just had to issue a call notice.

The trouble is, it sold a bond that is not callable. Still, the company has some things it can do. For example, it can go out in the open market and start buying the bonds. But this will cause a price squeeze, as the price will increase since the market knows that the issuer is buying back its bonds. The price of the bond will shoot right up. Another alternative is to do a bond defeasance. *Defeasance* just means that you buy strips of government bonds with the same coupons and the same maturity as the original bond. However, this is also an expensive proposition as the company that issued the bond is of a lower credit rating than the government. Other alternatives are just as expensive.

In crediting issuers callable bonds, buyers accept the fact that the bonds are priced more cheaply than similar noncallable bonds. This means that their yield is higher.

PUTTABLE BONDS

Let's look at the other side of the coin. Suppose the issuer is considering the sale of a puttable bond. A bond that is puttable may be sold to the issuer on certain dates at predetermined prices. That means that if, on the predetermined dates, the rates are too high, the bondholders can exercise the right to put the bond back to the issuer at the predetermined price, say par.

As an example, a puttable bond costs $102.548, and the nonputtable costs $100.907. With the puttable, the issuer gets about $1.60 more per $100 face value of bond issue. That seems like a better deal for the company. The issuer gets more cash in right now.

But now consider the situation of the issuer. If interest rates begin climbing, the holders of the bond will ask for their money back. The issuer must now refinance and find the cash to pay the bondholders back. In fact, this is what happened to several British pharmaceutical companies in the 1980s. They almost went bankrupt because people put their bonds. These companies had to refinance at much higher rates than originally intended.

Consider also that the issuer's credit can deteriorate. In this case, interest rates in general may stay the same, or even decline somewhat. On the other hand, the issuer's credit spread may widen by many basis points. In that case, the coupons, which are payable by the issuer, are no longer enough to compensate the investors for the credit risk associated with holding the bonds. So the holders of the bonds will put them back to the issuer. This is why the put option on a bond has been described as a credit derivative.

But in this situation, the issuer, whose credit rating is already deteriorating, now has to come up with cash to pay the investors back. This will likely cause a further deterioration in the credit rating of the issuer. As a credit derivative, the put option on a bond is quite weak since the issuing company is, in a sense, guaranteeing its own credit.

In summary, there is reason and motivation for callable and puttable bonds. Some bonds are, in fact, both callable and puttable. The issuer has the option to call in the bond, and the holder has the option to put it back to the issuer.

HEDGING OF BERMUDAN OPTIONS

Before we consider the delta hedging of Bermudan options, let us examine the delta hedge ratios of European and American options. We can begin by considering European and American put options, with strikes of $100, that are due to expire in six months. The interest rate is set at 5 percent, and the dividend rate is set at zero. Let the volatility be 30 percent. The delta hedge ratios of both options are compared under various spot prices in Figure 2.6.

We notice from Figure 2.6 that delta is higher in absolute value for the American option than for the European option. The hedge ratio is more extreme. A holder of an American option may decide on early exercise if the put is sufficiently deep in the money. So assume that the stock is $75. The holder of the American option is going to exercise it early. The writer of the option, who is doing the hedging, had better be ready with a short position in the underlying. So the writer of the option has to be ready with a delta hedge ratio of −1. On the other hand, there is six months to go until the holder of the European option can actually force the writer to accept delivery of the underlying. So the writer of the option actually has a lot of time to prepare. There-

| | European Put | | American Put | |
Spot	Price	Delta	Price	Delta
100	$7.18	−0.41	$7.39	−0.42
95	$9.48	−0.50	$9.77	−0.52
90	$12.28	−0.60	$12.70	−0.64
85	$15.57	−0.70	$16.20	−0.75
80	$19.34	−0.79	$20.29	−0.87
75	$23.52	−0.87	$25.00	−1.00

Figure 2.6   The delta of a European and an American put.

fore, even if the European option is way in the money, the delta is not quite −1 yet because there is still a long time to go.

Now consider a Bermudan option. The delta hedge ratio of a Bermudan option swings between the American and European. The Bermudan option resembles an American option more and more as the exercise date approaches. After the exercise date passes, it becomes more like a European option. Then, as the next exercise date approaches, the option begins to resemble an American option again.

SUMMARY

In summary, you can use a delta hedging approach for Bermudan options, but you must be aware of the fact that the delta hedge ratio can be much more severe with an American or a Bermudan than with a European.

Bermudan options have several exercise dates. These are typically set at regular intervals (e.g., annually or semi-annually). Bermudan options are used mostly in interest rate applications in which settlement occurs at regular intervals. For example, a bond might pay semi-annual coupons and may be callable on the coupon dates. Bermudan options give the holder more rights than a European option but less rights than an American option.

You can use a delta hedging approach for Bermudan options, but you must be aware of the fact that the delta hedge ratios can be much more severe with an American or a Bermudan than with a European option.

CHAPTER 3

Binary Options

INTRODUCTION

Consider a portfolio of European options all on the same underlying security and with the same expiration date. We can plot a
graph of the payout of the portfolio versus the price of the underlying at expiration. As shown in Figure 3.1, that graph looks like
a series of straight lines.

We can distinguish between a payout that looks like a slope
and a payout that looks like a vertical line. These are illustrated
in Figures 3.2 and 3.3.

A standard European option (Figure 3.2) pays out $S_t - X$ if
$S_t > X$; otherwise it pays out 0. The payout function can also be
written as $\max(S_t - X, 0)$. Here S_t is the spot price of the underlying on the expiration date, t, and X is the strike.

A binary option (Figure 3.3) pays \$1 if $S_t > X$; otherwise it
pays \$0. The binary option is also known as *digital* or *all or
nothing*.

THE DISTINCTION BETWEEN EUROPEAN
AND BINARY OPTIONS

The main distinction between European options and binary
options is simply this:

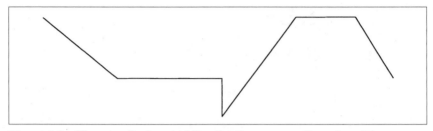

Figure 3.1   The payout of a portfolio of options versus the price of the underlying security.

- The payout of a European option is related to the difference between the underlying and the strike price.
- The payout of a binary option is determined by whether or not the underlying is above the strike price. The amount paid out is independent of the difference.

To illustrate: A European call option struck at $100 will pay $5 if the underlying ends at $105, $10 if it ends at $110, and $20 if it ends at $120. A binary call option struck at $100 will pay out $1 if the underlying ends at $101 and will pay out the same $1 even if the underlying ends up at $110, $120, or $150. This means that if the strike is $100, the binary option has a payout of $1 if the underlying is priced at $100.001. On the other hand, if the underlying price is $99.999, the binary option pays zero.

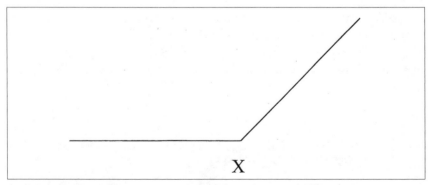

Figure 3.2   The payout of a standard European option. Its payout function is $\max(S_t - X, 0)$.

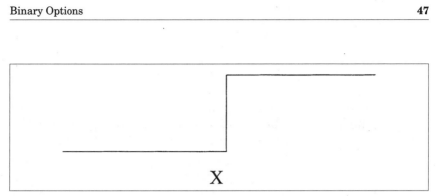

Figure 3.3   The payout of a binary option. It pays out \$1 if $S_t > X;$ otherwise it pays out 0.

The payout profile is called *binary, zero or one, all or nothing,* or *on or off.* At times the option is called *cash or nothing.* The principle is that the payout is either on or off, like a light switch.

BINARY CALL AND PUT OPTIONS

As mentioned above, a binary call option pays \$1 if the underlying, $S,$ is above the strike, $X.$ The same payout is given regardless of the difference between S and $X.$ The only requirement is that S be greater than $X.$ A binary put option pays \$1 if the underlying is below the strike price.

BACK TO THE PORTFOLIO

Let's take the graph in Figure 3.1. This graph represents the payout of a portfolio of options, all with the same underlying security and the same expiration date. Whatever the shape of the graph, we can achieve this payout with a portfolio of European options and binary options. If the graph contains a slope, then there are some European options. A vertical line means there are binary options.

VALUATION

The valuation of the binary option call is extremely simple. The valuation formula is the present value of the area under the lognormal distribution curve to the right of the strike price.

$$C = \exp(-r^*t) * N(d2)$$

Here C is the price of the binary option, $N(\ )$ is the cumulative standard normal distribution function, r is the risk-free interest rate and t is the time to expiration.

$$d2 = \frac{\log\left(\dfrac{S}{X}\right) + r - q - \sigma^2/2}{\sigma\sqrt{t}}$$

where

> S = spot price of underlying
> X = strike price
> q = dividend yield
> σ = volatility

Therefore, the price of the binary option is given by the area under the curve.

What is the probability of the underlying ending in the money, discounted to today's rate? Figure 3.4 shows a binary option struck at \$100. The current spot price is \$100. The price of the option is \$0.48. This can be regarded as the probability that the underlying will end up above \$100 (roughly 50 percent), discounted by one year. We notice that the option has virtually no theta.

Pricing the same option with only two weeks to expiration gives us a price of \$0.50. Of course, the probability that the underlying will end up above \$100 is still roughly 50 percent. With two weeks to expiration, we have just changed the present value somewhat.

ASSET OR NOTHING OPTIONS

An *asset or nothing* option has the following payout. If the stock ends over the strike, the owner of the option is going to get this stock. If it ends under the strike, the option ends out of the money and pays out a value of zero. The payout diagram is illustrated in Figure 3.5. The asset or nothing can be constructed as a combination of a European option and a binary option. The valuation formula is simply the sum of the two.

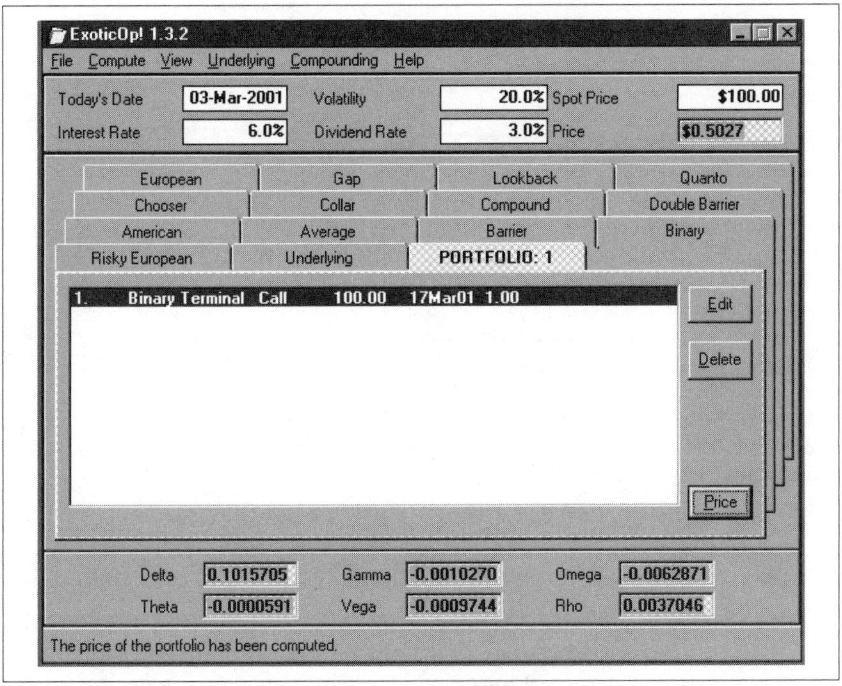

Figure 3.4 The pricing of a one-year binary option.

SUPER SHARES

Combine a long position in an asset or nothing struck at $X1$ and a short position in an asset or nothing struck at $X2$. Effectively, we created an option that entitles its holder to receive the stock if it ends in the range $X1$ to $X2$. Otherwise, the holder receives nothing. The payout diagram for the *super share* is illustrated in Figure 3.6.

Suppose the dealer buys a stock. The dealer now has a stock that she purchased and paid for. At the same time, the dealer sells super shares to her various clients.

- Client A buys an option and pays a premium for it. One year later, Client A is entitled to receive the stock if it ends above zero and below or equal to $10.

- Client B is going to get this stock if it ends above $10 and below or equal to $20.

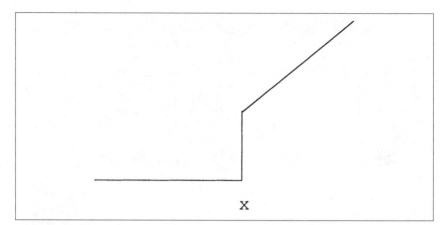

X

Figure 3.5   The payout of an asset or nothing option. It pays out S_t if $S_t > X$; otherwise it pays out zero.

- Client C will receive it if it ends above $20 and below or equal to $30.
- Client D will receive it if it ends above $30 and below or equal to $40. And so on.

Each client has purchased a super share.

Taken together, all the super shares add up to one position in the share. In the past, that is actually how some dealers made

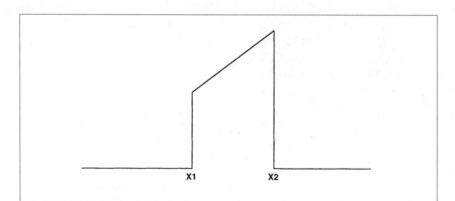

X1   X2

Figure 3.6   The payout of a super share. It pays out S_t if $S_t > X1$ and $S_t < X2$; otherwise it pays out zero.

money. They bought a share, and then they sold all these little individual super shares. The total premiums the dealers received were more than the current stock price and were more than they paid for the share. On expiration date, the dealers would just pass the stock certificate to that particular client whose super share expired in the money. In the meantime the dealers collected the dividends paid out on the share and kept it themselves.

THE STEP STRUCTURE

Consider a long position in a binary option struck at $90 combined with a short position in a binary option struck at $110. The holder of this position will receive $100 if the stock is above $90 but below $110. Figure 3.7 is the payout diagram of the step structure. It is obvious why the name *step* was chosen.

How do you price it? The pricing is basically the probability that the underlying will end up between $90 and $110, discounted to today. With a volatility of 20 percent, the price comes out to $37.35. That means that approximately 40 percent of the distribution is between $90 and $110 and then it is discounted to today.

How does a position in the step structure look before expiration? Figure 3.8 is a three-dimensional graphics of the step position. We are looking at the graph from a 45° angle. One axis represents time, and the other axis represents the spot price of the underlying. The height of the graph represents the price of the structure.

Consider the structure with the underlying priced today at $109.99 versus $110.01. The price of the step structure today

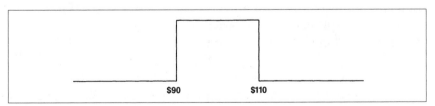

Figure 3.7 The payout diagram of a step structure. Receive $100 if the share closes between $90 and $110. Otherwise receive nothing.

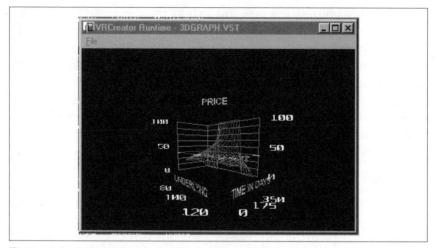

Figure 3.8   A three-dimensional graphics of a step structure.

should be pretty similar for these two spot prices of the underlying security. But note that:

- Should the underlying stay at $109.99 and not move at all, then as time passes, the step structure's price will approach $100.
- At $110.01 if nothing happens and time passes, the price of the step structure will go to zero.

In the graph two lines start at almost the same place but go to different places. One line moves up to $100, and the other moves down to $0. In physics this is called *bifurcation*.

The step structure has a very negative vega. As volatility increases, the chance of ending in the money decreases. The delta of the structure is quite small. It doesn't matter if the underlying moves in small movements, around $100. If it goes to $101 or $99, the price of the structure should pretty much stay the same. So long as the underlying is at almost equal distance from the edges of the step (e.g., $90 and $110), it has more or less the same probability of ending between $90 and $110.

When the underlying moves up close to one of the edges, say at $109, of course, the chances of ending out of the money have a higher probability. So at $109, there is a strong exposure to the underlying, and the client would like it to go down. However, at $100 there is only a small exposure to the underlying.

In Figure 3.9, we plot the delta profile of the step structure. There are only two "interesting" points on this chart. The entire chart is flat except for the two points. One point is at $90 and at expiration, and delta is infinity; and the other point is at $110 and at expiration, and delta is minus infinity.

Since the payout graph is vertical at $90 and at expiration, then delta is infinity. At $110, delta is minus infinity. As the underlying goes from $89.99 to $90.01, the digital option changes from paying zero to paying $100.

Delta is the slope of the payout graph. In this case, delta cannot be derived. It is in fact either positive infinity at $90 or negative infinity at $110. In our implementation the machine shows it as an arbitrary large number, say 64.8.

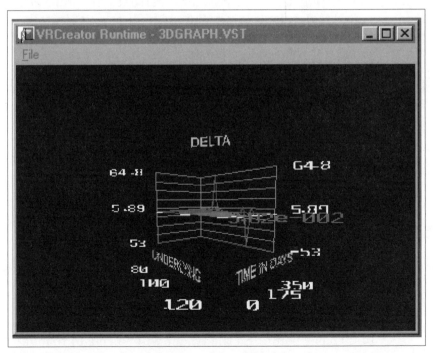

Figure 3.9   A three-dimensional graphics of the delta of a step structure.

Note that the 64.8 has no meaning; it is really infinity. The program is just trying to show an infinitely large number on the graph. As a dealer, delta is infinity because if the spot price is $90 today and if the underlying ends above $90 tomorrow, you have to pay $100; and if it ends at $89.99, you have to pay zero. There is no delta hedge ratio defined here.

MOTIVATION FOR BUYING DIGITAL OPTIONS

The manager of a proprietary hedge fund studied the German yield curve and noticed that it used to be quite steep. At the time of the study, the overnight rate was approximately 3 percent. The one-month forward on the overnight rate was 3.50 percent. The proprietary trader had the following idea. Often at times the market thinks that one month hence the overnight rate is going to go higher to 3.50 percent. However, most of the time nothing happens to the overnight rate; it stays at 3 percent. The proprietary trader wanted to develop a low-premium, high-payout strategy to make huge profits himself if he was correct. On the other hand, the trader did not want to lose much in case he was wrong.

The strategy was developed with binary options. The market determines the forward rate at 3.50 percent. The trader disagrees with the market and thinks the rate will stay down at 3 percent. Consider the following alternatives:

1. Engage in a short forward transaction. Although this is zero cost, it may be quite expensive if the trader turns out to be wrong and interest rates increase to 4 percent.

2. Assume the trader buys an at-the-money option. The trader buys an at-the-money put, struck at 3.50 percent. If interest rates stay at 3 percent, he is going to get 50 basis points times the notional amount. That's a very nice payout. However, there is a problem with this strategy, as the trader has to pay for an at-the-money European option for which the premium is quite expensive. In our case, the cost of the option is about 14.20 basis points. So the trader will "spend 14 to make 50."

3. To reduce the cost the trader can buy an out-of-the-money option. That is, the trader will buy a put struck at 3.05 percent. Since this is an out-of-the-money put, it's going to be a lot cheaper. In our case, the cost of the out-of-the-money put is about 1.36 basis points. On the other hand, the payout of the option is going to be much lower. If interest rates are at 3 percent, the payout will be only 5 basis points. Now the trader has to "spend 1.36 to make 5."

4. A digital put option struck at 3.05 percent can be made to pay 50 basis points if interest rates are lower than 3.05 percent. This option costs about 4.85 basis points. With the digital, the trader can "spend 4.85 to make 50."

Consider that the price of the option is the present value of the expected value of the cash flow. In an at-the-money European option, a large part of the expected value comes from interest rates that are just below 3.50 percent. Interest rates that are just below 3.50 percent are highly probable. On the other hand, rates that are just below 3.50 percent will result in a small option payout. For example, there is a non-trivial probability that on expiration of the option, interest rates will be around 3.40 percent. This will cause the payout of the option to be around 10 basis points.

Thus the region of interest rates just below 3.50 percent can be classified as a "high-probability, low-payout" region. It is this region which contributes most to the expected payout of the option and therefore to the price of the option.

Now consider the region of interest rates which are approximately at 3.00 percent. This is drastically below 3.50 percent. In this region, the option will pay out about 50 basis points. However, the probability that interest rates will end up around 3.00 percent is very low (as compared to the probability that they will end up at about 3.40 percent).

Thus the region of interest rates around 3.00 percent can be classified as a "low-probability, high-payout" region. This region contributes very little to the price of the option since it has such a low probability.

A binary option virtually eliminates the low-payout high-probability regions. It is therefore cheaper than a European option. In addition, the binary option is more suitable to the trader. This is due to the fact that the trader is not interested in getting paid if interest rates end up slightly below 3.50 percent. The trader took an extreme view and decided that he wants to receive a payout only if interest rates are around 3.00 percent, which is drastically below 3.50 percent.

There are other circumstances where an out-of-the-money digital option is appropriate. For example, real estate developers in Israel have been borrowing in Swiss francs or Japanese yen and investing in domestic developments. These realtors are worried that the Israeli currency will be devalued. They are not worried about changes in the currency which are in the range of 5 to 10 percent. These are considered to be within normal trading ranges. The realtors are worried about a 30 percent devaluation. Such realtors have found that the out-of-the-money digital option provided a good hedge.

REPLICATION

A European option can be approximated by digital options. It is possible to take a European option and to "build steps to the top of the mountain," as illustrated in Figure 3.10. We can have a series of digital options:

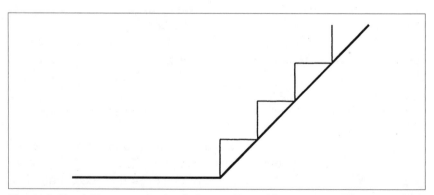

Figure 3.10   A European option being replicated by a series of digital options.

- One that pays a dollar struck at $100
- Another that pays a dollar struck at $101
- One more that pays a dollar struck at $102, etc.

An alternative structure is more precise. It is created with:

- One option paying $0.50 struck at $100
- Another paying $0.50 struck at $100.50
- Yet another option paying $0.50 struck at $101, etc.

We can make the steps as long or small as we wish, and so we can make the replication as precise as possible.

What is more interesting is the replication of a digital option with European options. The dealer sells a digital option to a client and now needs to hedge himself.

In Figure 3.11, we see a bull spread on top of a digital option. Consider a digital call option that pays $1 if the underlying is over $100 at expiration. Compare this digital option with a port-folio consistency of a long position in a call struck at $100 and a short position in a call struck at $101. Above $101 both positions pay out a dollar. Below $100 both positions result in zero. Between $100 and $101, the bull spread is not an exact hedge for the digital option.

An alternative hedge is to be long two European call options struck at $100 and short two European call options struck at $100.50. This bull spread mirrors the digital option exactly except for the region between $100 and $100.50.

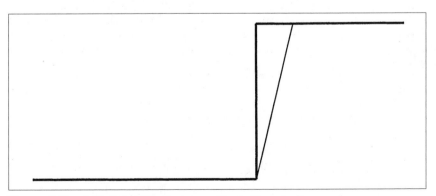

Figure 3.11   A digital option being replicated by a bull spread.

If the trader wants to be really aggressive, she can go long ten calls at $100 and short ten calls at $100.10. This bull spread mirrors the digital option exactly except for the small region between $100 and $100.10.

In the general case, the hedge for a digital option struck at X which pays $1 is:

- Long 1/e Europeans at point X
- Short 1/e Europeans at point $X + e$

In the three hedging alternatives examined above, e was $1, $0.50, and $0.10, respectively.

We can find e so that the hedge is correct within a certain probability by constructing the bull spread. Note that:

- If $S \leq X$, we are hedged.
- If $S \geq X + e$, we are hedged.
- If $X < S < X + e$, we are not exactly hedged.

Hence, we can choose e so that

$$P(X < S < X + e) < 1 - \text{prob}$$

where prob is the desired probability of being hedged.

Consider the following directive for exotic options traders:

Digital calls are hedged with a bull spread with a 20-tick difference, unless volatility is lower than 10 percent, in which case we move to a 10-tick difference.

Assuming that the underlying has a spot price of $100; if the volatility is high, then the chances of ending in the region between $100 and $101 are low. If the volatility is lower, there is a higher chance of ending in that central region and so we must tighten the hedge. In practice, the trader would like to use a wider hedge since the tighter hedge will result in higher transaction costs and bigger bid-ask spreads.

AN ALTERNATIVE HEDGE

In our case, if the bull spread did not match the European, then it underhedged it. A more symmetrical hedge can be constructed.

- Long 1/e Europeans at point $X - e/2$
- Short 1/e Europeans at point $X + e/2$

The dealer can be assured of overhedging by constructing the bull spread as:

- Long 1/e Europeans at point $X - e$
- Short 1/e Europeans at point X

However, it is unlikely that this hedge will cost less than the digital option.

It is clear that exact hedging, close to X and close to the time of expiration, is very, very difficult. Say that spot today is \$155, the strike is \$155, and the option expires tomorrow. The dealer will be hard-pressed to find an appropriate hedge.

THE FIRST EXOTIC

Digital options are probably the very first exotics that a lot of banks step into. A bank sells a digital and puts it on the books as a very aggressive bull spread. The system can already handle European options, and so the bank enters it in the books as long 100 call options struck at \$100 and short 100 call options struck at \$100.01. Since the bank already has the capability of pricing and hedging European options, it can replicate the digital with them. Since the payout of the digital and the bull spread is similar, so is the pricing. Delta and all other Greeks are pretty much the same. Thus it's the most natural exotic to get into because the system can almost already handle it.

TIMING MISMATCH

In Germany, digital options are determined according to the "fixing," normally at 1 p.m. German time. However, European options are determined at the close, 4 p.m. German time. Hence, there is a timing difference. The dealers construct the bull spread hedge in such a manner that the short leg of the call spread expires one day before the long leg. In this fashion, the maturity of the digital is captured.

MARKET MANIPULATION

A dealer who is short an at-the-money digital option that is going to expire tomorrow may be tempted to manipulate the market. The dealer would like to influence the market and move it so the option expires worthless. The motivation to do so is much higher in the case of a digital option than in the case of a European. A slight move of the underlying can save huge amounts for the writer of a digital option and yet it will only slightly impact the writer of a European option.

EXAMPLE: A DOG-LEG FORWARD

Here is a one-month trade that was offered to Canadian clients. These Canadian companies export into the United States and have U.S. dollar receivables. The one-month forward rate at the time of the trade was 1 U.S. dollar to 1.35 Canadian dollars.

In the dogleg forward, the client sells U.S. dollars forward for one month in exchange for Canadian dollars at the rate of 1.37. Right away, the client gets a better rate than the forward. However, there is a stipulation. Every day during the month that the U.S. dollar is below 1.30 Canadian dollars, the client receives 5 basis points in addition to the price; and every day that the U.S. dollar is higher than 1.40 Canadian dollars, the client gets 20 basis points deducted from the price.

The Canadian company receives U.S. dollars all the time. Some of these dollars are exchanged for Canadian currency in the spot market. Thus every day that the U.S. dollar is trading at a high rate, the company makes a profit in the spot market. In particular, if the U.S. dollar is trading above 1.40 in the spot market, the company makes a large profit in the spot market. In this case, the company may not mind receiving a bit less on the forward transaction.

On the other hand, every day that the U.S. dollar is trading low, the company loses money in the spot market. If the U.S. dollar trades below 1.30 Canadian dollars, the company loses a lot. In this case, the company wants to be compensated by receiving a high forward rate.

In this case, the client does a risk reversal. He buys a 1.37 put and sells a 1.37 call. This is obvious because the client has a synthetic forward at 1.37. But to this we add a string of digital options. There are two options that expire every day. The client is long one digital and is short the other digital. The client is long a U.S. dollar put struck at 1.30 Canadian dollars which pays 5 basis points, but he is short a digital call with a strike of 1.40 Canadian dollars which pays out 20 basis points.

In reality, the bank does not hedge itself with options that expire every day. This would involve too many transactions and would be too expensive for the bank. Alternatively, the bank may hedge itself with options that expire every other day (for double the notional amount). This will expose the bank to some timing risks but save on transaction costs. A more extreme variation would be to hedge every three days with triple the notional amount, etc.

DAILY ACCRUAL RANGE FLOATERS

Binary options are also sold with interest rates playing the role of the underlying. For example, several banks sold "Daily accrual range floaters." In one such note, the investor received Libor + 100 basis points for each day that Libor was between 5 percent and 6 percent. If Libor was outside the range, the investor did not receive a coupon for that day. At the end of three months, the issuer would count how many days the Libor had been in the pre-selected range and would compute the appropriate coupon. The name of this note comes from the fact that the coupon depended on the daily Libor fixings.

In this case, the client had a position in many step structures, which were analyzed above. The client was in effect saying that interest rates would remain stable. This type of daily accrual note is sold where the underlying security that determines the coupon payment is Libor, or spot foreign exchange rates, or credit spreads, etc. Many of these structures are sold by the banks and are very popular.

In Chapter 1 we noted that in most cases the client is long the option and the dealer is short. Clients buy exotics, but they rarely sell them, and so it's not a two-way market. As a result of this, the dealer is short options. This means that in most cases the dealer will develop a short volatility position. While the dealer can adequately delta-hedge the position with the underlying, the dealer still has a volatility exposure. The dealer would like to sell some structures in which the client is short volatility and thus purchase some of the volatility back. With the daily accrual structures, the client is short volatility. Now the dealer becomes long volatility. Once the dealer sells this structure, it equalizes the volatility exposures. This explains the enthusiasm of the dealers to sell these structures.

SUMMARY

Binary (or digital) options are useful in a variety of situations. They may be combined with European options to formulate specific strategies. It is not too difficult to price and hedge digital options unless they are very near expiration and very near the strike. In this case, hedging is close to impossible.

CHAPTER 4

Contingent Premium Options

INTRODUCTION

Companies need to protect themselves, and so they buy options. In addition, companies do not like to pay option premiums. Let's say that a particular company buys a call option. One possibility is to sell a put. The premium for the put option exactly matches the premium for the call. In this fashion, the company has entered into a synthetic forward position. Note that this is a dangerous position for a company to be in. If the underlying goes up, the company is protected; but if it goes down, the losses might be unlimited. An example of a loss: In 1997 Volkswagen hedged itself out of 1.3 billion German marks because it hedged its currency positions, specifically in U.S. dollars.

It is obvious that selling puts is a dangerous game. The company doesn't want to pay premiums for the call options. But it doesn't want its risk to be unlimited either. In this case, the contingent premium option is a good choice.

The contingent premium option is composed of a long position in a call option and a short position in a digital call with exactly the same strike. The resulting payout diagram is illustrated in Figure 4.1.

Below the strike price both the European call and the digital call options are out of the money and the payout profile is

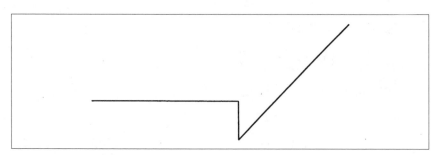

Figure 4.1   A contingent premium option.

zero. At the strike, the client is short a digital and has to pay the payout amount of that digital. But then the European call option begins paying a little. As the underlying moves higher and higher, the European call pays more and more until eventually the European will pay more than the client has to pay due to his short position in the digital option. In a sense, the short position in the digital option allows the client to "borrow" the premium for the European option from his future payout, whether it exists or not.

EXAMPLE

The client wants to buy a three-month at-the-money European call option struck at $100. The premium for this option is approximately $4.55. This is illustrated in Figure 4.2.

Now we add a short position in a digital option, also struck at $100. The first question is how much should the digital option pay out. It turns out that in order to create a zero premium position, the digital option must pay out about $8.80. This is illustrated in Figure 4.3.

Consider Figure 4.1 again. It is the payout profile of this structure. Under $100, both options are out of the money and no one has to make any payments. As soon as the underlying crosses $100, the client has to pay $8.80. Then, as the underlying climbs over $100 to levels such as $101 or $102, the European call begins to pay out and the payout graph climbs. Eventually at $108.80 the European call pays $8.80 back and there is no out-of-pocket expense to the client. As the underlying

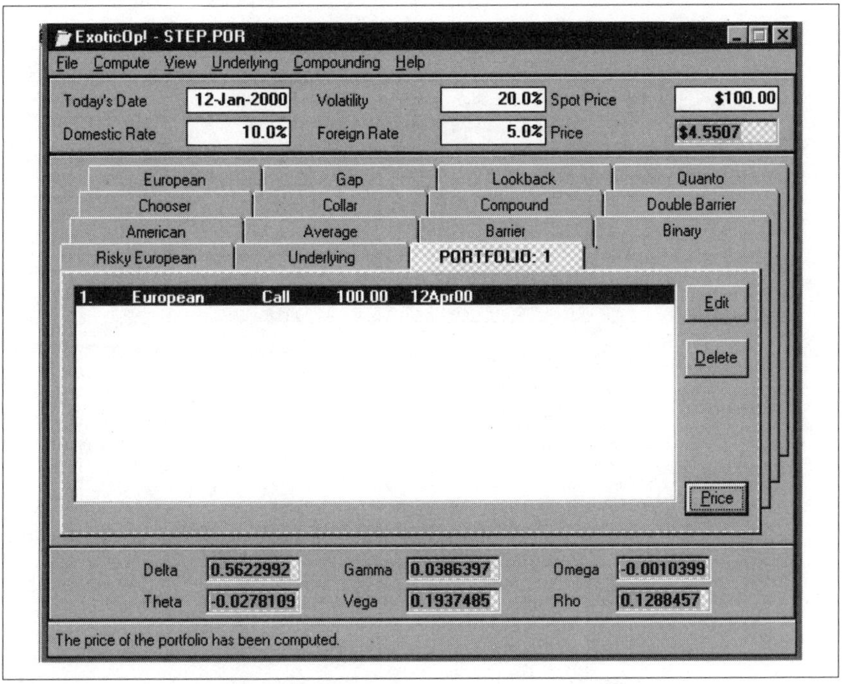

Figure 4.2   A European option.

climbs more and more, the client begins to get paid. The European option's payout is more than $8.80, and it begins to overshadow the digital.

The client has a problem. We started out with the premise that the client didn't want to pay $4.55 for the European option. But now the client is puzzled. If the underlying ends just over $100, the client will have to pay $8.80. Why is this such a high amount? Why is it not more like $4.55, or maybe the future value of $4.55?

The dealer receives that $4.55 in any case. This is a premium that the dealer collects. The $8.80, on the other hand, is not a certain cash flow. The dealer only receives it if the underlying is over $100. However, if the underlying ends below $100, the dealer will receive nothing. What are the dealer's chances of receiving the $8.80? More or less 50 percent because the underlying has to close above $100. Therefore we can expect that the

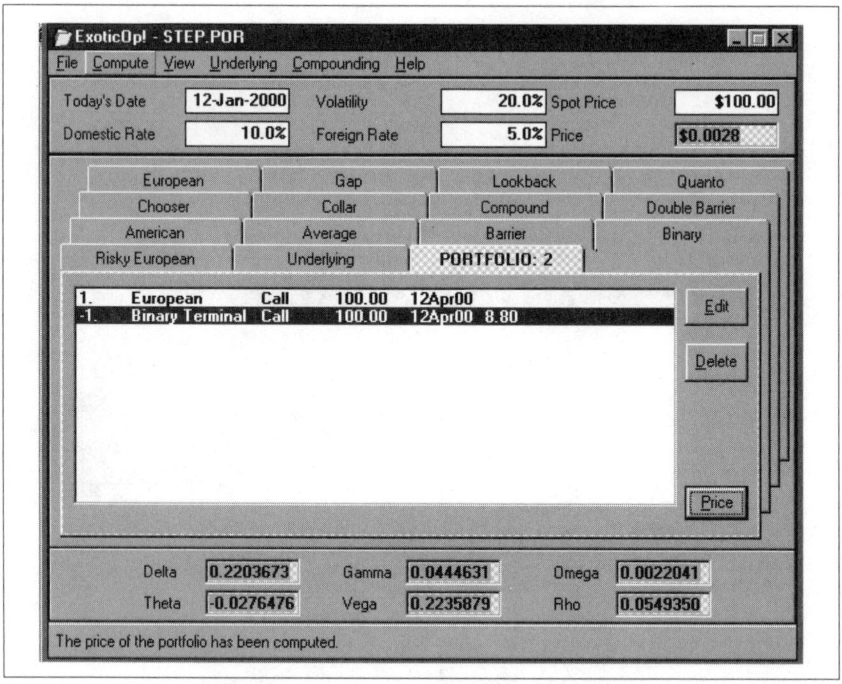

Figure 4.3   A contingent premium structure. It is made up of a long position in a European and a short position in a digital.

payout level of the digital option would be approximately twice the premium for the European option.

Note that when we compute the exact payout level, we need to take into consideration the forward curve, the present value of the cash flows, and the volatility. But, on an intuitive level, the payout of the digital option should be approximately twice the premium of the European option.

LOW-STRIKE DIGITAL

The client considers $8.80 to be a big potential liability. The client does not want to pay that much. That's not a problem since all kinds of structures can be created to avoid paying a high price. For example, we can move the strike of the digital a little bit to the left. There is no reason why the digital and the

ExoticOp! - STEP.POR

File Compute View Underlying Compounding Help

| Today's Date | 12-Jan-2000 | Volatility | | 20.0% | Spot Price | | $100.00 |
| Domestic Rate | | 10.0% | Foreign Rate | | 5.0% | Price | $0.0069 |

European	Gap	Lookback	Quanto
Chooser	Collar	Compound	Double Barrier
American	Average	Barrier	Binary
Risky European	Underlying	**PORTFOLIO: 2**	

| 1. | European | Call | 100.00 | 12Apr00 | | Edit |
| -1. | Binary Terminal | Call | 90.00 | 12Apr00 | 5.35 | |

Delete

Price

| Delta | 0.4521990 | Gamma | 0.0520917 | Omega | 0.0017280 |
| Theta | -0.0350122 | Vega | 0.2613539 | Rho | 0.1127249 |

The price of the portfolio has been computed.

Figure 4.4 A low-strike digital.

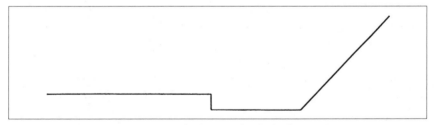

Figure 4.5   The payout profile of a low-strike digital contingent premium structure.

European options have to have the same strike. Keep the strike of the European call option at $100 and make the digital have a strike of $90. This is a low-strike digital. With this structure, the maximal level the client will ever have to pay is $5.35. This is shown in Figure 4.4. Figure 4.5 shows the payout profile of the structure.

SUMMARY

Contingent premium options are made up of a combination of a long position in a European option coupled with a short position in a digital. The premiums of both options offset each other exactly.

CHAPTER 5

Contingent Premium Caps: A Primer

INTRODUCTION

Contingent premium options are options that do not require the up-front payment of a premium. In some sense, they allow clients to "borrow" premiums from the payout at expiry. They are also a particularly appealing application of digital options. In this chapter, we discuss various topics pertaining to contingent premium structures and why they may be interesting to clients. Note that although we discuss caps, the same ideas apply also to floors.

WHAT ARE THEY?

Consider a regular cap. The holder of the option pays a premium to the issuer. After the premium is paid, the holder of the option enjoys protection against a rise (in the case of a floor it would be a decline) in interest rates. In a *contingent premium cap,* the holder does not pay an up-front premium. At the expiry of the option, the issuer may pay the holder of the option, or, alternatively, the holder of the option will be required to pay the issuer.

ADVANTAGES TO THE USER

Clients typically use caps in several types of scenarios:

1. When they want to be protected from interest rate hikes.
2. When they are legally required to do so (e.g., a leveraged financing deal).
3. When caps are perceived as a good strategy (e.g., when volatility levels are low).

However, like all options, regular caps require the payment of an up-front premium. But suppose a cash-poor client has a project that the client expects will be very profitable. The client is interested in purchasing a cap but has no funds to pay for the premium. A contingent premium cap may be a very helpful structure for such a client.

Another advantage of contingent premium caps is that, as we shall see, they are made up of a long position together with a short position. This combination has two positive effects:

1. It reduces the time decay. A cap, like any other option, suffers from time decay. All other things being equal, the value of the cap declines as time goes by. Contingent premium options are much better at retaining their market value.
2. It reduces sensitivity to volatility. A standard cap is sensitive to volatility. When volatility declines, so does the value of the cap. In contrast, contingent premium caps are much less sensitive to swings in volatility.

As a result of these two points, contingent premium caps retain their value through time even if there are volatility swings. Hence, it will be relatively painless for a client to get out of a contingent premium cap.

HOW ARE THEY CONSTRUCTED?

A contingent premium cap is composed of:

1. A long position in a standard cap
2. A short position in a digital (all or nothing) option

Let us reconsider the client who wishes to reduce her financing costs. One available strategy for her is to be short options. The short position will fund her long position. For example, the client who is long a cap may also be short a floor. However, when a client is short traditional floors, her potential liability may be unlimited.

This explains the popularity of the contingent premium cap. Since the short position is in a digital option, the maximal amount that the holder may have to pay out is capped. It is guaranteed to not be larger than the payout amount of the digital. On the other hand, the long position is in a regular cap. Thus the upside is unlimited.

To sum up the main points so far, a contingent premium cap eliminates the need to pay an up-front premium and reduces time decay and exposure to volatility. It has an unlimited upside but only a limited downside risk.

SEVERAL STRUCTURES

The structure is constructed so that the premium of the standard cap is exactly equal to the premium of the digital. Thus no premium need exchange hands at the initiation of the deal.

There is a wide latitude in the type of deal that can be constructed. After the details of the cap have been chosen, we need to choose the details of the digital. In particular, the strike of the digital and the amount that will be paid out may be chosen. Since the premium of the digital must match the premium of the cap, once we choose a strike for the digital, the amount that will be paid is determined.

Consider a quarterly cap whose strike is 5.25 percent. We assume a trade date of March 6, 2000, an effective date of September 6, 2000, and an expiry date of December 6, 2000. Figure 5.1 shows the payout of this cap and also the probability of receiving that payout. For example, if Libor at expiry is 8.25 percent, the payout of this cap is $(8.25 - 5.25) * 0.25 = 0.750$.

Intuitively, the graph in Figure 5.1 shows that there is a positive probability-multiplied payout. That's why a regular cap commands a premium, in this case about 4.90 basis points.

Now, consider several contingent premium caps. All of them are quarterly instruments with the same dates as the original cap.

We add a digital option with the same strike (5.25 percent). The first issue is to compute the payout of the digital. We already

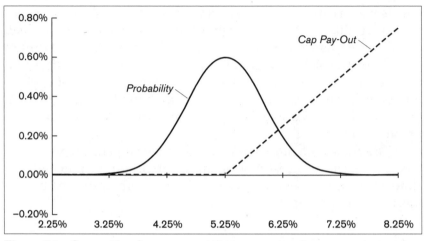

Figure 5.1 Conventional cap.

know that the premium of the digital should be 4.90 basis points. Thus, by working backward we can find that the annualized payout of the digital must be about 49 basis points. Figure 5.2 shows the payout profile of a standard contingent premium cap. Since these options are settled quarterly, the maximum penalty is about $^{49}/_4 = 12.25$ basis points per quarter. Intuitively, the graph in this figure shows that the probability-multiplied payout sums to zero. That's why a contingent premium cap does not require an up-

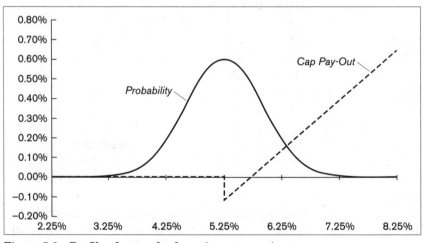

Figure 5.2 Profile of a standard contingent premium cap.

front premium. This graph also shows an interesting feature of digitals. If Libor ends at 5.24 percent, both the digital and the cap are out of the money so no money changes hands. If Libor closes at 5.26 percent, both options are in the money. The standard cap has a payout that is almost negligible. The writer of the digital option, on the other hand, is liable for the entire payout.

Suppose that Libor closes above 5.25 percent and the digital option expires in the money. In this case the holder, who has written the digital, will pay 12.25 basis points per quarter. This amount is payable by the holder and is deducted from the payout of the standard cap. The worst case for the client happens when the standard cap pays nothing and the digital option is payable. In this case, the client will be forced to pay 12.25 basis points per quarter out of pocket.

Can the client reduce his maximal exposure? Can we construct a structure in which, at the worst case, the client will have to pay less? The answer lies in adjusting the strike of the digital. If we lower the strike of the digital, we can use a lower payout and achieve the same premium.

The next graph, Figure 5.3, shows a contingent premium cap in which the strike of the digital was set at 4.75 percent, way below the strike of the standard cap. In this structure, the annualized payout of the digital is only 28 basis points. Per quarter, this comes out to 7 basis points which is the maximal exposure of

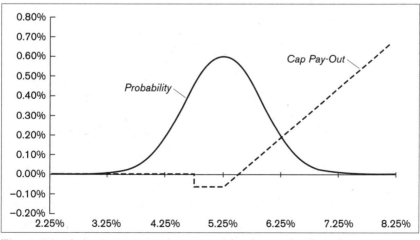

Figure 5.3   A contingent premium cap with a low strike digital.

the client. By "pulling" the strike of the digital downward, we reduce the payout of the digital and the maximal exposure of the client. On the other hand, we increase the probability that the client will have an out-of-pocket expense. We can see that the area where the payout chart is negative corresponds to the high-probability region.

A low-strike digital lowers the maximal exposure of the client. What about a high-strike digital? Figure 5.4 shows a contingent premium cap with a digital struck at 5.75 percent, well above the strike of the standard cap.

We've determined that the strike of the digital is 5.75 percent. The annualized payout amount of the digital is 123 basis points. However, in this case, the client will never be required to pay the full amount. In the worst case, Libor closes just above 5.75 percent. The client will be required to pay 123 basis points for the digital. However, the same client also receives 50 basis points from the standard cap. The computation is 5.75 percent − 5.25 percent = 0.50. Thus the client has to pay 73 basis points (50 − 123 = −73 basis points) over a period of 3 months, or 18.25 basis points per quarter.

This last structure is very interesting. The payout of the digital is 123 basis points. However, the client will never have to pay the entire cost out of pocket. On the other hand, if Libor

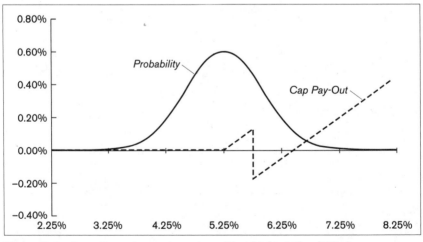

Figure 5.4   A contingent premium cap with a high-strike digital.

TABLE 5.1

Type	Annualized Payout of Digital	Quarterly Maximum Penalty	Quarterly Payout at 8.25%
Standard contingent	49 basis points	12.25 basis points	$(300 - 49)/4 = 62.75$
Contingent with low-strike digital	28 basis points	7 basis points	$(300 - 28)/4 = 68$
Contingent with high-strike digital	123 basis points	18.25 basis points	$(300 - 123)/4 = 44.25$

becomes very high, the holder will receive less money than in the other structures.

Table 5.1 summarizes the payout of the digital, the maximal out-of-pocket penalty payable by the holder of the contingent premium cap, and the payout that would be received by the holder of the cap if Libor closes at very high levels (e.g., 8.25 percent).

In a contingent premium cap the holder, in a sense, borrows the up-front premium from the future payouts. Unfortunately, if no future payouts exist, the holder will have to pay. This is the maximal penalty presented in the Table 5.1.

SUMMARY

Contingent premium caps are instruments that allow clients to defer payment of the premium. In addition they have the following traits:

- Small time decay
- Reduced sensitivity to volatility
- Tremendous flexibility in their creation

CHAPTER 6

Forward Start Options

INTRODUCTION

Forward start options are options whose strike will be determined at some later date. For example, one could buy an option today to expire in one year. The strike of the option will be determined in three months according to the price of the underlying security then. Of course, the strike of the option could be determined according to any pre-agreed-upon formula (e.g., at the money, 10 percent out of the money, etc.).

MOTIVATION

Case 1

Consider an employee working for a software firm. The firm decides that this person is a valuable employee, but not valuable enough to pay in cash. The firm also wants the employee to stay employed and not resign in the midst of a project. The firm makes the following offer to the employe: "If you stay until the end of December, we will give you a large number of one-year call options. The strike price of the options will be determined to be equal to the price of the firm's shares as of January 1." That is, if the employee stays employed until the end of the year, the employee will receive some at-the-money options, with an expiration date of one year later.

As an example, assume that today is March 4, 2000. If the employee stays with the company until December 31, 2000, the company is going to give the employee at-the-money options whose price will be determined then. These options will expire on December 31, 2001. If the price of this company's stock as of January 1, 2000, is $100, the employee will get options with a strike price of $100. If the share price will be $110, the strike of the options will be $110. If the share price will be $90, the strike of the options will be set to $90, etc.

Note that the employee cannot use European option pricing formulas to determine the value of such an option. This is because the value of the option depends on its strike. And as of today, the strike price is still unknown since it has not yet been set. The employee can't just put it into the Black-Scholes formula because in fact he doesn't know the strike.

Case 2

Consider a corporate treasurer who will need some at-the-money options as of January 1 of next year. This need will arise due to a deal that will close at the end of this year. The treasurer has determined that the implied volatility of such options will rise by a substantial amount between now and the end of the year. In this case, he may be motivated to purchase the options now and pay for them today. The strike price of the options will be determined on January 1 of next year. This will be a profitable transaction if the volatility that is projected today for the period at which the options will be activated (the forward volatility) is in fact lower than the actual implied volatility of such options at the end of the year.

EMPLOYEE OPTIONS

These types of options are often given as bonuses to key employees. They are known as "golden handcuffs" since the employee cannot leave the firm until the end of the year without forfeiting the options. Current accounting practices in the United States permit firms to value many types of employee options at cost and not at fair value. These valuations typically utilize the spot price of the stock as of the date at which the options were given rather than the current stock price. As most share prices have increased substantially, such options are evaluated at a large discount to their fair value. Since these are a liability to the issuer, the liability is valued at less than its actual value. This has the effect of making many balance sheets look prettier than they really are. If such options would have been evaluated at their fair market value (marked to market), the valuations of many U.S. firms would have to be reduced substantially. Allowing firms to value employee options with the original stock price rather than the current stock price represents a major loophole in accounting principles. There are constant ongoing discussions on this particular topic between the regulatory authorities, the accounting groups, and the corporate consortiums.

DISCUSSION

The forward starting option could be struck at the money at some future date. Alternatively, it does not have to be at the money; it could be 20 percent out of the money, 20 percent in the money, etc. The main difference between a forward start option and a normal option is that the formula for the strike has to do with the underlying as of some future date and not as of today.

These types of forward start options are used in a very popular equity product that is being sold in many countries. The *rachet* or *cliquet* option gives its holder all the rises in an equity index. It locks in all the rises of the equity index but does not penalize the investor if the equity index falls. The investor gets the participation in the equity as it goes up from month to month (or from quarter to quarter). On the other hand, the investor does not lose when the market declines. These products are generally sold through the retail network to retail clients. Even insurance companies sell them. These investment products guarantee the client the return from month to month or from quarter to quarter. The next chapter will discuss how these are built with forward start options.

Such products also can be created on interest rates. A rachet swap, for example, is an interest rate swap in which the client pays a fixed rate and receives a floating rate (e.g., Libor). The client is guaranteed that the level of the floating rate received can never fall beneath its previous level.

THREE DIFFERENT TYPES

We can consider three different types of formulas to determine the strike price.

Type 1. The client and the dealer agree on the strike and the number of options today. This is just like buying regular options.

Type 2. This is the case that is discussed above. The dealer sells the client 100 at-the-money options whose strike will be determined at a later date.

Type 3. On a future date the dealer will give the client at-the-money options. In this case both the strike and the number of the options will be determined at a later date. For example, the dealer will provide the client with at-the-money options on $1,000 worth of stock. So if the stock is at $20, the client will get 50 options. If the stock is at $25, the client will get 40 options. In this case, the notional value of the entire deal is fixed.

In Type 1 the client gets 100 call options struck at $100. In Type 2, the client gets 100 call options whose strike will be determined at some future date. If the spot price of the underlying on that date is $110, the client will receive 100 options struck at $110. In Type 3, both the number of options and the strike price will be determined at a future date. Assume that the notional value of the deal is $10,000 worth of shares. If the share price on the determination date is $100, the client will receive 100 options struck at $100. If the share price is $110, the client will receive 90.9090 options struck at $110, etc.

VALUATION

Case 1

In this case both the strike and the number of options are fixed. If we fix both the strike and the number and the option is a

European-style option, then it is just like buying a regular European option to December 31, 2001.

If the option has an American-style exercise, then it is just like buying an American option that cannot yet be exercised. The American option can only be exercised in the period from January 1, 2001, until December 31, 2001. Therefore, it is really like a Bermudan option in that it cannot be exercised before January 1, 2001 and can be exercised at any moment afterward. After January 1, 2001, it can be exercised at any time. Note that this is *not* like being long an American option with an expiration on December 31, 2001, and being short the American option with an expiration of January 1, 2001.

Case 2

In this case, we have true forward start options. The client will receive 100 one-year at-the-money options whose strike will be determined as of January 1, 2000. The strike will actually be determined at some future date.

How do we price this option? Let's suppose that the price of the underlying share the determination date is $100. So the price of this option, on that determination date, is going to be simple to compute. It will be the price of an at-the-money option struck at $100; the price of the underlying is $100, and the maturity of the option is in one year. Obviously, we can price a one-year option from that determination date. The only difficulty is that we don't actually know the price of the underlying share at the determination date. It could be $100, or $110, or $90, or $80, or whatever other price the underlying share will have on that date.

Let $P(S,X,T)$ be the price of an option in which the strike price is X, the time to expiration is T, and the underlying is currently priced at S. Obviously,

$$P(S/c, X/c, T) = 1/c * P(S,X,T)$$

where c is an arbitrary constant. This means that the price of an option in which the share price and the strike are both divided by a constant is the price of the original option divided by the same constant. Thus the price of an option whose spot is $200 and whose strike is $200 is the same as two options with the stock at \$100 and the strike at \$100. This is exactly what happens in the case of a two-for-one stock split. Instead of owning one option, the holder receives two options whose strike is half.

Let t be the determination date and T be the expiration date. Now, let $S(t)$ be the price of the stock at the determination date and $S(0)$ be its price today.

$$P[S(t), S(t),T - t] = S(t)/S(0) * P[S(0), S(0),T - t]$$

Suppose one buys $P[S(0),S(0),T - t]/S(0)$ units of stock today. In three months, these will also be worth $S(t)/S(0)*$ $P[S(0),S(0),T - t]$ at time t since the price of the stock has moved from $S(0)$ to $S(t)$.

But the owner of the shares also receives a dividend rate of q. Thus the expected value of $S(t)$ is

$$S(t) = \exp[(r - q)*t] * S(0)$$

At the determination date t, the price of the option is given by

$$\exp[(r - q)*t] * S(0)/S(0) * P[S(0), S(0),T - t]$$
$$= \exp[(r - q)*t] * P[S(0), S(0),T - t]$$

The price of the option today is given by

$$\exp(-r*t)* \exp[(r - q)*t] * P[S(0), S(0),T - t]$$
$$= \exp(-q*t) * P[S(0), S(0),T - t]$$

Conclusion: The forward start option has the same price as an at-the-money European option, discounted by the dividend rate.

Case 3

In this case, the notional value of the underlying is fixed. The client asks for three-month options starting in three months on \$1,000 worth of stocks. Let $S(t)$ be the price of the stock on the determination date t. In time t, when the option is issued, it will be worth

$$P[S(t), S(t),(T - t)]$$

The amount of options to be issued is

$$1,000/S(t)$$

The price (as of time t) is

$$1,000/S(t) * P[S(t), S(t),(T - t)] = P[1,000,1,000,(T - t)]$$

The price today is

$$\exp(-r*t) * P[1,000,1,000,(T - t)]$$

Conclusion: This type of forward start option has the same price as an at-the-money European option, discounted by the risk-free rate.

Note: All these analyses assume that volatility and interest rates are static.

In foreign exchange, if we fix the amount of the foreign currency, it means that we discount back at the foreign currency rate, and if we fix the amount of the domestic currency, we discount back at the risk-free rate.

APPLICATION

An options trader in Brazil says that he charges his clients for a forward start option more than the price of a European option. People in Brazil are accustomed to escalating prices. There is a high inflation rate there and the price of everything rises. For example, if you want to buy a car in Brazil, it's going to be more expensive the next month. A client has some cash now and wants to buy an at-the-money European option. But the client does not want the option to begin today. She wants to buy it so that it starts in three months from today. On the other hand, she wants to pay cash now. As we've just seen the fair value of the option is one that is discounted by either the dividend rate or the risk-free rate. So the forward start option has to be cheaper than a normal option. The trader justifies the higher price by telling the client that there is volatility risk, stock price risk, interest rate risk, etc. The trader mentions to the client that if the spot price of the underlying moves up, the option will be more expensive than what it was sold for. What the dealer doesn't tell the client is that if the underlying moves down, the option will be cheaper than what it was sold for.

POSITIONS IN VOLATILITY

Forward start options are an excellent way to take positions on volatility. The client thinks that beginning in 2001, volatility is going to increase by a lot. The market perceives that volatility will stay constant. The client can buy forward start options. The volatility that will be used to price them is the forward implied volatility as of today. If, indeed, volatility increases in 2001, the price of the options will be much higher then. This is similar to doing a forward rate agreement (FRA) on volatility. The client buys the option today at a forward rate volatility. On the determination date, the price of the option depends on the actual implied volatility in the future. Instead of doing an FRA on interest rates, this is similar to doing an FRA on volatility. Forward start options are a good way to bet on volatility rising.

A similar situation occurs when the client has some information about a company. Consider a client with a view on a greeting card company. The stock price is going to be depressed until the beginning of February, but then the company is going to market its Valentine's Day cards and it is going to do so well that the price of the stock will shoot up. A forward start option would be a reasonable way to deal with this situation. The advantage of buying a forward start option rather than a normal option is that the price is lower for the forward start.

IMPLIED VOLATILITY SWAP

The forward start option is similar to an instrument known as an *implied volatility swap*. If the implied volatility of an at-the-money option goes up more than expected by the forward curve, the buyer of the forward start makes money. On the other hand, if implied volatility is lower than the forward, the client will lose money as compared with buying an at-the-money option on the forward date.

The bank that sells the forward start option has to hedge against the implied volatility of the at-the-money option. The bank can do this by purchasing straddles and strangles. As the underlying moves, the at-the-money point moves. Thus this is a dynamic hedge that has to be continuously adjusted.

CONTINGENT NOTIONAL FORWARD START

Consider the following situation. A client sells a structured note and wants protection from the bank. For example, the client sells a warrant on a stock. The client does not know in advance what the strike price will be, because this will be determined by the market on the actual date of the sale. The strike price of the warrant will be equal to the spot price of the underlying on the specific sale date.

The client can buy a forward start option for protection. As the market moves up or down, so does the strike of the structured note. The forward start option will replicate those movements. One can see this process on term sheets. Some term sheets include a clause that says "the strike will be determined on the pricing date."

But now there is another problem. The bank does not know in advance how many structured notes the client will sell. The maximal amount on offer is $10 million. Based on past experience, the minimal amount that will sell is $5 million. The exact amount depends on the market's appetite and on the success of the structured note program. Therefore, the client wants to buy *contingent notional forward start*.

If the bank prices the structure for $10 million and assumes that the client will buy only $5 million, the bank will quote double the original price. But if it does, the client will not purchase the structure from this bank. The bank has to somehow determine a price that is a combination of a fixed cost plus a price per option. The bank will then just allocate the fixed cost among $5 million worth of structures. If the client ends up buying more than that, the bank makes extra money.

By selling forward start options, the bank assumes volatility and interest rate risks. The price of a normal European option is dependent upon the risk-free rate. When the bank prices a forward start option, it computes the price of that option taking into account the forward interest rates. Assume the bank sells the forward start and interest rates shoot up. Then the price of the option will be more expensive than what it was sold for. So the bank has to protect itself against the interest rate risk when it does that.

The bank has to buy a cap to protect itself against interest rates rising between the time the forward start is sold and the date that the option is fixed. The cap has a notional of $10 million. The bank prices the forward start as described above and obtains the cost per option. Then the bank adds the cost of a cap on $10 million and amortizes that cost over $5 million. Thus the contingent premium is sold for a little bit more than a normal forward start option. The extra price reflects the fact that the client has a choice. The client did not commit to buy $10 million. The client only promised to buy at least $5 million, and he has the option to buy as much as $10 million. Therefore, the contingent notional is more expensive.

Why doesn't the bank enter into a swap or an FRA? The FRA would include a free interest rate cap. However, when the bank enters into an FRA, it has to lock itself in for the entire $10 million amount. Now assume that interest rates have declined. The bank will owe on a $10 million FRA. If the client purchases $10 million of the structure, then the bank is hedged. On the other hand, if the client only purchases $5 million, the bank will lose on a $10 million FRA and will earn on a $5 million forward start. The bank will not be hedged.

SUMMARY

Forward start options are used in situations where it is impossible to determine the strike price in advance. In practice, they are most often used to create long-term option structures in the equity and interest-rate markets. In some cases, fixing the strike price in advance would cause the option to be very expensive. Letting the strike be determined by the level of the underlying may make for a cheaper option. Forward start options are the basic building block in rachet options (see Chapter 7).

Ratchet Options

INTRODUCTION

The *rachet option* has become quite popular with retail investors. These options were first developed in France on the CAC 40 equity index and were called *cliquet options*. The structure starts out as a normal call option, and then, on every fixing date, the owner gets the increase of the underlying. The underlying security of these options is typically an equity index.

APPLICATION

The ratchet option is extremely useful for fund managers (or retail investors) who wish to profit if the index keeps rising, but who do not want to lose if the index declines. Increases in the index from one fixing date to the next are locked in. In case of a drop in the equity markets, the investor does not lose the gains that have already been made.

EXAMPLE

The ratchet option has a set of fixing dates, set apart at equal intervals. Assume the fixing dates are three months apart.

The first fixing date is typically the settlement date. Suppose that on the settlement date the price of the underlying index is $100.

Three months later, on the second fixing date, the underlying climbs to $102. At that point, the investor locks in a gain of $2.

Three months after that, on the third fixing date, the index falls to $101. The investor does not lose when the index drops.

Three months pass by, and on the fourth fixing date the underlying is at $105. The investor locks in $4, which is the difference between $105, the current level of the index, and $101, the previous level.

On the final fixing date, the index is at $106. The investor will lock in another $1 and will be paid out $7, the sum of all the locked-in amounts: $2 + $4 + $1 = $7

A COLLECTION OF FORWARD START OPTIONS

It is clear that the ratchet can be considered to be a collection of forward start options. Consider the previous example, owning the ratchet is equivalent to owning the following portfolio of options:

- A three-month European option struck at $100
- A forward start option that begins in three months and expires in six, a 3 × 3 option
- A forward start option that begins in six months and expires in nine, a 6 × 3 option
- A forward start option that begins in nine months and expires in twelve, a 9 × 3 option

For the previous example:

The underlying starts at $100, and this is the strike of the first European option. Three months later, the European option expires and pays out $2.

At that precise moment, the 3 × 3 forward start option begins. Its strike is set to the at-the-money rate of $102.

Three months later, the underlying has dropped to $101. The forward start option, which was struck at $102, expires worthless. The 6 × 3 forward start begins, and its strike price is set to $101, the at-the-money rate.

At the nine-month point, the underlying has climbed to $105. The 6 × 3 option expires and pays out $4. The 9 × 3 option begins, and its strike is set to $105.

At the one-year point, the underlying is at $106. The 9 × 3 option expires and pays out $1.

From the above discussion it is clear that the collection of forward start options is equivalent to the ratchet except for one detail. Each forward start option pays out when it expires. The investor would receive $2 at the end of three months, $4 at the end of nine months, and $1 at the end of the year. The ratchet would pay out the entire sum of $7 at the end of the year.

To equate the ratchet with a series of forward starting options requires some time-value-of-money calculations.

ANOTHER VERSION

There is another version of the rachet. In this version, if the underlying falls down, it doesn't reset the strike. So in our previous example, as the underlying drops from $102 to $101 between the three- and six-month reset dates, the strike price is not reset downward. In this case, the strike stays at $102. So at the nine-month point, when the underlying is at $105, the option would only pay out $3. At the end of the year, the investor would receive a payout of $6.

BONUS COMPUTATION FOR PORTFOLIO MANAGERS

Many portfolio managers (PMs) receive their bonuses according to their quarterly performance. So if a PM does well the first quarter and doesn't do well the second quarter, the PM will still get an annual bonus based on the first quarter's performance. For example, a certain investment management group was known to lose during the first three quarters of the year. But during the last quarter, it would have a stellar performance and would outperform the market. This happened several years in a row, year after year. Thus despite their losses during the first three quarters, the PMs in this group would still receive a bonus, as their final bonus would be computed taking into account the last quarter's positive performance.

A similar thing often happens in school. A particular student does poorly the first semester and then performs well during the second semester. The teacher gives that student an award: "The most improved student." Make sure you distinguish between the "best student" and the "most improved one."

PRICING

Since the ratchet is a set of forward start calls, we already know how to price it. In the previous chapter we have shown how to price a single forward start call. To price the ratchet we sum the prices of the individual forward start options, making sure to adjust for the time value of money. As discussed above, the individual forward start options would each pay out when they expire, but the ratchet would save the payment until the end of the entire period.

RATCHET SWAPS

Ratchet swaps are interest rate swaps. In an interest rate swap one party pays fixed and the other pays floating. The ratchet swap guarantees that the floating rate can never go down. The floating rate can only be reset upward. Of course, the fixed rate paid on such a ratchet swap would be higher than that of a normal swap.

STICKY FLOATERS

Another example of a structured note is the *one-way collared note,* also called a *sticky floater.* This kind of note becomes popular with investors who are concerned with drops in interest rates. The sticky floater is a floating-rate note in which the investor obtains protection against declining rates in return for giving up rises in rates. One type of floating-rate note guarantees that coupon levels will not fall below the previous coupon. In return, the coupon level will not rise by more than 25 basis points above the previous coupon. For example, assume that on the first coupon determination date the Libor is at 5 percent. A particular note offers investors Libor plus 65.5 basis points. The first coupon is thus set at 5.655 percent.

In addition, the next coupon level is locked. It's guaranteed to be between 5.655 and 5.905 percent which is 5.655 percent plus 25 basis points.

What about the following coupon? If Libor drops to 4 percent, then the second coupon level should be set at Libor plus 65.5 basis points. But the investor is guaranteed that the coupon will stay above 5.655 percent. In this case, the third coupon will be set between 5.655 and 5.905 percent. The minimal coupon can be guaranteed in this fashion since the coupon also cannot rise by very much. If Libor really climbs up to 8 percent, the second coupon will still be set at 5.905 percent, which is the upper bound. The third coupon cannot be set above 5.905 percent plus 25 basis points, or 6.155 percent.

With this note, the investor is purchasing a normal floating rate note paying Libor plus 65.5 basis points. In addition the investor is also selling a portfolio of path-dependent forward start interest rate options and simultaneously buying a corresponding portfolio of path-dependent forward start interest rate options. On each coupon date, the investor becomes long an interest rate floor and simultaneously becomes short an interest rate cap. The strikes of the options are set on the coupon date for expiration on the next coupon date. For example, when the first coupon was set at 5.655 percent, the investor also becomes long an interest rate floor struck at 5.00 percent. The investor also becomes short an interest rate cap struck at 5.25 percent. If, on the next coupon date, interest rates were to fall to 4 percent, the normal floating rate note would pay 4 percent plus 65.5 basis points or 4.655 percent and the floor would pay 5 − 4 percent = 1 percent. Thus the coupon that will be received by the investor is 5.655 percent. On the other hand, if Libor rates were to climb to 7 percent, the floating rate note would pay 7.655 percent. However, the investor's short position in the interest rate cap would expire in the money and the investor would have to pay 7 − 5.25 percent = 1.75 percent. The investor's total coupon would be 7.655 percent − 1.75 percent = 5.905 percent.

Thus the coupon level is set to a floating rate subject to a minimal coupon and a maximal one. The coupon cannot fall below the previous level, nor can it rise above the previous coupon plus 25 basis points.

The sticky floater is, thus, an example of a floating rate note with an embedded interest rate floor coupled with an embedded cap.

In general, floating rate bonds that contain embedded floors are difficult to sell. The interest rate floors are quite expensive and their price must be accounted for somehow. Floating rate notes with embedded floors are typically issued interest rate with far away maturity dates and only when the yield curve is upward-sloping. This is illustrated in Figure 7.1.

Figure 7.1 depicts an upward-sloping yield curve with a fixed-strike interest rate floor. The floor is in the money over the short term and gradually becomes out of the money in the long term. In the short term the floor is expensive and it becomes cheaper over the long term. By amortizing the cost of all these floors, the notes have reasonable prices. There are times when the yield curve is not upward-sloping or perhaps the investor requires a shorter-term note.

The sticky floater incorporates embedded floors but has two mechanisms to reduce the price of these floors:

1. The floors are composed of forward starting options rather than fixed strike options.
2. The investor also has a short cap position.

The premium of the forward start options is cheaper than those of a fixed strike option. In addition, the short cap position helps pay for the premium of the floors.

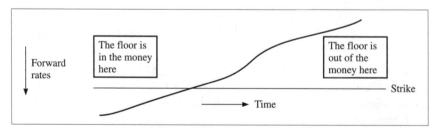

Figure 7.1   An upward-sloping yield curve with an interest rate floor.

This note is also interesting to study from a duration point of view. If interest rates decline, the note behaves like a fixed-rate bond. If interest rates rise rapidly, it again behaves like a fixed-rate bond with step-up coupons. This is because on each coupon payment date, coupon rates would rise by 25 basis points. Hence for interest rates which are either falling or rising rapidly, the note would have a high duration, similar to a fixed coupon bond. If, on the other hand, interest rates were to only fluctuate slightly and stay within a 25 basis point band, the note would mimic a floating-rate note with a low duration.

EQUITY-LINKED INDEX ANNUITIES

Insurance companies have been offering their retail clients *equity-linked index (ELI)* annuity products. These products have been marketed with a variety of features:

- Some products offer a straight-through participation in the rise of the index over the term of the ELI. These would be hedged with normal European options.
- Some products offer the maximal price the index has ever attained and thus contain an embedded lookback option.
- Yet other products have a reset feature that is then hedged with a ratchet option.

For example, Lincoln Benefit Life, a division of the Allstate insurance company, has marketed more than $500 million of a structure called the *savers annuity index*. It works like this:

Clients invest for seven years. Each year the clients receive an interest rate based on the increase of the S&P times a participation rate. For example, assume that the S&P increased in one year by 10 percent. If the participation rate is 0.80, then the clients would receive an interest rate of 8 percent on their money for that year. In these structures, the maximal interest rate is usually capped. So whatever the S&P does, the annuity won't pay more than a fixed rate for the year. In some structures, all payments are made at the maturity of the ELI. In others, interest is paid out yearly. After seven years the clients can withdraw or stay for another seven years. Should the clients need their money before the seven years are over, they can withdraw their funds, but they will have to pay an early-withdrawal surrender charge for that privilege.

The reset structure is sold to clients who believe that the market, in general, is going up. Still they want to be protected in case of a crash in the middle of the period. With this product, at least the clients will not be hurt that much. Every time the index goes up, the clients will receive a benefit based on that up move. But if there is a drop in the middle, the structure will cushion the fall.

SMALL DIFFICULTY IN HEDGING

There is a small difficulty in hedging if the starting value is not equal to 100. The insurance company pays the client an amount related to the relative appreciation of the index. The forward start option, on the other hand, pays the difference between the strike and the spot price of the underlying at expiration.

For example, assume that the underlying index is at $101 when the forward start option is set and is at $105 when it expires. The forward start option pays the difference, $105 − $101 = $4. So the insurance company has to pay the client ($105 − $101)/101 = $3.96 percent. To sum it up, the insurance company needs to pay the client 3.96 percent, and it receives 4 percent from its hedging instrument.

Now consider the situation where the underlying is at $70 when the forward start is set and at $120 when it expires. The forward start will pay $50 to the insurance company. On the other hand, the insurance company is obliged to give the client an interest rate of amount of ($120 − $70)/70 ≈ 71 percent which is about $71 assuming a notional of $100. In other words the amount that the insurance company has to pay is larger than what it receives— not exactly an ideal situation. This is one of the reasons that most structures include a cap on the maximal interest paid.

SHORTENING MATURITIES

The biggest difficulty with ELIs is the liquidity of the hedging equity options. Most derivative dealing firms would not offer liquidity in long-term equity options or else would sell them at very expensive rates. Liquidity is such a concern that most firms that sell these structures to the public have actually started to shorten the maturity profiles of the ELIs that are offered. For example, rather than seven-year ELIs, there are ELIs with maturity dates ranging from one to three years.

Most retail clients don't fully understand pricing, and so they just keep looking at the participation rates. From the point of view of the clients, a high participation rate means higher potential interest rates. Most retail clients don't realize that the price they are paying is quite prohibitive. Since the hedging equity option is so expensive, the insurance companies only offer the ELI structures to the retail clients with a participation rate less than 1. The longer the term of the indexed product, the higher the participation rate that can be offered. The price of the hedging option must be paid for by the issuing insurance company. The insurance company amortizes the premium for the hedge over the life of the ELI structure. The premium for the options is paid for by the difference between the market interest rates and the minimal guaranteed rates. For example, if rates are at 7 percent and the minimal guaranteed rate is 3 percent, then the insurance company has 4 percent per annum for the duration of the ELI to use as premium for the equity options. If the structure will exist for a long time, then the insurance company can give the clients a reasonable participation rate. From the clients' point of view, the price that is amortized over a long time looks like a nice participation rate that is slightly lower than 1 (e.g., 80 percent in the case of the seven-year structure discussed above). The long-term structures don't look that bad from the clients' point of view, and the clients need not be made aware of the high cost of hedging. On the other hand, short-term structures are amortized over a shorter time period. The participation rate becomes smaller and the structure becomes harder and harder to sell. In short-term structures, the participation rates are lower than in long-term structures. So clients would prefer to buy long-term ELIs from the insurance companies. On the other hand banks are reluctant to sell long-term hedging instruments.

HEDGING WITH SHORT-TERM OPTIONS

Another solution to the lack of liquidity in long-term equity options was attempted by several insurance companies. Even though they sold long-term ELI products, they tried to hedge them by buying short-term options and then rerolling the hedge. That is, an insurance company would purchase a one-year at-the-money call option. Then, a year later, it would roll the hedge over and purchase another one-year at-the-money call option. So long as volatility does not increase, this is not an unreasonable hedging strategy. Safeco Corporation, based in Seattle, Washington, was, until the beginning of 1999, a major issuer of equity-linked index annuities. However, in January 1999, Safeco announced that its earnings were negatively affected by the equity-linked annuity business and that it was discontinuing the product. Because Safeco was buying one-year options as a hedge on the long-term product, it was badly hurt by the rising prices of call options.

In 1998, stock market volatility increased substantially, and, at the same time, there was a drop in interest rates. Both of these occurrences had a negative impact on the attractiveness of the product. With high volatility the options became very expensive. Low interest rates compounded the problem since insurance companies take the present value of the difference between the current interest rates and the minimal return guarantee (say 3 percent) and use it to buy options. In a situation where interest rates drop from 7 to 5 percent and the minimal guarantee stays at 3 percent, participation rates come down. Indeed, in 1998, participation rates fell to around 50 percent for nine-year structures. In order to be able to sell reasonable-looking ELI structures to clients, companies have started to use "back ending." At the final year, the participation rate of the client will be determined by the *average* level of the index. The insurance company could use Asian options to hedge the last part of the structure. The Asian option effectively dampens the volatility of the returns, for both the client and the insurance company. Oddly enough, many clients perceive the Asian as a welcome feature. They are concerned with the possibility that the market might climb for a long time and then have a correction toward the end of the nine-year ELI. If the market falls at the very end of the ninth year, the returns would be disappointing. Since the Asian is cheaper, a higher participation rate may be offered. Other strategies are also available—for example, offering a 100 percent guarantee on only 90 percent of the capital invested.

However, the insurance companies are careful not to offer too many features in the product. For one thing, retail clients may find it confusing. Another reason is that the Securities and Exchange Commission, the SEC, may insist on registering the ELI structures as investment products if it is determined that the client takes on too much market risk.

THE MARKET

Here are the top ten U.S. equity-linked index annuity vendors as of the first three quarters of 1998. Numbers are in millions of U.S. dollars. The figures represent the amounts of equity index annuity sales.

1. American Life and Casualty, $589.0
2. Safeco (estimated), $484.0
3. Jackson National, $367.9
4. LifeUSA, $221.3
5. Keyport, $207.8
6. National Western, $175.4
7. Lincoln Benefit, $134.7
8. Life of the Southwest (LSW), $133.7
9. Name withheld, $113.3
10. American Equity, $104.7

Source: *Risk Magazine*, March 1999.

INTEREST RATE EXPOSURE

The insurance company, which issues the ELI, is also exposed to interest rates. Assume that the surrender charge is 5 percent. Subsequently, interest rates have climbed to 10 percent. Clients may be tempted to cash out and reinvest elsewhere at high interest rates. Some insurance companies hedge the interest rate risk by buying interest rate caps or swaptions.

LONG TERM VERSUS SHORT TERM

To summarize, several effects are involved in creating the ELI structure:

- Increasing the maturity of the ELI makes more funds available for hedging. The guaranteed interest rate is below market rate. The difference between the guaranteed rate and the market rate is used to purchase options. Longer-term ELI structures would generate more available premiums. With more available premiums, the insurance company could purchase more equity options and increase the participation rate.
- On the other hand, the cost of long-term options may be prohibitively expensive. In addition, the insurance company will have to hedge its interest rate exposure, which also adds to the cost. These factors will drive the maturity down.

INVESTOR'S PERSPECTIVE

Obviously, the guaranteed equity-linked annuity product is attractive to retail clients. They receive a guarantee on their capital coupled with a minimal interest rate. In addition, they participate in the rise of the equity markets.

OTHER ACRONYMS

Similar structures have also been called multi-period strike reset options (MSRO). Other firms offer stock market annual reset term (SMART).

SUMMARY

The ratchet option is used to hedge resetting ELI annuities, which have been marketed aggressively to retail clients. They have also been used to create ratchet floaters and other long-term instuments.

CHAPTER 8

Chooser Options

INTRODUCTION

Chooser options are options in which the investor gets to choose between a call and a put at a later date. In essence, the investor receives a certificate. On the *choice date* the investor turns in the certificate and receives a put or a call, whichever the investor chooses. The strike prices and expiration dates of the call and the put are prespecified in advance. If the strike price and expiration date of the call are equal to those of the put, the instrument is a *simple chooser.* If the strike prices or expiration dates are not the same, it is a *complex chooser.*

EXAMPLE

Figure 8.1 is an illustration of a chooser. An investor purchases the option on February 11, 1999. The choice date is July 15, 1999. This means that on July 15, 1999, the investor will be obliged to choose between a put and a call.

The call and the put have a strike of $100 and an expiration date of December 15, 1999. We assume that the trade date is labeled 0, the choice date is labeled $T1$, and the expiration date is labeled $T2$. For example:

February 11, 1999: Purchase the chooser, time 0.

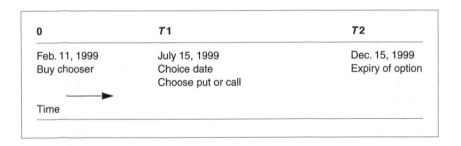

Figure 8.1   A chooser option.

July 15, 1999: Choose between a $100 call and a $100 put,
time $T1$.

December 15, 1999: The options expire, and the investor
will get paid if the option is in the money, time $T2$.

0	$T1$	$T2$
Feb. 11, 1999	July 15, 1999	Dec. 15, 1999
Buy chooser	Choice date	Expiry of option
	Choose put or call	
Time		

The call and the put have identical expiration dates and
identical strikes.

INVESTOR'S STRATEGY

The strategy of the investor on the choice date is quite clear. On July 15, 1999, the investor will compare the price of a $100 call option with the price of a $100 put. The investor will redeem the chooser certificate for the option with the highest price. In general the investor will proceed as follows:

- If the underlying is high, the investor will choose the call.
- If the underlying is low, the investor will choose the put.

APPLICATION: CHOOSER VS. STRADDLE

Consider the following situation: Boeing might get a contract from United Airlines to supply a huge number of Boeing 767s. If it does, the stock price will go up. If it doesn't receive the contract, the stock price will go down. As soon as the contract is decided, the stock price of Boeing will move in the anticipated direction.

In the following case, which would be better, a chooser or a straddle? Most investors would buy a straddle. They would buy a put and a call. If Boeing stock moves either way, they are going to make money. If Boeing stock stays the same and does not move at all, the investors would lose. Figure 8.2 shows an at the money straddle.

You're long a call and long a put, and you have a straddle. The straddle is very nice but it is expensive because you have to pay two option premiums, one for the call and one for the put. So in this case the straddle will cost $10.68. The $10.68 is the sum of the price of a call, which in this case is $6.12 and the put price, which is $4.56. This is very expensive because you have to pay for both options. Also, two options means you suffer from time premium twice. That is to say, every day that passes, you lose time premium for the call and also time premium for the put. The reason a straddle is so expensive is because the investors are going to get paid either way. Wherever the underlying is, they will get paid. The only way that the investors will receive nothing is if the underlying closes exactly at $100. Note that the straddle costs $10.68, in comparison with the chooser which costs $9.15.

As soon as the United Airlines purchase decision date arrives, the investors know whether they want a put or a call. So

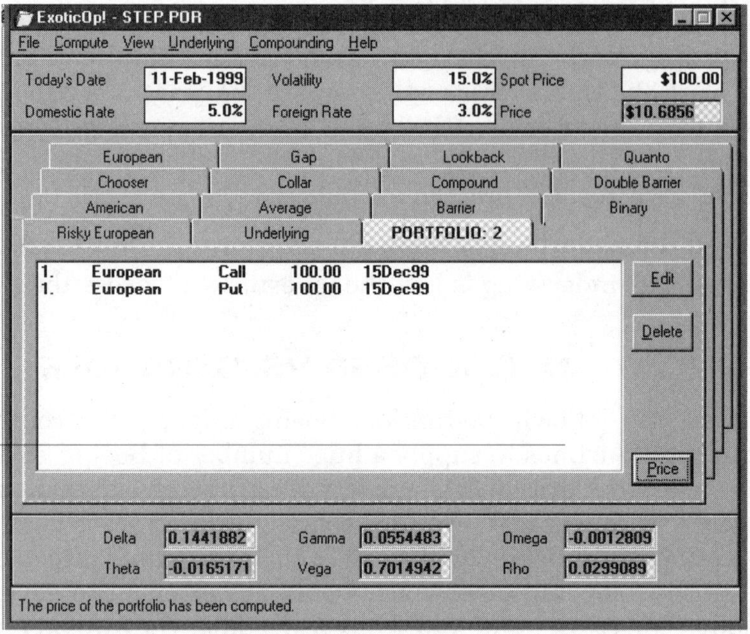

Figure 8.2   An at the money straddle.

why do they have to wait until the end? Instead of purchasing a
straddle, the clients purchase a chooser and receive a blank piece
of paper. On July 15, 1999, they will have to choose if they want a
put or a call. The chooser costs $9.15. That is better than paying
$10.68. The chooser is cheaper than the straddle. So on July 15
the clients have to trade their piece of paper for a $100 put or a
$100 call. It is their choice.

Note that the client is also taking a risk with the chooser.
The client made a choice on the choice date, but it could be the
wrong choice. For example, on the choice date the underlying was
high, and so the investor chose a call option. Then, the underlying
went down and ended at $90, and so the call expired out of the
money. The client received nothing at expiration. With a straddle
the client is guaranteed to receive some payout—either the payout of the put or the payout of the call. With the chooser there is
no guarantee. Just because there is a choice does not mean that
life will turn out as expected.

Of course the more you wait the less chance of a decline. If the choice date is one day before expiration and the underlying is at 120, it will probably stay around $120 and will probably stay in the money.

EXTREME VALUES

Assume you are the client. Which one do you want, the put or the call? If the underlying is expensive, you will choose the call. If the underlying is cheap, you will choose the put. And you will choose between them on the choice date.

Suppose the choice date is today. Obviously you want the more expensive option. How much can the dealer charge you for the chooser? The dealer can charge you, at maximum, whichever is more, the put or the call. The call costs $6.12 and the put costs $4.56. Thus the dealer can charge you no more than $6.12.

Assume that the choice date is at expiration. Then the chooser is exactly equivalent to a straddle. With the straddle, one option is in the money. If you own a $100 straddle, either the price is below $100, in which case you will choose the put, or the price is above $100, in which case you will choose the call. So if the choice date is equal to the expiration date, the price of the chooser is exactly equal to the price of the straddle, which is the sum of the call and the put. The later the choice date, the higher the price of the chooser. The more you wait, the more information you have. If your choice date was July 15, 1999, would you ever choose early? No, you would wait until the last possible date to make your choice because then you would have more information.

On July 15, 1999, the price of the underlying was high so you chose a call. But the price can go down, and the call can expire out of the money. For example, on July 15, 1999, the underlying was at $120 and you chose a call. Then the underlying declined and on December 15, 1999, it ended at $75. Of course it is not guaranteed that the price will go up. In this case, the chooser expired out of the money. The chooser can be cheaper than the straddle because its price goes up as you move the choice date into the future. We understand two things. If you choose today the dealer can charge you the maximum between a put and a call. If you choose on the expiration date the dealer can charge you the put plus the call.

EFFECT OF THE CHOICE DATE
ON THE PRICE OF THE CHOOSER

Consider a six-month chooser. Assume that the stock price is at $40; the strike is at $40; and there is 20 percent volatility, a 6 percent risk-free rate, and a 2 percent dividend rate. Figure 8.3 shows the price of the chooser as we vary the choice date.

The left end of the graph in Figure 8.3 shows the price of the chooser when you choose today. It is the maximum of the put and the call, or $2.62. The right end illustrates what happens when you choose at the end. The price is the sum of the put and the call, or $4.46. The graph is concave, that is to say that if the choice date is three months, you have to pay more than the average of $2.62 and $4.46.

In Figure 8.4 the parameters stay the same except the stock price changes to $45. So you get to choose between a call at $40 and a put at $40. Note that the entire shape of the graph changes when the stock price changes. The graph is now a convex graph.

How can we explain the different shapes of the two graphs? If the underlying is at $40 and the strike price is $40, as in Figure 8.3, both options are currently at the money. The dealer faces a lot of uncertainty about which of the call, or the put the client will

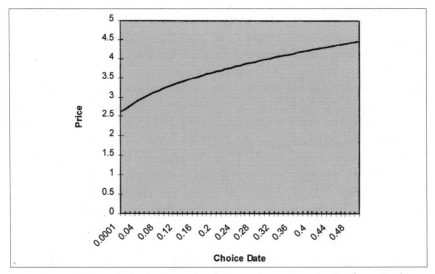

Figure 8.3   Effect of choice date on the price of the chooser, $S = \$40, X = \$40$.

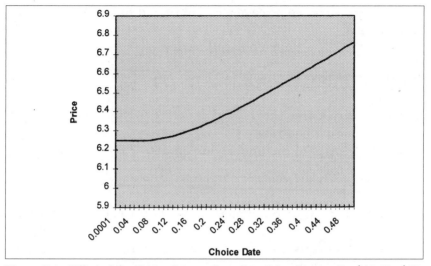

Figure 8.4   Effect of the choice date on the price of the chooser, S = \$40, X = \$45.

choose. So even if the choice date is very soon, e.g., within a few days, the dealer has to hedge himself. On the other hand, assume that the stock price is \$40 and the strike is at \$45, as in Figure 8.4. The put option is \$5 in the money, and the call is \$5 out of the money. The dealer is pretty much guaranteed that the client will choose a put option. So the dealer does not face any uncertainty.

Only if the dealer allows the client to wait a long time before choosing will there be a possibility that the client will choose a call.

PRICING VIA A FORMULA

There are two methods to price the chooser. The first method relies on some sort of put-call parity. The chooser is equivalent to being long a call option and long a put with a special spot and strike price. That put will allow you to trade the \$100 call option with a \$100 put option using the put-call parity.

We label today as 0, the choice date as $T1$, and the expiration date as $T2$.

At time $T1$, the price of the chooser is

$$\max[C1(S, X), P1(S, X)]$$

where $C1(S, X)$ is the price of a call option at date $T1$ with spot S and strike X.

At time $T1$, we have put-call parity

$$P1(S1,X) = C1(S1, X) - S1 \exp[-d(T2 - T1)] + X \exp[-r(T2 - T1)]$$

where r = risk-free rate
          d = dividend rate
          $S1$ = price of the underlying on date $T1$

At time $T1$, the chooser can be written as

$$\max\{C1(S1, X), C1 - S1 \exp[-d(T2 - T1) + X \exp[-r(T2 - T1)]\}$$

This is true for any value of $S1$. In particular, if we substitute S instead of $S1$, we will have the value of the chooser

$$C1 + \max\{0, X \exp[-r(T2 - T1)] - S \exp[-d(T2 - T1)]\}$$

So a chooser is equivalent to:

- Long a call with a spot price of S, a strike price of X, and time to expiration $T2$.

- Long a put with underlying spot price of $S \exp[-d(T2 - T1)]$, a strike of $X \exp[-r(T2 - T1)]$, and a time to expiration of $T2$.

PRICING VIA QUADRATURE

Another way to price the put is to use a numerical integration or quadrature. The price of any financial instrument is the present value of the expected value of the cash flow. Assume that you knew that on the choice date the underlying is at 110. In this case, you could evaluate the price of the call and the price of the put. If the underlying is at 110, then you know how to price a 100 call option and a 100 put option, and you know how to take the maximum. The maximum will be the call. The idea here is that for every underlying level on the choice date that you can price a call, you can price a put, and you can take the maximum and choose which one you want. So given a particular level of the underlying on the choice date, you know the value of the chooser on that choice date.

In fact, you don't know the level of underlying on the choice date, as it is in the future. But you do know the volatility, and so you can put a probability distribution on the level of the underlying on the date. There is a certain probability for it to be $110, and you know the maximum of a put struck at $100 and a call struck at $100, and you know how to price it by taking the maximal value. You know the probability distribution of the underlying on the choice date for each of those underlying levels.

Since you know the distribution of the underlying at the choice date, and for each level of underlying you can price the chooser, you have the expected value for the chooser as of the choice date. All you have to do is simply discount that price to today.

COMPLEX CHOOSER

There is no law that says that the strike of the call and the put in the chooser have to be the same. In this case, the chooser is a complex chooser. The regular chooser was $9.15 and allowed you to choose between a call struck at $100 and a put struck at $100.

If you can choose between a $95 put and a $105 call, it will be cheaper, because both the call and the put are out of the money. Now you are doing the chooser on a strangle, not on a straddle. This is a way to make your chooser cheaper. This chooser is illustrated in Figure 8.5.

VOLATILITY

To price the chooser, we will use the forward-forward volatility. This will be discussed in a later chapter on compound options.

HEDGING

The dealer can hedge the chooser with a position in a $100 call and a position in a $100 put. If, according to the numerical integration, there is a 52 percent probability that the investor will

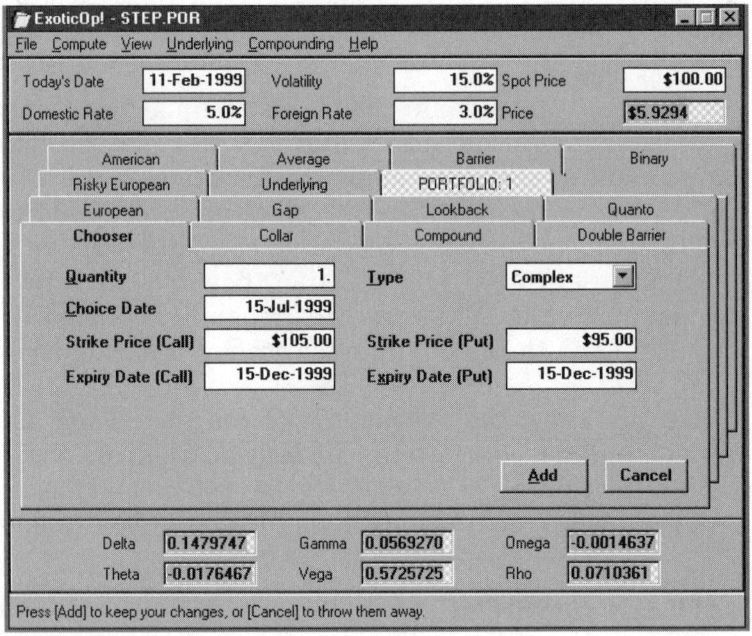

Figure 8.5   A complex chooser.

choose a call and a 48 percent probability that she will choose a put, the dealer can hold a position of 52 percent calls and 48 percent puts. As the underlying moves up and down, these distributions change, and the dealer will have to modify his position accordingly. As the choice date approaches, the investor's choice becomes clearer and clearer. The dealer's position will come to resemble a 100 percent call and 0 percent put. Thus, the dealer will be perfectly hedged.

THE GAMMA OF A CHOOSER

The gamma of a chooser option is greater than that of a straddle, especially if the choice date is soon. For example, the gamma of the straddle in Figure 8.2 is approximately 0.05. In Figure 8.6 we examine a similar chooser with a choice date in one week. Its gamma is approximately 0.16. The higher gamma is due to the fact that in one week the chooser will turn into either a call with

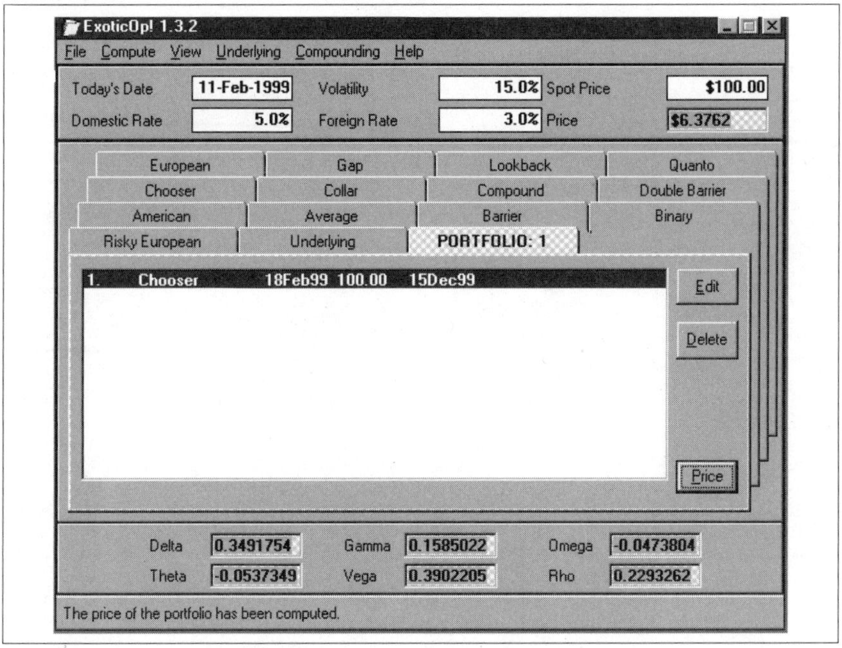

Figure 8.6   A chooser option with a choice date in one week.

a delta of about 0.5 or a put with a delta of about −0.5. The straddle will also become a call or a put, but that will happen only on December 15, 1999.

SUMMARY

The chooser option can be considered as an alternative to a straddle or a strangle strategy. It is useful when there is some "event" after which you will know, with high probability, the direction of the underlying.

We have seen two pricing methods. The simple pricing method can be used on the regular chooser. You can use a put-call parity and price the chooser as a combination of a call plus a special put. Alternatively, you can use the numerical integration (quadrature) method that works in every case, whether it is European or American, or whether or not they are the same strikes or expiration dates.

CHAPTER 9

Shout Options

INTRODUCTION

The shout option got its name because the client has to actually call the dealer and trigger the option. The act of triggering the option is called *shouting*.

An example illustrates the process. Assume the underlying starts with a price of $100. Then the price of the underlying moves up and down, this way and that. One moment, when the underlying is priced at $105, the client calls the dealer and "shouts." By shouting, the client locks in $5, which is the difference between $105 (the current spot price) and $100 (the original strike). On expiration, the client will receive at least $5 but may receive more.

What happens at expiration? Let us consider two scenarios.

1. On expiration the price of the underlying is at $104. In this case, the client will receive $5 on expiration. This is because the client has already locked in $5 on the shout date.

2. On expiration the spot price of the underlying is $108. In this case, the client will actually receive $8 on expiration.

To summarize, as soon as the client shouts, she receives a guaranteed $5 on expiration, plus she gets a call option struck at $105.

MOTIVATION

What is the motivation behind this type of structure? Everyone would like a lookback option. This is obvious. Who wouldn't want the right to sell at the maximum? But the lookback option is quite expensive. The shout option imposes on the holder of the option the responsibility of locking in. If the holder of a shout option actually shouts when the underlying is at its maximum level, then the shout option becomes equivalent to the lookback. On the other hand, if the holder shouts at a time when the underlying is not at its maximal price, then the shout option will probably pay less than the lookback. The shout is a very ego-building option. It is sold to a client who thinks that she can determine when the underlying has reached its maximal level. "I know a top when I see one." The dealer sells this option by telling the client, "You are such a good reader of the market. You know how to recognize the high. So when you think the market's reached its peak, just call us and we will lock your profits."

Assume that the highest price the underlying has reached is indeed $105. At that precise moment the client shouted. With the shout option, the client would receive $5 at expiration, which is the same as she would have received with a lookback paying max $(M - X, 0)$, where M is the maximal price of the underlying and X, the strike, is $100.

On the other hand, assume that the underlying actually reached $120 sometime during the life of the option and then ended lower. The shout option will pay either $5 or $8 (as in cases 1 and 2 above), while the lookback will actually pay $20.

Thus the maximal price is determined automatically in the lookback option, whereas the shout option places the onus of determining the maximal price on the holder. Because of this, the shout option is cheaper.

The shout option allows the client a single opportunity to shout. Once the client shouts, she is not allowed to shout again. We can write the payout formula as

$$\max[S(T) - X, S(H) - X]$$

Here $S(T)$ is the price of the underlying on expiration, $S(H)$ is the price of the underlying at the moment the investor shouted, and X is the original strike.

ACTIVE AND PASSIVE STRUCTURES

In exotic options, it is possible to make a distinction between active structures and passive structures—structures in which the client has to do something versus structures in which things just happen. The shout option is an active structure since the client has to shout. As such, it is suitable for a market professional who sits in front of a live quote screen and watches the market all day. The shout option is not suitable for a retail investor who goes on a cruise for several weeks and is out of touch with the market.

PRICING AND HEDGING OF THE SHOUT

How does one price the shout option? As soon as the client shouts (at $105 say), the shout becomes equivalent to a portfolio consisting of both:

1. A cash payment of $5 to be paid at expiration
2. A call option struck at $105

So upon shouting, the value of the shout is the present value of $5 plus the price of an at-the-money call option, struck at $105. After shouting, the price of the shout is still the same: the present value of $5 plus the price of a $105 call option. So once the investor shouts, it's a no-brainer to price it because we know how to take $5 at expiry and calculate the present value of it for today. We also know the price of a call option struck at $105. We therefore know how to price the shout option. We can also hedge it. The dealer has to bring the client $5 at expiry and also replicate a call option struck at $105. So after shouting, pricing and hedging are trivial.

The difficulty is how to price the shout option before the investor shouts. The investor has some choice here. In this respect, the shout option is very similar to an American option. With an American option, the holder has an option of early exercise; and with a shout option, the holder has the option to lock in a profit. Once the holder exercises the American option, he immediately gets $5. With a shout option, the holder receives $5 at expiration, plus a call option struck at $105. It stands to reason that we should be able to use some American option pricing techniques to price this option.

We will use American option pricing techniques to answer the following three questions:

1. How do you price the shout option before the investor shouts?
2. When should the investor shout?
3. How should the dealer hedge the option before shouting?

THE SHOUT AND OTHER OPTIONS

The shout option has to be cheaper than a lookback option. The reason is that the most an investor can hope to do with a shout is to capture the maximum. The investor can't do any better but can perhaps do worse. So the shout option cannot be more expensive than a lookback.

The shout option is more expensive than any one-rung ladder. The one-rung ladder will automatically be triggered should the underlying hit the level of the rung. The holder of the shout can leave instructions to automatically shout if and when the underlying reaches that level. That is, the investor can leave instructions with the bank to shout automatically at $105 or $108 or whichever other level he chooses to.

The shout is more expensive than any one-date ratchet. This is true because the holder of the shout can leave instructions with the bank to shout at a specific day, e.g., June 26, regardless of the price of the underlying security. A one-date ratchet option with a ratchet date of June 26 will have exactly the same payout as the shout option in which the client shouted on the same date. For example, assume that the price of the underlying security is at $105 on June 26. Both the ratchet and the shout would lock in $5 to pay at expiration and whatever upside there is above $105. Since the shout option allows you to choose the moment at which you shout, and the one-date ratchet fixes that date in advance, the shout option must be at least as expensive as any one-date ratchet.

One can price all one-rung ladders and all one-date ratchets. The price of the shout option must be greater than all these ladder and ratchet options.

WHEN SHOULD THE INVESTOR SHOUT?

Many investors shout emotionally. They shout when they think they see a high; therefore, the bank makes extra money. The "correct" method of determining when to shout is analogous to the method of determining when to exercise an American option. Most investors have become adequately familiar with American options. They recognize when they should exercise and when they should not. For example, American call options are only candidates for early exercise just prior to the payout of a dividend. If there are no dividends, American call options are not to be exercised early.

At this point in time, investors are quite aware of the rules regarding rational early exercise of American options. The situation is quite different with shout options. Holders of shout options might not be aware of when to shout since they are not aware of the rational rules for shouting. Many investors just shout when they think the underlying security is at a high price point. Of course, that might not be the right thing to do.

American options are typically analyzed using trees. Consider a binomial tree for pricing an American option. One would build a tree of underlying security prices. The tree is built forward in time all the way to expiration. Then, we price the option beginning on the expiration date and going backward in time. We know how to fill the final level of the tree. It is simply the intrinsic value of the option. Then, we fill the one before the last level. Each node is the present value of the weighted average of the nodes in the next level. For example, let p be the probability that the price of the underlying will go up and A be the price of the option in the next period under the assumption that the underlying price moved up. We will label the price of the option B under the assumption that the price of the underlying has moved down. In a binomial tree, the probability of that event is given by $1 - p$. Then, the price of a European option at our current node is given by

$$\exp(-r * dt) * [p * A + (1 - p) * B]$$

Here r is the risk-free rate and dt is the time period between successive leaves in the tree. The term $\exp(-r * dt)$ is thus a present value operator.

If this were an American call option, we would change the calculation at each node to

$$\max\{S - X, \exp(-r * dt) * [p * A + (1 - p) * B]\}$$

This means that the holder of the American option may choose to receive its intrinsic value at any time by exercising early.

A tree to analyze a shout option utilizes very similar logic. The only difference is that we like to do all of our analysis in terms of expiration-date dollars.

At each node, the holder may choose to shout. If the holder shouts, he will receive an amount of $S - X$ at expiration. He will also receive any appreciation of the underlying above its current price. This is equivalent to receiving an at-the-money European call option. We are interested in the value of that option at expiration. This is called FV of ATM. The future value of an at-the-money option can be computed by taking the Black-Scholes price of the option and performing a future value computation on it.

$$\exp\{r * [T - t(k)]\} * \text{BS}$$

Here T is the expiration date and $t(k)$ is the current date. Thus $[T - t(k)]$ is the time left from the current node until expiration. The term BS is used to denote the Black-Scholes price of an at-the-money European call option beginning at the present date, $t(k)$, and expiring on the original expiration date, T.

In the tree to analyze the shout option, the calculation at each node is

$$\max\{((S - X) + \text{FV of ATM}), [p * A + (1 - p) * B]\}$$

In a typical note if the holder does not shout, then the expected value of his option is

$$[p * A + (1 - p) * B]$$

If the holder does shout, then he receives the locked-in cash value at expiration plus any appreciation of the underlying security beyond its current price. This is the expected future value of an at-the-money European call option. The cash value to be received is $S - X$, and the expected future value of an at-the-money European option is denoted by FV of ATM. So when the holder shouts, he receives

$$(S - X) + \text{FV of ATM}$$

At each point, the holder of the option will try to maximize its value, and so the computation becomes

$$\max\{((S - X) + \text{FV of ATM}), [p * A + (1 - p) * B]\}$$

We keep repeating this computation and fill the tree backward in time. At the initial node, we get the value of a shout option. This is the expected payout of the shout option at expiration.

To find the price of the shout option at the present date, we just calculate the present value of the expected payout to today. This is done by multiplying the final result by

$$\exp\{-r * [T - t(0)]\}$$

where $t(0)$ is today's date.

The rational shout decision will be made according to this tree. One should shout only at points where the tree indicates that this is the appropriate choice of action.

Note that the fixing is done on a certain date; that is, the shout is performed on a certain date. The dealer pays at expiration so the currency is very important. The interest rate of that currency will be the one used to discount the expected value of the payout back to the settlement date.

DELTA OF A SHOUT

The delta of a shout option is higher than that of its European counterpart. If the underlying goes up by a dollar before the shout, then the expected amount to be locked in is higher. The locked-in amount increases. A similar increase does not occur with a European option. Assume that the underlying is at $104. If the holder of the option were to shout, $4 would have to be locked in. If the underlying climbs to $105 before the holder shouts, the dealer may have to lock in $5. In both cases, the client will still receive an at-the-money option. Therefore, the delta of a shout is higher than that of a European. Of course, after the shout occurs, the holder has a European option with a delta to match.

REPLICATION

We now consider the replication of a shout option.

Step 1. On the settlement date, the dealer just buys a regular European call option struck at the money (e.g., at $100).

Step 2. Let's suppose that on a particular day, the underlying goes to $105 and the investor shouts. In response, the dealer:

- Sells short the underlying at $105.
- Buys an at-the-money call, that is, a call struck at $105.
- Sells a put struck at $100.

To see whether this works, we examine three cases:

1. On the expiration date, the underlying is at $108. The shout option has to pay out $8.

   The dealer exercises the original call struck at $100 to receive $8.

   The dealer loses $3 because of the short underlying position undertaken when the underlying was at $105. But the dealer also recovers the $3 because of the call option that was purchased at $105. The final put option, struck at $100, expires worthless. Hence the dealer ends up with $8, exactly what is required to pay the holder of the shout.

2. On expiration date, the underlying is at $102. The shout option has to pay out $5

   The dealer exercises the original call struck at $100 to receive $2.

   The dealer makes $3 because of the short underlying position undertaken when the underlying was at $105. The call option, which was struck at $105, expires worthless. The final put option, struck at $100, also expires worthless. The dealer ends up with $5, which covers the payout of the shout option.

3. On expiration date, the underlying is at $98. The shout option has to pay out $5.

The original call, struck at $100, expires worthless. The dealer makes $7 because of the short underlying position undertaken when the underlying was at $105. The call option, which was struck at $105, expires worthless. The dealer has to pay out an additional $2 to satisfy the final put option, which was struck at $100. The dealer ends up with $5, which covers the payout of the shout option.

It is clear that the dealer does not need to sell the $100 put on the shout date. In that case, the dealer will forgo the premium of the put option but may be overhedged. The dealer will, in fact, receive more than is required if the underlying ends below $100 (as in case 3).

To summarize, the replication involves two stages. The first stage is undertaken the moment the client buys the shout option. The second stage occurs when the client shouts. Once the client shouts, the dealer is hedged until the expiration date.

LIMITED-PAYOUT CAP

The traditional shout option allows its holder one opportunity to shout. The holder has only one choice. An example of a structure that has many choices is the *limited-payout cap.*

Let us revisit an example from Chapter 1. Consider a plain vanilla interest rate cap. The duration of the cap is five years, its strike is 6 percent, and it has quarterly fixing. Thus the cap is composed of 20 caplets. Such interest rate caps have become widespread. In the United States, the price competition is so severe that deals are won or lost on the basis of 0.1 basis points. In London, the price competition is within 0.25 basis points. The marketplace for standard interest rate caps is very competitive because many banks can sell them. Since these are standard structures, clients can shop around for the best prices.

A limited-payout cap is a similar product. Its strike is also 6 percent, its maturity is five years, and it also has quarterly fixing. It differs from a standard cap in that it has only ten caplets. On each fixing date, the holder of the caplet may decide that she requires interest rate protection and use up one of the caplets.

Suppose a salesperson approaches his client, say the CFO of a company, to make a case for buying limited-payout caps. He reminds his client that five years ago, she purchased a standard interest rate cap. During the last five years there were many quarters in which interest rates were quite low and the cap was out of the money. For example, if the cap has a strike of 6 percent and interest rates are now at 3 percent, then this caplet is out of the money. Since there were long stretches of time, quarter after quarter, in which the cap wasn't even utilized, the limited-payout cap, with ten caplets, would be a cheaper way for the CFO to go.

It would work like this. Every three months the CFO calls the dealer and tells him whether she wants to utilize one of the caplets. Even if interest rates are higher than 6 percent, it is not clear that the CFO should exercise one of the caplets. The CFO may be better off to wait and use it in the future when interest rates will become much higher. Obviously, should the CFO use one of the caplets and collect a payout, she will have one less caplet for the future. The limited-payout cap is like a half-full shotgun. You have to choose when you shoot very carefully since you have a limited supply of bullets.

Note that there are other variations of this structure. In one variation, the client is obliged to choose where to place the ten caplets at the very beginning of the trade. On the settlement date the client will specify that the caps are to be placed in quarters 1, 2, 5, 8, etc. This is a much simpler variation. The recommended strategy for the client is to examine the price of each caplet and find the ten most expensive ones. In general, the most expensive caplets are the ones placed toward the end of the five years when the uncertainty is highest.

Another variation is the automatic exercise cap, in which the first ten caplets that are in the money are automatically exercised. This type of cap presents no choice to the client.

In the limited-payout cap discussed above, the client (the CFO) does not have to choose the timing of the caplets in advance. Rather, the client gets to decide every three months whether she needs protection or not.

Let's look at the limited-payout cap from the point of view of the CFO who is being offered this type of deal. First, the structure is priced at a discount of about 15 percent to a normal cap. But, still, the client is hesitant.

The client can easily determine the market price of a normal cap. The client can check with six banks. All would quote prices that are within 0.1 basis point of each other. The client can be quite sure that this is a reasonable price for the vanilla cap. However, for the limited-payout cap, the client likes the 15 percent discount, but no other dealer can verify the price of this highly esoteric structure. Nor does the client have any idea how to price it herself. The client cannot verify whether 15 percent is a reasonable discount; maybe it should be 20 or 25 percent. The client doesn't know whether the dealer is charging other clients a similar price. Perhaps the other client paid much less.

It is this lack of competition that's the source of interest in exotic options to the dealer. The very first dealer to develop a certain ability and offer this structure to clients can determine the size of the discount almost single-handedly. That dealer can determine the 15 percent discount, and his clients have no other choice. However, this situation will change very rapidly as other dealers quickly catch up and begin to offer that same structure at competitive prices.

The limited-payout cap is related to the shout option in that the client has opportunities to make a decision. As with a shout option, a tree can be used to price the limited payout cap.

For a normal shout option, at each node in the tree there is an "if" statement that represents the client's choice of whether to shout or not. However, suppose the client has two opportunities to shout. One is to utilize two trees, a tree on top of a tree. The bottom tree represents the case in which the client has one shout opportunity left. And the top tree represents the case in which the client has two shouting opportunities. Another strategy is to use a single tree with a state variable. The state variable can be divided into three states: The client has two shout decisions left, the client has only one shout decision left, and the client has no shout decisions left.

A structure in which the client has ten opportunities can be thought of as a tree on top of a tree on top of a tree—or, alternatively, a tree with a state variable with eleven possible states. When pricing options on interest rates, the effects of correlation between the different points on the curve must be carefully considered.

SUMMARY

The shout option and its variations are a form of a cheap look-back option. The lookback automatically chooses the "best" decision the client could have made. In the shout option, the onus is placed on the client to make the decision. Similar to American options, shout options are often priced using a tree. The shout is an "active" option, not generally suited to the retail market.

CHAPTER 10

Compound Options

INTRODUCTION

The compound option has been sold very successfully, even to retail clients. It is basically an option whose underlying is itself an option. Sometimes the compound is called *an option on an option.*

EXAMPLE

Assume that on March 23, 2000, a client wants to buy one at-the-money call option to the end of the year. The call has a strike of $100 and an expiration date of December 31, 2000. The price of this call option is $11.31 (see Figure 10.1).

Now consider the following problem. On June 15, 2000, the client would like the right to buy that same call option for $5. The client has to pay something today for the right to pay $5 on June 15, 2000, and receive a $100 call option to expire on December 31, 2000 (see Figure 10.2).

Basically, today the client is buying a call struck at $5 with an expiration of June 15, 2000. However, the underlying security of this call option is not a stock, or an index, or a currency. Rather, the underlying instrument of the call is a call option itself. The client wants the right to buy the $100 call with expiration on December 31, 2000, for $5—the *right* but not the *obligation* to purchase the call.

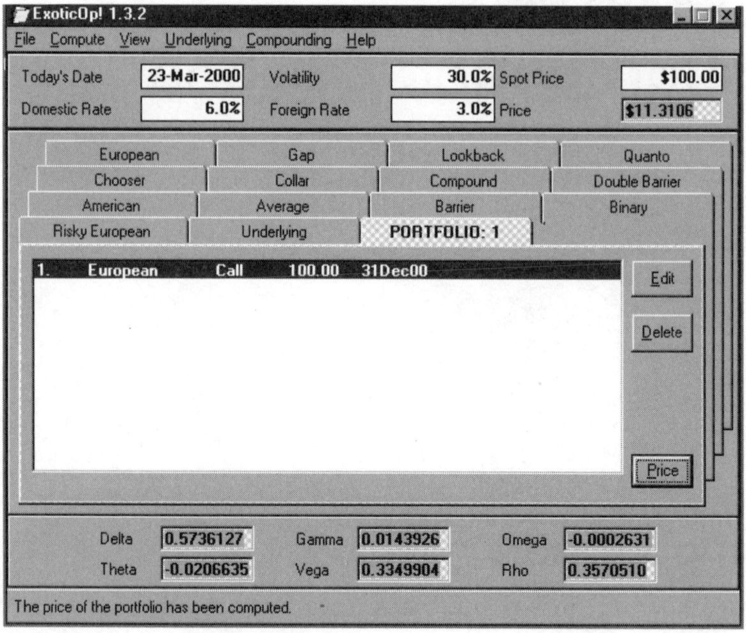

Figure 10.1   A European call option.

The call option struck at 100 with an expiration of December 31, 2000, is called the *underlying option,* and the right to buy that call on June 15, 2000, for $5 is called the *compound option.* Some authors refer to these as *mother* and *daughter* options.

PRICING INTUITION

How much should the dealer charge for this option? Would the dealer sell it for $6? Why not? If the price of the European today is $11.12, then the price of the compound call has to be at least $6.12. If the price of the compound would have been cheaper than $6.12, then nobody would buy the original European option. For example, suppose the price of the compound was $5.50. The clients would buy the compound for $5.50, wait until June 15, 2000, pay another $5, and obtain the original option. It is clear that under these circumstances no one would purchase the original European option. As you can see from Figure 10.3, the price of the compound option is actually $6.92.

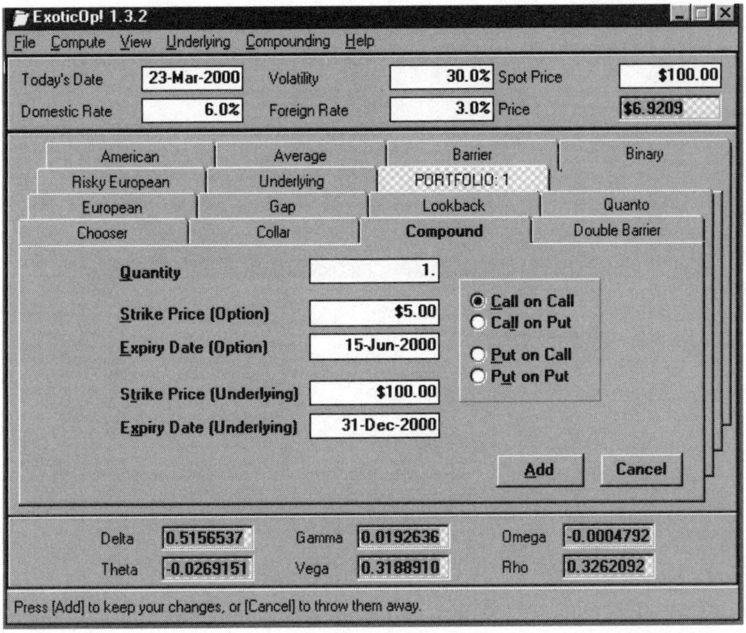

Figure 10.2   The details of the compound.

INTEREST RATE RISK MANAGEMENT

Suppose that a company has a deal that is waiting for approval. Perhaps it's a takeover bid that must be approved by a regulator. Or perhaps it's a competitive bidding situation in which the company doesn't know if it is going to win the project. Once the project receives the green light to go ahead, the company will have to borrow money to finance it. The company may wish to buy an interest rate cap to secure the financing costs, but it is not sure if it will need the cap since the regulator may not approve the project. If the company just buys the cap, it will have to pay an expensive premium. If the regulator doesn't approve the project, maybe the company can sell that cap. But since it is a company, and not a derivatives dealer, it may not be interested in selling options. Also note that the cap has suffered from time decay. In addition, maybe the volatility is lower and the price of the cap is cheaper than it was when the company bought it.

One alternative to buying an interest rate cap is to wait until the deal is approved by the regulator. But by that time

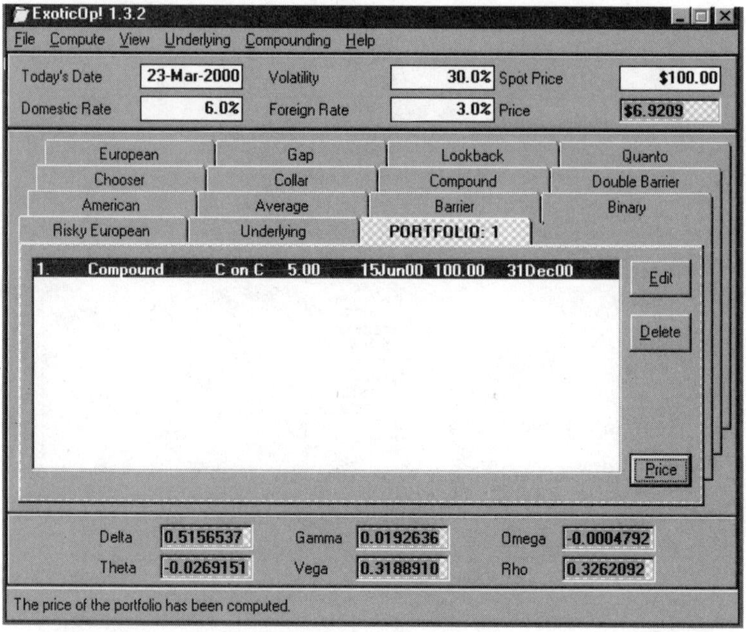

Figure 10.3   The price of a compound call on a call.

interest rates may have climbed so much that the financing costs on the project will be prohibitive.

A better alternative is for the company to pay a small premium now for the right to pay another premium later and then receive the cap. An option to buy a cap is called a *caption*. Similarly, an option to buy a floor is called a *floortion* or *floption*.

TYPES OF COMPOUNDS

The compound option is typically European. The client does not want to pay its $5 anytime before it has to. In any case, the client will not be able to exercise the underlying option before June 15, 2000, so there is no need to pay the $5 before then. But the underlying options can be American or European. Once the $5 has been paid on June 15, 2000, the client may exercise its option at any time. Therefore, it is possible to have a European on a European or a European on an American.

One also has to distinguish between the four possible types:

- A call on a call
- A call on a put
- A put on a call
- A put on a put

However, since clients are mostly interested in buying options from the dealer, not in selling options, most of the compound options in the market are going to be either a call on a call or a call on a put. Very rarely do we find that a client wants to buy a put on a call or a put on a put. Most clients want to buy options from the dealer in order to protect themselves, not to sell options.

A COMPARATIVE TABLE

It is instructive to see just how much the amount that you have to pay later on affects the amount that you have to pay today. The three columns in Table 10.1 illustrate this point. The first column shows the option premium payable today for the compound option. The second column contains the premium payable

TABLE 10.1

A Compound Option

Payable Today	Payable Later	Sum
$11.30	$0.01	$11.31
$10.82	$0.50	$11.32
$10.33	$1.00	$11.33
$9.39	$2.00	$11.39
$8.50	$3.00	$11.50
$6.92	$5.00	$11.92
$5.57	$7.00	$12.57
$3.98	$10.00	$13.98
$2.20	$15.00	$17.20
$1.18	$20.00	$21.18

on June 15, 2000. This is the strike of the compound option. The third column is the sum of the first two.

Consider Table 10.1. The more the client can pay later, the smaller the amount he has to pay today. Also, the higher the sum of both amounts. This has a little to do with the time value of money. But what is more important than that is the fact that the more the client can pay later, the more decision power the client has and the more uncertainty the dealer has. Intuitively, the more the client can postpone paying until later, the higher the sum of both payments will be.

Consider the company that is not sure if it will obtain the approval by the regulator. The more sure it is of winning the deal, the more toward the top of Table 10.1 it will want to be. The more unsure it is, the more it will move toward the bottom. Uncertainty is expensive.

PRICING METHODS

The first to price compound options was Bob Geske. In a 1979 paper ("The Valuation of Compound Options," *Journal of Financial Economics*, 7, 1979, pp. 63–81) he used a very interesting method. Consider the value of a firm. The firm's value is its assets minus its liabilities. So we can write

$$V = A - L$$

where A denotes assets, L denotes liabilities, and V denotes the value of the firm.

If the liabilities are bigger than the assets, the firm becomes bankrupt. As the firm's value cannot become negative, we can refine this and write

$$V = \max(A - L, 0)$$

For most companies, the liabilities are fixed. The companies have to pay certain interest rate expenses, as there are certain bonds outstanding, etc. The assets change from day to day. Either the company makes a sale or it doesn't. If the assets are changing and the liabilities are fixed, then the value of a firm looks very much like a call option on the assets of the firm with a strike set to the liabilities of the firm.

A stock's price is given by

$$S = V/n$$

where n is the number of outstanding shares.

When we view it this way, we can consider a stock to be almost like a call option on the firm. And if the stock is like a call option on the firm, then a regular call option is a compound option (call on a call) on the firm. Geske used the Black-Scholes formula for a call option on a stock and said that this was a compound option on the firm.

He modified the Black-Scholes formula to solve for a call on a call. Mark Rubinstein later generalized this method to work for all four cases: a call on a call, a call on a put, a put on a call, and a put on a put.[1]

Rubinstein's method worked in the case of a European on a European. Also, it was based on solving a nonlinear equation via an iterative process.

In 1993, I applied the numerical quadrature method to compound options.[2] As an example, consider the compound option described in the case above. If one were certain that on June 15, 2000, the underlying would be priced at $110, then we could price a call option struck at $100 to expire on December 31, 2000. If the price of that call option is above $5, then the holder of the compound would exercise his option and the value of the compound would be

$$C(110,100) - \$5$$

where $C(S,X)$ is the Black-Scholes price of a call option with a spot price of $110 and a strike of $100.

In general, if the price of the underlying on June 15, 2000, is S, then the value of the compound is

$$\max [C(S,100) - \$5, 0]$$

We now multiply the value of the compound at S by the probability of getting to S. We use a numerical integration scheme that is numerically very stable. This is the expected value of the com-

---

[1] Rubenstein, "Double Trouble," *Risk Magazine,* December 1991–January 1992.

[2] Nelken, "Square Deals," *Risk Magazine,* April 1993.

pound on June 15, 2000. To find its price today, we discount that expected value from June 15, 2000, to today by the risk-free rate. In this fashion, we can price compound options. With this method we can price European options on European as well as European options on American.

FORWARD VOLATILITY

We need the volatility from March to June to create a probability distribution for the underlying. However, to price the options from June to December, we need the volatility for that time frame. The volatility from June to December is called the *forward volatility*.

How does the dealer figure this volatility out? The dealer knows the implied volatility from today to June 15, 2000, and also from today until December 31, 2000. The formula for the forward volatility is based on the fact that variances add up.

Let L be the long time frame and σL be the long-term volatility. Let S be the short time frame and σS be the short-term volatility. The time between them is X, and the forward volatility is σX.

In our case, L is the time from today until December 31, 2000, and S is the time from today until June 15, 2000.

Obviously,

$$X = S - L$$

Since variances add up, we have

$$S * (\sigma S)^2 + X * (\sigma X)^2 = L * (\sigma L)^2$$

From this we obtain,

$$\sigma X = \sqrt{\{[L * (\sigma L)^2 - S * (\sigma S)^2]/(L - S)\}}$$

Theoretically, one could have an inverted volatility curve. It is possible for the short-term volatility to be so high compared with the long-term volatility that the number inside the square root will be negative and the formula will not give a solution. In case of an inverted volatility curve, it's possible that the formula doesn't work.

In practical situations, this never happens; and while the short-term volatility can be higher than the long-term volatility, there is a limit to how much higher it can go, as there is always more uncertainty associated with longer time frames.

HEDGING

A compound option is hedged with the underlying option. Which hedge ratio should the dealer use?

Let the underlying option delta be $D1$ and the compound option delta be $D2$. The compound option hedge ratio with respect to the underlying option is $D2/D1$. From Figure 10.1, we have $D1 = 0.57$. From Figure 10.3 we have that $D2 = 0.51$. We hedge the compound option with 0.89 European option.

An alternative hedging strategy is to hedge the compound with the underlying instrument. If the client exercises the compound option, continue hedging the European option with the underlying instrument.

APPLICATION

In 1994, Banker's Trust Canada issued installment warrants. In these warrants, you paid \$2.50 today for the right to pay \$2.50 one year later. If you made the second payment, you would receive an option on the Canadian index TSE-35. This option was marketed to retail investors. They were already familiar with making payments. Such investors make payments on their car loans, credit card bills, home mortgages, etc. So why not make payments on an option? The retail clients were also happy with the lower up-front premium required.

SUMMARY

Compound options can be interesting to companies which are unsure of their hedging needs. In such cases, they may be interested in buying an option to buy an option—a compound. In many situations, though, the total price which will be paid for the compound is prohibitively expensive and the company declines the deal. Other compound structures have been created for the retail market.

CHAPTER 11

Barrier Options

INTRODUCTION

Barrier options are the most successful type of exotic option. They're the most widely used. Because they're so widely used, the premium on barrier options has almost disappeared. The bid-ask spread for barrier options used to be 10 times what it is on European, but now it is only 1½ to 2 times. Barrier options have become like vanilla—that is, they are very commonplace and everyone knows how to do them.

TYPES OF BARRIER OPTIONS

What is a barrier option? The option is basically a European option (just like a regular call or a regular put), except with one more element, the barrier. The option is European, but the barrier is American. In our example, the strike is at $100 and the barrier is at $110.

Two things can happen when the underlying crosses the barrier:

- *Knock-in options.* The options become activated (or "alive") if the underlying crosses the barrier. So long as the underlying has not crossed the barrier, these options are not in effect.

- *Knock-out options.* The options become extinguished (or "die") if the underlying crosses the barrier. These options start out as normal European options. However, should the underlying cross the barrier, the option immediately gets knocked out.

What does it mean to cross the barrier? Does the underlying price have to go to $110, or does it have to go above $110? How many trades have to be done? How many trades have to be done at that level? We will examine all these questions shortly.

DISTINGUISHING BETWEEN UP AND DOWN OPTIONS

The first question we address is this: Does the underlying price have to cross the barrier from below (e.g., the current level of the underlying is $100 and the barrier is at $110), does it have to cross it coming up, or does it have to cross it coming down?

If the underlying has to cross the barrier coming up (see Table 11.1), the option is:

- Up and in
- Up and out

If the underlying has to cross the barrier coming down, the option is:

- Down and in
- Down and out

In addition, you have to specify a call or a put.

TABLE 11.1

Barrier Options

	Down	Up
Out	*Down and out*—dies if the underlying crosses the barrier coming down	*Up and out*—dies if the underlying crosses the barrier coming up
In	*Down and in*—becomes activated if the underlying crosses the barrier coming down	*Up and in*—becomes activated if the underlying crosses the barrier coming up

"NASTY" AND "NICE" BARRIERS

Consider two call options (see Figures 11.1 and 11.2):

An up-and-out call with $B > X$ is a "nasty" barrier.

A down-and-out call with $B < X$ is a "nice" barrier.

Why do we say that? Assume that $B > X$; that is, the barrier is above the strike. Then a regular European call would be in the money when the spot reaches the barrier. It will have a high

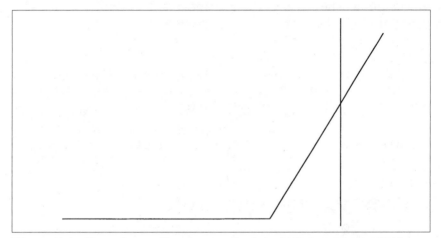

Figure 11.1   Up-and-out call option—strike is at $100; barrier is at $110.

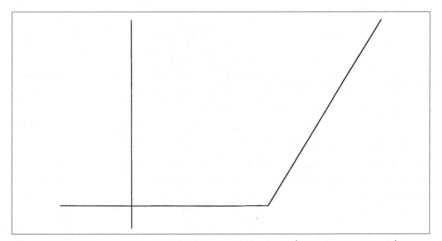

Figure 11.2   Down-and-out call option—strike is at $100; barrier is at $90.

intrinsic value and a high price. Therefore, the existence of the barrier really hurt the European call option.

On the other hand, assume that $B < X$; that is, the barrier is below the strike. Then a regular European call will be out of the money when the spot reaches the barrier. It will have no intrinsic value and a low price. Even if this were a European option, its price would be so low at that out-of-the-money point that we would not lose very much. In this case, the existence of the barrier did not interfere too much with the European call option.

Consider a one-year European call option struck at $100. In our example, the price of the European call option is $6.71. The down-and-out (D&O) call with a strike at $90 is priced at $6.14, and the up-and-out (U&O) call with a strike at $110 is priced at $0.25.

Why the big difference in prices? The most you can earn with the U&O is $10. To do that, the underlying has to climb to $110 but never touch it. With the D&O option, however, you can earn unlimited amounts (similar to the European call). In fact, if the underlying just keeps climbing, the D&O will behave similarly to the European.

A VERY BULLISH INVESTOR

Consider a D&O call option with a strike of $100 and a barrier of $90. Assume that the spot price is $100.

- If the underlying never falls below $90, the investor has a call option.
- If the underlying ever declines to below $90, the investor has nothing.

This would be a useful option for an investor who is very bullish and expects the underlying to just increase in price. The D&O is cheaper than a standard call ($6.14 versus $6.71).

D&O call options are often used as bonus packages for executives. Assume that the board of a company gives the executive a normal call option. The executive is expected to make the stock price go up. This may be difficult to do. What if the executive just increases the volatility of the stock? With a European option, the value of the bonus would increase. So the board tells the executive that the stock price has to rise and then he will get his bonus. However, if the stock price falls to below 90 percent of its value, the executive will lose his entire bonus.

Obviously, if we were to move the barrier to $95, the option would become cheaper ($4.32 in our case). This is because the probability of losing the option has increased.

A MODESTLY BULLISH INVESTOR

Consider a modestly bullish investor. Such an investor may think that the underlying will rise up, but not by a lot. This investor may be interested in a bull spread (see Figure 11.3). The bull spread provides the same benefit as the call option so long as the underlying price ends below $120. If it climbs above $120, the investor will collect only $20.

Consider an up-and-out call option with a barrier at $120 (see Figure 11.4). Is it priced the same as a bull spread, cheaper than the bull spread, or more expensive?

Of course, the U&O is priced cheaper than the bull spread. The price of $1.92 reflects the fact that with the U&O, the investor loses everything if the underlying climbs to $120. With the bull spread, the investor collects the $20.

To make the U&O more similar to the bull spread, we include a rebate. The rebate is paid out in the event that the U&O option is knocked out. So let's add a rebate of $20 to our up-and-out option. If the underlying crosses the $120 barrier, the investor will lose the option but will receive $20.

How does the price of the up and out compare with the bull spread now? Now the up and out is priced at $6.55, more expen-

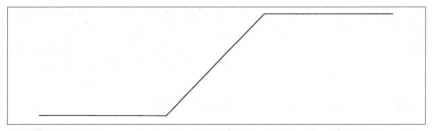

Figure 11.3   Bull spread—long a call at $100, short a call at $120. Price of the bull spread, $5.61.

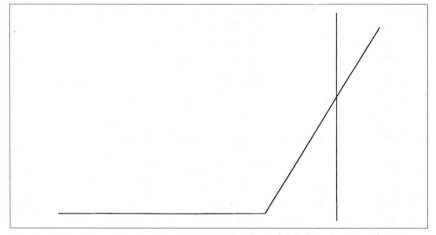

Figure 11.4   Up-and-out call option—strike is at $100; barrier is at $120.

sive than the bull spread. We still have the same maximal amount of $20. But the probability of earning the $20 is much higher with the barrier option than with the bull spread. If the underlying shoots up and then declines, you will not earn much with the bull spread. However, the barrier option will pay out the $20.

In addition, there is the time value of money. With the knock-out option, you will receive the rebate as soon as the option is knocked out. With the bull spread, you will have to wait until expiration.

REBATE

If a knock-out option gets knocked out or fails to materialize, then the investor will receive a cash rebate. Note that with a knock-out option, the rebate can be paid immediately upon being knocked out. With a knock-in option, we have to wait until expiration to know whether or not the option was knocked in.

GODZILLA VERSUS KING KONG

Consider again the up-and-out call option with a strike at $100 and a barrier at $120. Assume there is no rebate. In this example, we use a volatility of 15 percent. On one hand, we have a call option. We are long the underlying and long volatility. Thus our position has:

Delta—positive

Theta—negative

Vega—positive

Gamma—positive

On the other hand, we have the barrier, which may cause us to lose the entire position. The barrier causes the opposite effect:

Delta—negative

Theta—positive

Vega—negative

Gamma—negative

Which of these effects "wins" at any one particular time is a matter of how far we are away from the barrier, from the strike, and from expiration. In any case, since we have two opposing forces, the Greeks of a barrier option cannot be determined intuitively.

At one year to expiration, we note the strong power of the barrier (see Table 11.2). Remember that the barrier is American and the strike is European. Thus even when the underlying is at $100, and we would expect an at-the-money option with a delta of about 0.50, we see a delta of almost zero. As the underlying continues to climb, we expect to have an in-the-money option. However, the barrier negates that effect and we have a negative delta.

TABLE 11.2

A Year to Expiration

Underlying	Option Premium	Delta	Gamma	Vega	Theta
$90	$1.20	0.09	−0.0006	−0.01	−0.0001
$95	$1.65	0.07	−0.007	−0.11	0.001
$100	$1.92	0.02	−0.01	−0.21	0.004
$105	$1.86	−0.04	−0.01	−0.25	0.005
$110	$1.46	−0.11	−0.01	−0.22	0.004
$115	$0.78	−0.15	−0.004	−0.13	0.002
$120	0	0	0	0	0

The negative delta signifies that as the underlying increases in price, so does the probability of it crossing the barrier and of the option being knocked out. When the underlying is low, theta is negative (similar to a European option). But as the underlying keeps climbing, theta turns positive. The positive theta indicates that with every passing day we have one less day to cross the barrier.

With just two weeks to expiration and the underlying at $115, theta is positive and large (see Table 11.3). In this case, the option is $15 in the money. Every day that passes increases our probability of receiving the $15. On the other hand, delta is negative. We do not want the underlying to climb any more. It is close enough to the barrier, and if it climbs some more, we might get knocked out.

Note that at $110, delta is positive, and at $115, delta is quite negative. Somewhere around $113.60, delta becomes zero. But we also obtain a gamma of –0.46. This is not a "nice relaxed" zero of a delta-hedged position. Rather it is the zero of two opposing forces that just happen to be at a weak equilibrium.

Gamma helps us distinguish between two inherently different cases in which delta is zero. In the first case, delta switches from positive to negative territory passing through zero. Two deltas are shown in Figure 11.5. The first delta chart is stable at zero and gamma is also close to zero. The second delta chart rapidly declines through zero. Its gamma is negative.

We see similar effects with volatility. At one year to expiration, set the underlying price to $100 and the volatility to 5 per-

TABLE 11.3

Two Weeks to Expiration

Underlying	Option Premium	Delta	Gamma	Vega	Theta
$90	$0.0003	0.0004	0.0009	0.0003	0.0001
$95	$0.07	0.05	0.04	0.02	–0.01
$100	$1.29	0.51	0.11	0.08	–0.04
$105	$5.15	0.94	0.03	0.02	–0.01
$110	$9.95	0.89	–0.09	–0.06	0.02
$115	$11.50	–0.78	–0.59	–0.56	0.27
$120	0	0	0	0	0

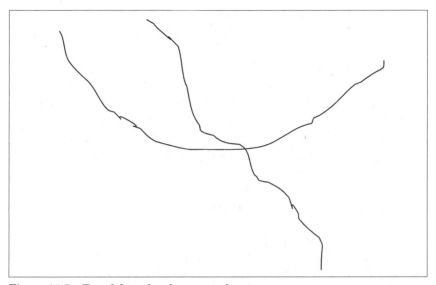

Figure 11.5   Two deltas that happen to be at zero.

cent. The option is priced at $2.95, and its vega is 0.31 (a positive vega). However, as we've already seen, at 15 percent volatility, vega is −0.21 (negative). At an intermediate volatility of about 7.6 percent, vega is zero.

⠀⠀If you have very little volatility, you likely just want a little bit more to increase your chances of ending in the money. The probability of being knocked out is kind of small at this stage. So increasing volatility a little bit helps you to be in the money. But if you increase it too much, the barrier comes to knock you out.

⠀⠀Observe the negative vega at $115 two weeks before expiration. What does this mean? In a European option, when the volatility falls, so does the price. But in this case, when the volatility falls, the price rises.

⠀⠀In a delta-hedging regime, the dealer makes money to stay equal to the increase in the price of the option by buying and selling the underlying security. For a European option, when volatility rises, the dealer has to make more money. But the underlying moves more and so the delta-hedge ratio can be kept constant. In the case of the barrier option, the dealer has to make more money just as volatility is falling. How can you make more money when the underlying is not moving? The only answer is to "double up your bet," also known as "increasing your hedge ratio."

Two weeks before expiration, consider a situation where reduced volatility is and the underlying moved to $118. The delta-hedge ratio is now –3.50! That is, the dealer has to hedge by selling short 350 percent of the underlying notional amount of the option. In some cases, we will see delta ratios of 1,000 percent or more. This will mean hedging with an underlying position ten times as large as the option position.

But now think of the dealer. It is in the dealer's interest to see the underlying price climb just a little bit from $118 to $120 so that the option will be knocked out. However, the dealer has to hedge by selling short, which puts a downward pressure on the price of the underlying. This will make the underlying cheaper, not more expensive. Thus the dealer "is going against himself."

HAS THE UNDERLYING TOUCHED THE BARRIER?

Obviously this is a very important question for both the dealer and the client. Consider a U.S. dollar–Japanese yen U&O call option, with a strike of $110 and a barrier at $124.85.

Let's look at the following scenarios:

1. One Friday at 5:15 p.m. New York time, it is rumored that Japan has defaulted on one of its bonds. As a result, the dollar-yen rate is quoted at 124-127 and $100 million trades at 127. Then it is announced that the rumor is false, and the rate falls back to 124.50

2. One million U.S. dollars trades at 124.90, and the market falls back to 124.50.

3. A stop-loss order to buy $5 million at 124.85 that you left with a third dealer was executed. However, in the brokers' market, the highest trade was 124.80.

4. A total of $50 million trades at $1 = DM 1.7, and the German mark–yen rate is quoted at 73.45 – 73.55; so the implied rate for the dollar-yen is 124.87 – 125.03.

These scenarios were chosen since they fall in the "gray" area.

In the interbank market, the market-making dealer is usually the *barrier event determination agent*. Some market participants have suggested using a third party as an agent. However, this causes difficulties: legal exposure to the third-party bank and loss of confidentiality in the barrier positions.

If a dealer is selected as the barrier event determination agent, which employee should it be? Most people tend to use the spot trader because the spot trader is more connected to the market than the exotic options trader. So the spot trader is usually the one to decide if the barrier has reached the spot. Also, it stands to reason that the spot dealer is more impartial than the exotic options trader.

When can a barrier event occur? Is a weekend trade considered? Some dealers consider all the trades because a model is based on the log-normal distribution, which doesn't stop over a weekend unless you devise a special model. Other dealers only consider specific times when the markets are liquid (in general this is Monday 6 a.m. Sydney time to Friday 5 p.m. New York time). In this case, the first scenario is not a barrier breach because that trade happens at 5:15 p.m. New York time when the market is not very liquid.

Do you use quotations or transactions? The option pricing models are based on log-normal distributions of quotations. Transactions, especially in illiquid markets, occur only once in a while. What if there were no transactions? When something doesn't trade, it's illiquid. Does that mean the barrier can never be breached? Other dealers use transactions because transactions are really more indicative that something has occurred. It is not like someone just put a quote on the screen and then took it off. Transactions are more indicative of market prices and less prone to manipulation. Also they can be backed by evidence—for example, Reuters dealers' conversations, an EBS tape log, or a note from a spot broker or an interbank counterparty confirming the trade. Some barrier options require that a confirmation of the trade be supplied by three independent broker-dealers.

The Federal Reserve Bank of New York foreign exchange committee association and the British Bankers Association (BBA) have adopted standard option confirmation guidelines. These guidelines require that transactions be used rather than quotations. But there is no worldwide consensus on the topic. And not every dealer abides by these recommendations.

If transactions are used, then what size? As markets tops and bottoms, only small amounts trade at the extreme levels. By its very nature the extreme level was reached only for a short time and only a small amount was traded. In such cases, the barrier may have been hit but only with a small volume of trading. The question then becomes: "Do we need a minimal size to declare a barrier hit?" Most dealers do not specify a minimal size. The BBA recommends a size that is generally accepted by the foreign exchange dealers for that currency but does not specify an amount. Some dealers will specify a consistent minimal amount (e.g., 3 million U.S. dollars by SBC Warburg). Consecutive transactions, which are close in time, are totaled and considered a single transaction. There is no barrier event in scenario 2 since only $1 million was traded. Barrier options with a large notional (Jumbos) may have higher transaction amount requirements.

Most dealers and end users agree that transactions done at off-market rates do not count as barrier events. An off-market rate is "Generally defined as a rate that is substantially more favorable or substantially less favorable than what is available to a professional spot dealer at the time of the transaction." An off-market rate is sometimes the result of a mistake or collusion. Also, we have to consider transactions with internal counterparties or with customers. Small retail trades are often done at larger bid-ask spreads. The price may not reflect the true market price. Internal transactions may be subject to special deals and agreements between different departments of the same bank. One approach is to count only transactions between independent interbank counterparties. Here, the term *independent* means the dealer has no control over the transactions, and *interbank counterparty* means a professional market maker in the foreign exchange market, not a customer or a client.

One difficult problem when using transactions is this: Suppose that A is the barrier determination agent and B and C have transacted. In all likelihood, A is not even aware of the transaction (see Figure 11.6).

One solution: Restrict the trades to the ones that the barrier determination agent, A, can reasonably observe:

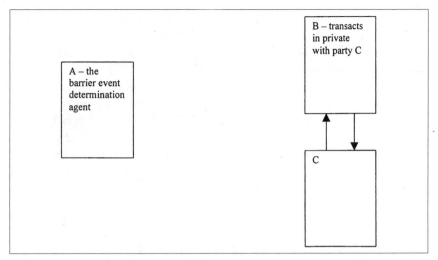

Figure 11.6   A does not even know that B and C have transacted.

- Transactions between the dealer (A) and an independent interbank counterparty either directly or through a broker
- Transactions between two independent counterparties done at a broker that normally reports these trades to the dealer

There would be no barrier event in scenario 3. The barrier determination agent could not have seen the trade.

Crosses

A barrier in an illiquid currency presents special problems. Transactions in such currency pairs are done via a cross. For example, a French franc–Japanese yen transaction is normally done through the Deutsche mark:

- First, French franc—Deutsche mark
- Then, Deutsche mark–Japanese yen

If there are no transactions in the illiquid currency, how can a barrier event be determined? Most confirmations either are silent on this question or permit barrier determination based on quotations or transactions on the cross. Most confirmations that allow uses of the cross are badly written. From them you can infer that a barrier event on a liquid currency may be determined based on trades in an illiquid currency pair. This is quite absurd. For example, a dollar-yen option may be determined by a trade in Thai bhat-yen and in dollar-bhat.

A solution is to restrict the crosses to illiquid currency pairs. Liquidity is a matter of judgment and depends on the activity in a particular time zone. The U.S. dollar–French franc is liquid during European hours but not liquid during U.S. hours. According to SBC Warburg conventions, there must be two transactions in the cross, each one for at least $3 million. Scenario 4 would not be considered a barrier breach since there was only a single trade.

KNOCKING OUT THE BARRIER

Barrier options are a good motivation for the dealer to try and manipulate the markets. Barrier options have achieved much publicity due to George Soros. He claims that they cause too much market manipulation by dealers. Indeed, if the underlying is at $119, there is a great temptation for the dealer to try and push the underlying up through $120 and knock the option out.

Some banks (e.g., SBC Warburg) have the following policy:

> No employee shall place or execute an order or initiate a spot transaction for the purpose of causing or preventing the occurrence of a barrier event. A violation of this policy is a serious offense that could result in dismissal.

AN ERROR BY J. P. MORGAN

> An article from *Derivatives Week* of May 19, 1997 confirms that it may have been J. P. Morgan who took a $20–$40 million hit on its forex exotic option book. The dealer sold a USD 800 million notional dollar/yen option to an Asian counterparty, a division of the Chinese state bank. The dealer sold a dollar call/yen put struck at JPY 123 or 124 with a knock-out at 127.30 (up and out call) that was set for expiration on May 1 in the Tokyo market. The expiration time ("cut") was at 3 p.m. Tokyo time. The dealer hedged itself by buying an identical option in NYC with a cut set at 10 a.m. local time. A lot of times in the market we see back-to-back deals. Usually back-to-back deals work out just fine. Everything is exactly the same with one exception. At expiration, 3 p.m.

local time in Tokyo, the dollar yen was trading at JPY 127.10, deep in the money. The client exercised the option. After the Tokyo close, the dollar rallied beyond 127.30 and the offsetting position of the dealer in NYC was knocked out.

The six-hour exposure mismatch may have resulted from

1. Lack of liquidity in the Tokyo market—so they had to hedge in NYC
2. A mistake

Even a large sophisticated dealer may occasionally stumble. Many exotic option traders remember the first weekend in May 1997. They spent it at the office confirming that all their back-to-back traders are done either NYC-NYC or Tokyo-Tokyo. Mismatches were flagged and dealt with.

Estimated size of the forex barrier option market
(It is instructive to look at the phenomenal growth of the barrier option market in foreign exchange.)

1992—$123
1993—$348
1994—$812
1995—$1333
1996—$2041
Estimated value of notional of barrier option trades in $ billions

Source: SBC Warburg.

As can be seen from the above data, the barrier option market has had phenomenal growth in recent years. From esoteric options written by a handful of "rocket scientist" option traders, barriers have turned into a commodity, much like European options. At the same time, the bid-ask spreads on barrier options were reduced from 10 times the spreads on European options to 1½ times the spreads on Europeans.

BARRIER OPTION FUNDAMENTAL EQUATION

The most basic barrier option equation (see Figure 11.7) is

Knock-in + Knock-out = European

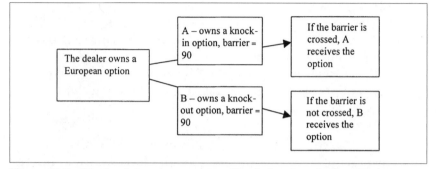

Figure 11.7   The basic barrier equation: Knock-in + knock-out = European.

Suppose a dealer owns a European option. He sells a knock-in to party A and a knock-out to party B. What happens? Either the knock-in option was knocked in and A receives a European option while B's knock-out option was knocked out. Or the option belongs to B since it wasn't knocked out. In that case, A did not get knocked in.

In the old days, the dealers used to make money. They purchased a European option and sold a knock-in and a knock-out to different parties. The sum of the prices paid for the knock-in plus the knock-out was greater than the European.

Once we include rebates, the situation becomes slightly more complicated. The down and out pays the rebate immediately upon knocking out. With a down and in, you must wait until expiration time to ascertain that you were not knocked in and are entitled to a rebate.

REGULATORY CAPITAL ARBITRAGE

In some regulatory regimes, there is a regulatory capital arbitrary. The European options are modeled by the Black-Scholes formula, which according to the regulator is an approved model. Therefore, the European option attracts a low regulatory capital. A down-and-out option, on the other hand, is evaluated with an unapproved model. It therefore attracts high regulatory capital that is computed with a formula. The formula is essentially a multiple of delta plus a multiple of gamma plus a multiple of rho plus a multiple of vega. The down and in is not an option yet. So it attracts no regulatory capital.

Assume that the dealer wants to sell a down and out option. This would attract a lot of regulatory capital. Instead, the dealer sells a European and purchases a down and in. This can be done because a down and out is the same as a European minus a down and in. By doing that the dealer reduces their regulatory capital charges by quite a lot.

PRICING

For continuously monitored barrier options, pricing can be done under the Black-Scholes framework. Closed-form formulas have been developed and are available.

One trick in the formulas has to do with the fact that for out options, we do not know when the barrier will be hit. So how can we assign a present-value to the rebate? It turns out that under risk neutrality, the stock grows at the risk-free rate. The rebate is discounted at the same risk-free rate. And so the interest rate drops out of the equation.

PRICING BARRIERS IN THE PRESENCE OF THE VOLATILITY SKEW

Assume that we have a volatility skew given by the following implied volatility parameters. The implied volatility of a $100 option is 14 percent, and the implied volatility of a $120 option is 12 percent (see Figure 11.8).

The trader wishes to price an up-and-out call option with a strike of $100 and a barrier at $120. Which volatility should the trader use? Here are a few possible answers:

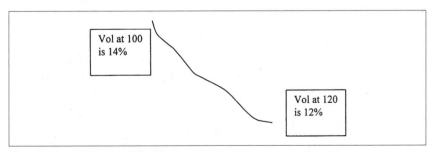

Figure 11.8   The volatility skew.

1. Use the volatility that will give the highest premium.

   At 12 percent the barrier is priced at $2.62.

   At 14 percent the barrier is priced at $2.14.

   In this case, the trader will use the 12 percent volatility and will sell the barrier at $2.62.

2. Use the $100 volatility for the call, and use the $120 volatility for the knock-out. That is, use a combination of the two (a weighted average).

   The trader may decide to use equal weights for both volatility numbers, price the option at 13 percent volatility, and obtain $2.38.

3. In this technique we rely on the barrier option equation. Recall that

   $$U\&O = European - U\&I$$

   The European is priced at 14 percent to give $6.33.

   The U&I is priced at 12 percent to give $2.94.

   The U&O is then priced as $3.39.

4. Use a more sophisticated model that can price barrier options given the shape of the implied volatility smile— for example, the Derman & Kani implied volatility trees.

5. Another strategy is to book the barrier at a different level (more conservative) than you actually sold it. This would force you to take corrective action before the barrier is hit. Also, it improves your hedge ratios. So you would:

   Sell the barrier at $120.

   Book it at $122.

   A $122 barrier option is priced at $2.61 using a 14 percent volatility and at $3.10 using a 12 percent volatility. So if you can sell the option for $3.10, you have the following advantages:

   - You receive more premium.
   - The client got knocked out at $120. You have room until $122 to execute your trade.

- When the underlying reaches $120, you know that you owe nothing to the client (since the client was knocked out). However, you have until $122 to liquidate your position.

Note that this technique may not be approved by your internal guidelines and risk management practices.

DISCRETELY MONITORED BARRIERS

To alleviate the problems of monitoring whether barriers were hit, some firms prefer to use discretely monitored barriers. These are monitored once a day (or once a week) at the close. As the closing prices are easily verified, the difficulties of assessing whether the barriers were hit disappear.

For example, the capped S&P index options (CAPs) that are traded on the Chicago Board Option Exchange are

Up-and-out calls with rebate $= B - X$

Down-and-out puts with rebate $= X - B$

The underlying is monitored once a day at the close. These were popular with retail clients as they could easily verify the barriers, since closing prices are widely distributed. On the other hand, it was difficult for the dealers to hedge using the closing price. The dealer does not know whether or not the barrier will be hit until the close. There was too much of an "event risk" in these options.

PRICING OF DISCRETE BARRIERS, I

A reasonable idea is to price discretely monitored barrier options with a tree (e.g., a binomial tree). But it turns out that trees lead to large errors in the prices (see Figure 11.9). A tree may overestimate or underestimate the price since the nodes of the tree may be above or below the barrier. Errors in the range of 10 to 15 percent have been reported. Errors may decrease and then increase as a function of the number of time steps.

In this case, special trees must be constructed—the nodes are "moved" to hit directly on the barrier.

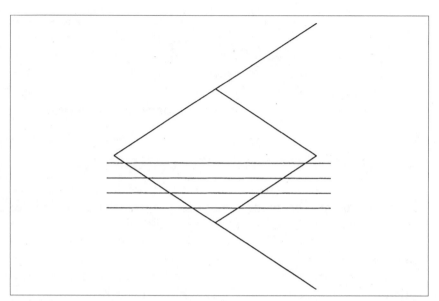

Figure 11.9　In this tree, all the illustrated barriers would produce exactly the same price. The tree does not differentiate between the four barriers.

PRICING OF DISCRETE BARRIERS, II

Let B represent the price of a continuously monitored barrier, and let $B(n)$ represent the price of a discretely monitored barrier with n observation dates. Ed Levy proposed using the following formula:

$$B(n) = B + a^*h + b^*\sqrt{h}$$

where h is the time slice between observation dates.

For $n = 1$ it is possible to solve exactly and obtain the value of $B(1)$. This is a barrier option with only one chance to hit the barrier, exactly at the midpoint to expiration.

For $n = 2$ we can solve exactly and obtain $B(2)$. We use the values for $B(1)$ and $B(2)$ to create a 2-by-2 system of linear equations and solve for a and b. These a and b values are then used in an approximate formula for the general case of $B(n)$.

HEDGING BARRIER OPTIONS

Traders found that a good way to hedge a down-and-out call is with a combination of a European call and a European put.

Let's consider an example: Suppose you sell a down-and-out call with a strike of $155 and a barrier at $145. The price of this option is $5.60. The domestic rate and the foreign rate are equal. What is a good hedge for this? If you buy a regular vanilla call at $155, you're hedged. A vanilla call will always pay even if the barrier gets knocked out. As a matter of fact, you're overhedged. A $155 call always hedges you, but the cost is $6.40. Selling an option at $5.60 and obtaining a cover for $6.40 is not such good business.

What if you also sell a put? You don't know what the strike is, but what you do know is that you want the put price to be the difference between $6.40 and $5.60. Find the strike price of the put so its premium will be $0.80. It turns out that the put struck at $136.15 is priced at $0.80. The combination of long a call at $155 and short a put at $136.15 is priced at $5.60, similar to what the trader received for the barrier option. Therefore, the total position is entered into with zero cost (see Figures 11.10 and 11.11).

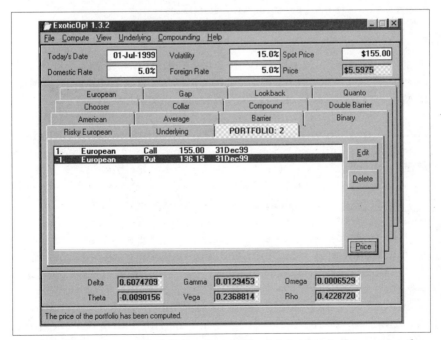

Figure 11.10   Long a call and short a put. The total value is the same as the barrier.

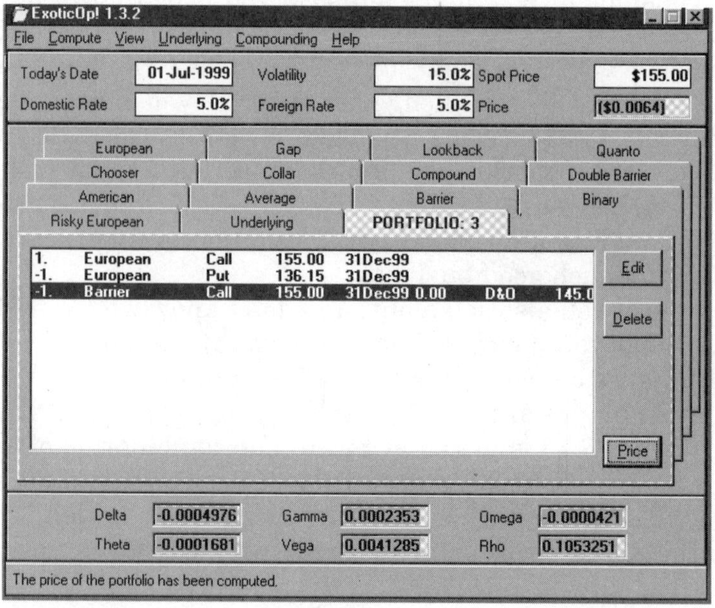

Figure 11.11   Hedging a barrier with Europeans.

So long as the underlying keeps climbing above $155, the European call hedges the barrier call and the trader is secure. However, what happens if the underlying declines?

As soon as the underlying hits $145, the barrier option gets knocked out (see Figure 11.11). The trader must now liquidate the corresponding position in European options. In this case, the $155 call costs $2.50 (as the underlying declines, so does the price of the call). The $136.15 put also costs about $2.50 (since it has become more in the money). So it is possible to sell the call and buy the put for close to zero-cost.

The danger in this strategy is based on some assumptions we made that may be unfounded. For one thing we assumed that the risk-free rate was equal to the dividend rate. We also assumed that volatility did not change. But the most important assumption, which could lead to the most difficult situations, was that we could actually get out of the European position when the underlying was at $145. What if the underlying gaps? What if it moves from $155 directly to $120? In this case, the trader will find that she is short a put option struck at $136.15 and the put is very much in the money.

HEDGING BARRIER OPTIONS

For summary we find that hedging barrier options is very simple in most cases since the gamma is lower than the gamma of European options.

Now consider the up-and-out call option. Hedging it is very difficult when you are right near the barrier and close to expiration. The gamma becomes very large, and the delta changes signs. A model is needed to compute the delta; it is very difficult to figure it out intuitively. You may have to suddenly reverse your position from long underlying to short and vice versa. In this scenario, when volatility is reduced, everything will blow up. As we've seen before, the delta-hedge ratios will become very large. We already saw that the volatility exposure is also tricky. At some points you are long volatility, and at others you are short. In these situations, barrier options become notoriously difficult to hedge.

RISKS IN KNOCK-OUT OPTIONS

What are the risks in knock-out options?

- Execution risk is due to the very high gamma ratios. You may suddenly have to reverse your position from long to short and vice versa.
- Monitoring activities must be carried out diligently to ascertain whether the options were knocked out.
- Even back-to-back trades pose special problems (as we've seen in the J. P. Morgan example).

DIVERSIFY THE BARRIERS!

If the trader is managing a book of options, it is in the trader's best interest to diversify the barriers.

- Diversification mitigates the execution risk since you will have high gammas on a small part of the book.

- Monitoring the barriers is done one by one, achieving economies of scale. That is, you can use one system to monitor hundreds of barriers.

- The trader can place automatic sell (or buy) orders at the knock-out barriers and reduce exposure. Before the barrier, the trader builds a position. Then, when it is hit, the trader has to immediately get rid of it.

- Barriers may be set at prices that cannot be traded—be careful with jumps. Make sure that enough liquidity exists close to the barrier and close to expiration, as you may have to suddenly reverse your position.

In our examples, we focused on a single option and saw the difficulties caused. However, if the big delta swings are only on a single option that is a small part of the portfolio, the problem is not as serious as we've illustrated. In a portfolio setting, where the trader has many barrier options at different strikes and varying barriers, the problems do not appear so serious.

In practice, these recommendations are difficult to carry out. Many clients set identical barrier levels. For example, in mid-1999, many clients requested U.S. dollar-Euro options with a barrier set at exactly $1.00. Diversification of the barriers was difficult.

STATIC HEDGING

Because of all the difficulties in dynamic hedging, some professionals have turned their attention to static hedging. Derman uses static hedging and builds a portfolio of European options. The static hedge consists of some European calls and some European puts with different expiration dates and varying strikes (see Figure 11.12). The trader is long some options and short others. The approach is to build a binomial tree and then buy and sell different European options so that at each level of the tree the delta is neutralized.

As the three-dimensional graph in Figure 11.13 shows, at high levels of the underlying and close to the expiration date, the holder of the portfolio is essentially short the calls. So if the market gaps upward close to the expiration date, the trader is far from being perfectly hedged.

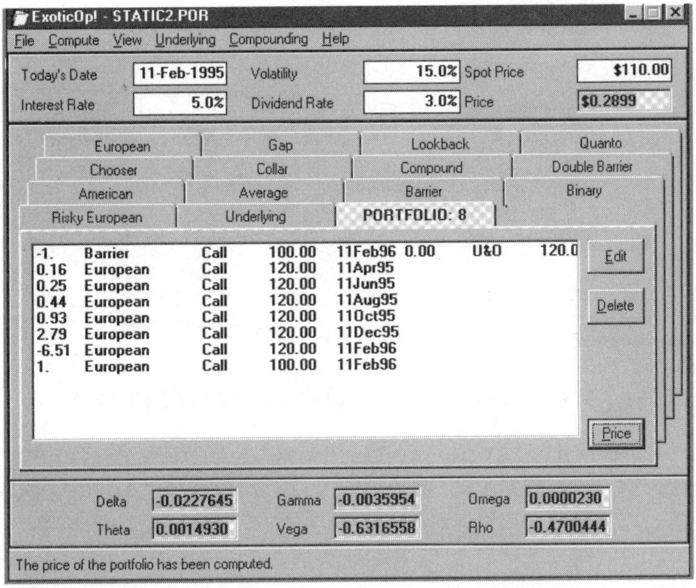

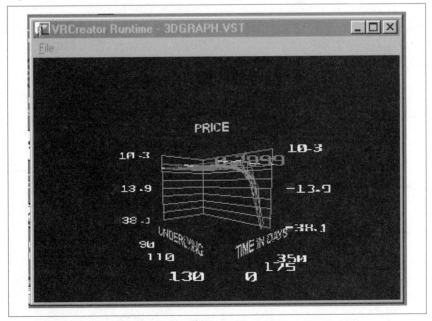

Figure 11.12 Static hedging example: details of portfolio.

Figure 11.13 Static hedging example. A 3D graph.

TABLE 11.4

A Comparison of Several Options at Different Volatility Levels

Type	Vol = 15%	Vol = 60%	Difference in Prices Expressed as %
European	$6.71	$23.58	251
Knock-in option, barrier at 90	$0.60	$14.71	2,350
Knock-out option, barrier at 95.70	$4.26	$4.26	Small

VOLATILITY-INSENSITIVE STRUCTURES

With barrier options one can create structures with no exposure to volatility. For example, consider the following three options:

1. A European option
2. A knock-in call option
3. A knock-out call option

Table 11.4 shows the relationship between their volatility and their payoff. With a knock-in option, the higher the volatility, the higher the expected payoff. Also, there is a higher propensity to receive the payoff. Both of these effects work in unison to give a very high sensitivity to volatility.

With the knock-out option, the higher the volatility, the higher the expected payoff. On the other hand, there is a lower propensity to receive the payoff. Both of these effects work against each other to give a very low sensitivity to volatility. Structures with low sensitivity to volatility are useful in situations where volatility cannot be determined accurately—for example, an initial purchase offering.

OPTIONS ON A SINGLE STOCK

Single-stock barrier options present special challenges. Dividends are paid out in lump sums on definite dividend dates. On the ex-dividend dates the stock price declines by the amount of the dividend. That decline may cause a barrier breach. Special care must be taken to consider the impact of the dividends paid on the barrier.

EXPLODING OPTIONS

Exploding options are up-and-out call options in which there is a rebate. The rebate is equal to the barrier minus the strike. An example of such a structure is the Goldman Sachs E-Signs (Enhanced Stock Index Growth Notes). These are six-year zero-coupon structures with the S&P 500 underlying index.

- If the index value closes at less than 200 percent of the initial index value on all the trading days, the holder will receive a redemption amount calculated as

Redemption amount

$$= \left[100\% + 111\%*\max \left(\frac{\text{final index value}}{\text{initial index value}} - 1,0 \right) \right]*\text{face value}$$

- If the index value closes at above 200 percent of the initial index price on any trading day, the holder will receive a redemption amount of

Redemption amount = 211%*face value

Assume the face value of the note is $25 and the S&P 500 is trading at $654.75. Also assume that the S&P 500 index stays below 1,309.50 throughout the entire life of the deal. If the S&P 500 closes at 800 at the maturity of the note, then at the end of the five years the investor will receive $31.15.

The most that the investor can receive under any circumstances is $52.75. Note that even though this is a knock-out option, the rebate is paid out at the end of the life of the option.

APPLICATION

Consider a German corporation that is long U.S. dollars against Deutsche marks, value six months from now. Let's suppose that the spot price is DM 1.6000 and that the corporation has a downside limit of DM 1.5500. The corporation has also decided to sell its dollars if the rate ever gets to DM 1.6500.

Consider the following two strategies:

- Buy a six-month European put with a strike of DM 1.5500. This option costs 380 points (1 point = DM 0.0001). If DM 1.6500 is reached, the corporation will sell its dollars and also sell the put option. It will get little for the option, as the option is out of the money and also suffered from time decay.
- Buy a six-month up-and-out put with a strike of 1.5500 and a barrier of 1.6500. This option only costs 230 points, 39 percent less. If 1.6500 is reached, the corporation will sell its dollars. The option "dies" automatically.

APPLICATION
Barrier Option with Rebate

Consider an up-and-out call option on a certain index. If the index rises by a lot, the investor will lose the option but will receive double the initial premium back.

The price of this structure is $3.08. If the investor gets knocked out, she receives $6. This is cheaper than purchasing a European option at $5.42 and may be quite attractive to bullish hedge funds. In fact, there is a growing use of rebates within barrier options (see Figure 11.14). This helps mitigate the event risk of being knocked out. The rebate varies. Examples include anything from the premium paid to half the intrinsic value at the barrier. Of course, large rebates would make it more expensive than a European.

APPLICATION

It is quite common for a corporation to buy a call option and finance the purchase by selling a put. In this fashion it establishes a synthetic long forward position (see Figure 11.15). In our example, the company buys an eleven-month call option and sells an eleven-month put option. This is a zero-cost position.

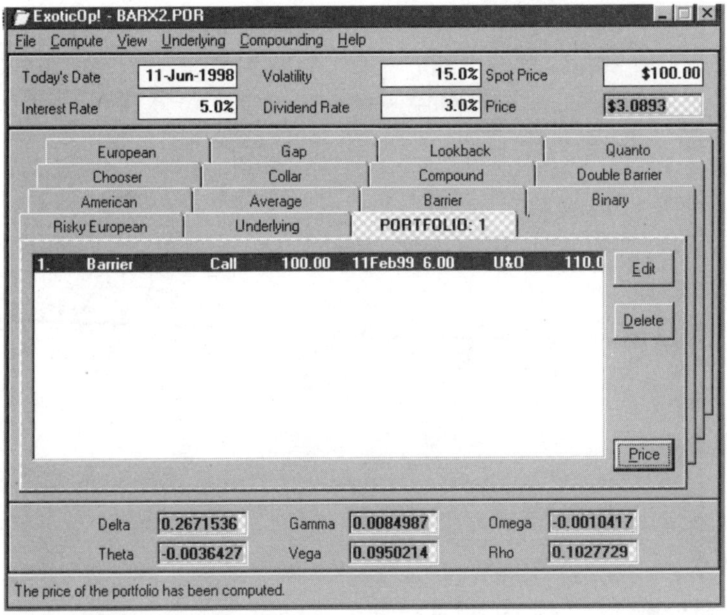

Figure 11.14   A barrier option with a rebate. The rebate is twice the option premium.

The strike levels of both the call and the put are identical at $101.77.

As an alternative, let the company enter into a similar position. It purchases a call and sells a barrier put with a knock-in with a barrier below the spot. This can also be a zero-cost structure.

In our example, the company is long a call option struck at $105 and short a put option also struck at $105 with a knock-in barrier at $84.30 (see Figure 11.16). If the underlying goes up and does not breach the barrier, the client gets a "free" option. If the underlying breaches the barrier, it becomes a forward. The company is now long a forward at $105 rather than at $101.77.

The two strategies are shown in Table 11.5.

Table 11.6 shows several scenarios. To summarize, with the barrier structure you "pay $3.23 to save $11.77." That is, the barrier structure may end up costing $3.23 more but may save $11.77.

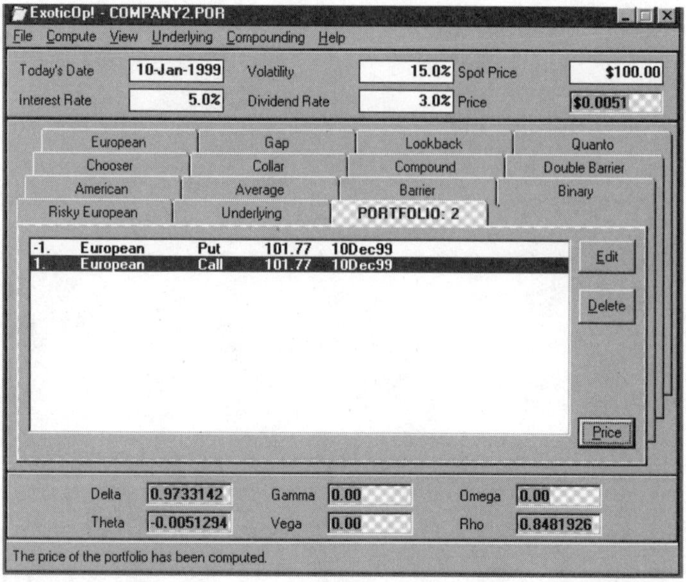

Figure 11.15   Long call, short put. This position mimics a forward.

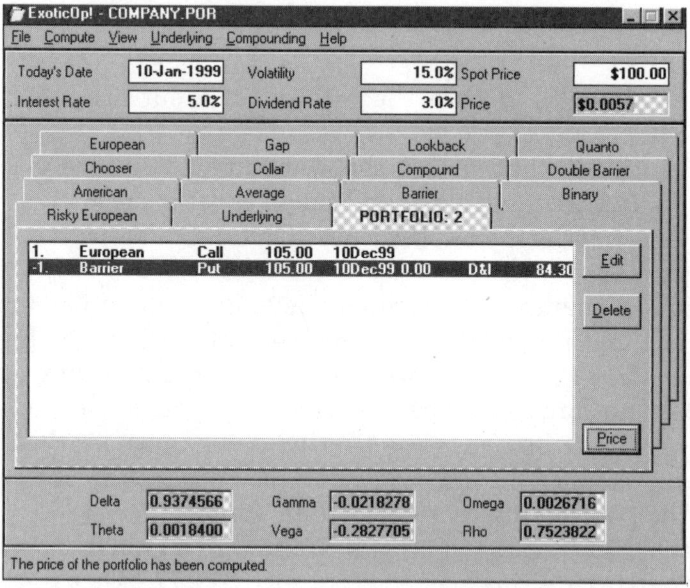

Figure 11.16   Long call, short a knock-in put. The put has not yet become activated.

TABLE 11.5

The Two Strategies

Synthetic forward	Long call at $101.77	Short put at $101.77
Barrier "forward"	Long call at $105	Short knock-in put at $105 with a barrier at $84.30

TABLE 11.6

Underlying	Synthetic Forward	Barrier Forward	Relative Advantage of the Barrier
Climbs up to end at $110	Client receives $8.23	Client receives $5	−$3.23
Declines to $90 but does not touch $84.30	Client has to pay $11.77	No payments are required	+$11.77
Declines to $80	Client has to pay $21.77	Client has to pay $25	−$3.23

OUTSIDE BARRIER

In this case, the barrier is on a different underlying. *Example:* In October 1993, Banker's Trust issued a call option on a basket of Belgian stocks, which got knocked out if the Belgian franc appreciated by more than 3.5 percent.

DELAYED-START BARRIER

A barrier that doesn't start immediately will make the option more expensive if it is a knock-out:

> 0   barrier starts   expiration
>
> Time →

Christophe Chazot, a Banker's Trust vice president and head of currency options in London, mentions that in 1996, investors considered barrier options, with a barrier to start after the U.K. elections, as something esoteric. Now they have become more commonplace.

With a delayed barrier, the client cannot be sure whether the underlying will be above the barrier or below it at the beginning of the window. Therefore, the client may end up with an up-and-out or possibly a down-and-out option. For example, suppose that the barrier is to start three months from today and that the barrier level is set at $100. If the underlying is at $90, the client will receive an up-and-out option. On the other hand, if the underlying is at $110, the client will end up with a down-and-out option.

Some clients would prefer to know the type of option they will end up with. In order to satisfy this request, the derivative dealers have created the *forced delayed start*. This option can only become active if the underlying is on one side of the barrier. For example, a forced delayed start up-and-out call with a strike of $100 and a barrier at $110 will only exist if the underlying is below $110 on the start of the barrier. If it is on the other side, the option is simply terminated, with or without a rebate.

Other structures, called *early termination barrier options*, are possible in which the barrier ends early. Some options are designed so that the barrier is only active in specific, predefined periods, the "windows":

```
0                                      expiration

      xxxxx     xxxxx     xxxxxx
   Time →
```

The barrier is only active in the periods denoted by the x's.

EUROPEAN-STYLE BARRIERS

Another development is the use of European-style barriers, which are not really barriers (see Figure 11.17). They consist of a call spread minus a digital. A regular barrier option struck at $100 with a barrier at $120 costs $1.92.

The European construction is:

- Long a call at $100
- Short a call at $120
- Short a digital call at $120 that pays $20

The price is $3.27. (See Figure 11.18.)

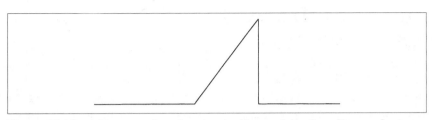

Figure 11.17 A European knock-out actually consists of a call spread minus a digital option.

The European structure costs more, but it alleviates the problem of barrier options. Even though a client might be correct in choosing the barrier and the underlying expired beneath it, the client could still be knocked out due to a temporary rally in the underlying.

ExoticOp! - COMPANY.POR			_ □ ×

File Compute View Underlying Compounding Help

Today's Date	01-Jan-1999	Volatility	15.0%	Spot Price	$100.00
Interest Rate	5.0%	Dividend Rate	3.0%	Price	$3.2785

European	Gap	Lookback	Quanto
Chooser	Collar	Compound	Double Barrier
American	Average	Barrier	Binary
Risky European	Underlying	**PORTFOLIO: 3**	

1.	European	Call	100.00	31Dec99		Edit
-1.	European	Call	120.00	31Dec99		
-1.	Binary Terminal	Call	120.00	31Dec99	20.00	Delete

Price

Delta	0.1551172	Gamma	-0.0075291	Omega	-0.0013354		
Theta	0.0019527	Vega	-0.1133259	Rho	0.1161902		

The price of the portfolio has been computed.

Figure 11.18 A "European" barrier.

SECOND-GENERATION EXOTICS

Another new concept is a barrier that pertains to the average. Suppose you have a barrier option dollar put–yen call struck at $120, with a barrier at 125. For the barrier to be breached the average value of the exchange rate has to be higher than $125. In this option you can get paid more than $5. The underlying price could stay low for a while, and so the average remains below $125. Then the underlying shoots up so that the terminal price is quite high and you receive a high payoff. This is an example of a second-generation exotic option. It used to be that a trader could hedge exotic options using the underlying and some European options. However, to hedge the second-generation exotic options you need first-generation exotic options. It is very difficult to hedge them with normal options.

SUMMARY

Barrier options have become the most popular type of exotic option. They are so popular, in fact, that they are no longer considered exotic. This is due to their cheap price, as compared with a European, as well as the fact that they allow efficient focusing on the client's specific needs.

CHAPTER 12

Double-Barrier Options

INTRODUCTION

A double-barrier option is a knock-out-style option with two barriers. Typically, one is an "up" barrier and the other a "down" barrier.

Figure 12.1 is a $100 call option that gets knocked out if the underlying reaches $110. It also gets knocked out if the underlying drops to $90.

PARAMETERS

Figure 12.2 illustrates the many parameters required to value the option:

- The strike, in this case $100
- The upper barrier, in this case $90
- The bottom barrier, in this case $110
- A rebate for the upper barrier, set to $0
- A rebate for the bottom barrier, set to $0

THE DOUBLE-BARRIER BOX TRADE

It is interesting to combine two double-barrier options. Let us combine a double-barrier in-the-money call with a double-

167

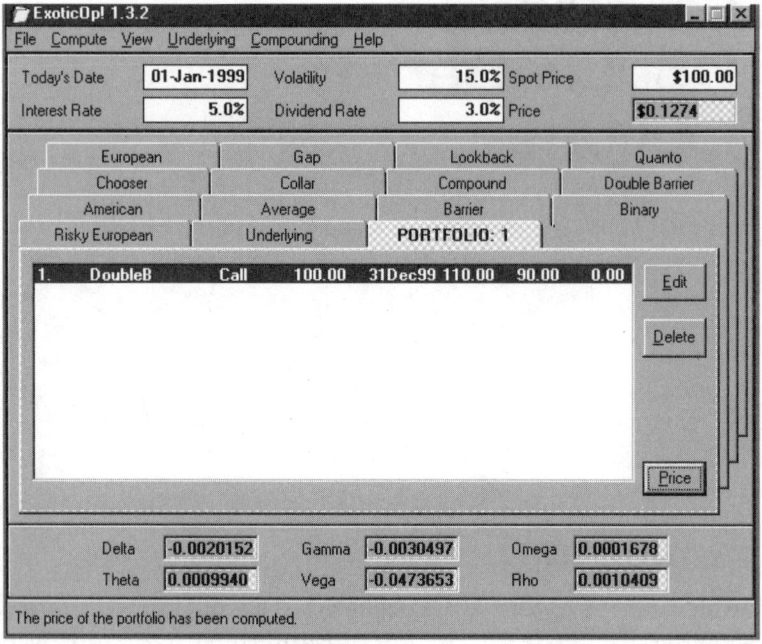

Figure 12.1   A double-barrier call option.

barrier in-the-money put. We have what is known as the *double-barrier box trade.*

Figure 12.3 illustrates what happens when you buy an in-the-money call struck at $145 and an in-the-money put struck at $170. As long as the underlying stays between $145 and $170, then the payout is always $25. You can always buy the underlying at $145 and sell it for $170. But if the underlying crosses either barrier, then both options get knocked out and the entire structure gets canceled.

Note that the price of the structure is approximately $4.55, and that you have the possibility of making $25. The saying is, "Pay $5 to make $25." Also note the Greeks of the structure in Figure 12.3. Delta and gamma are very small. The buyer of the box trade does not care if the underlying moves a little, so long as it stays far enough from both barriers. If the underlying moves from 158 to 157, say, it is still far enough from both barriers, and so the holder of the box trade is indifferent. The only

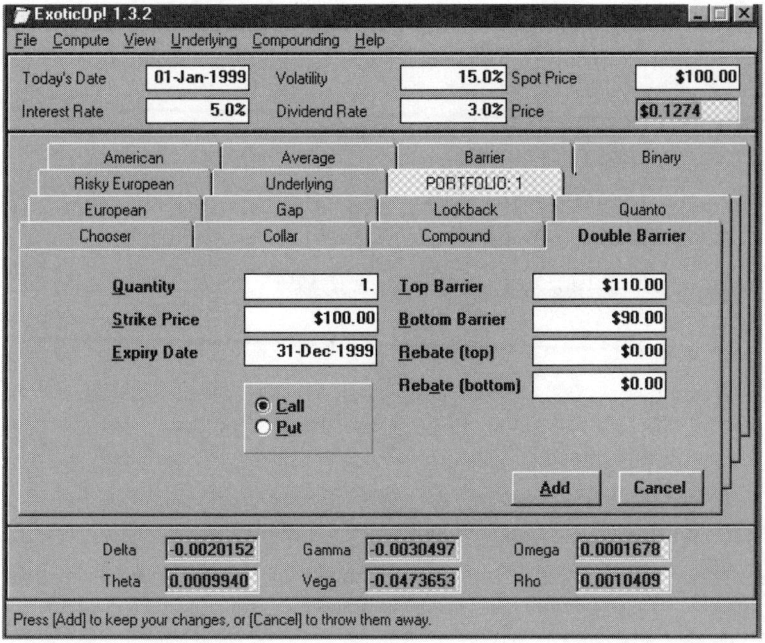

Figure 12.2   The many input parameters of a double-barrier option.

Greek with a nonzero value is vega, the sensitivity to volatility. The holder of the box is short vega. If volatility decreases, then the chances that the box will finish in the money are very much increased. If volatility increases, then the chances of ending in the money are very much lower and so the price drops.

THE DEALER'S POINT OF VIEW

Now consider the dealer. As an exotic options trader, the dealer constantly sells options—Asian options, chooser options, ratchet options, and other types of structures. While the dealer can adequately delta-hedge her position, her main concern is volatility. As the dealer is short options, she is also short volatility. The clients of these options are all long volatility. As volatility increases, the price of the options goes up. The dealer sold these options with a low volatility and a low price, and now the price has increased.

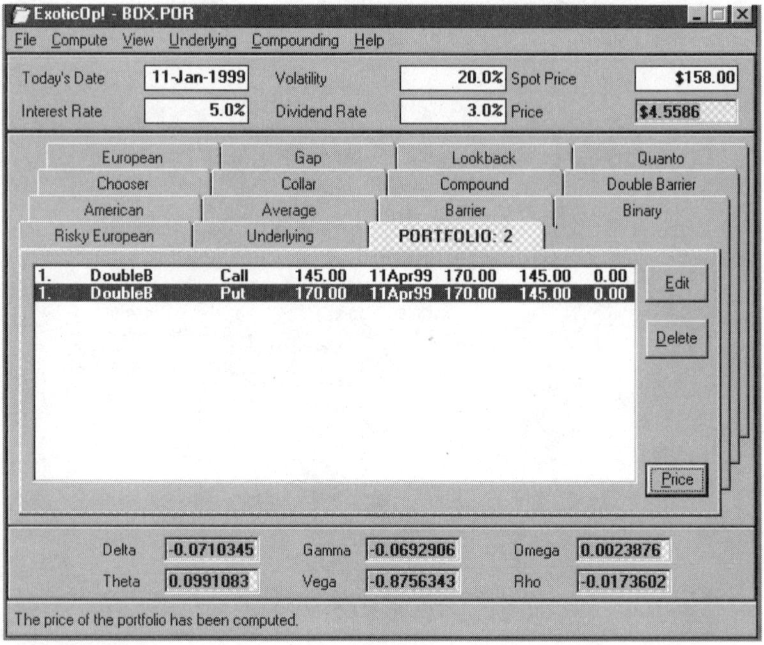

Figure 12.3   A double-barrier box trade.

The double-barrier box allows the dealer to sell options that are short volatility. As volatility increases, the price of the options decreases. Thus the dealer is now long volatility. This long volatility exposure helps to equalize the dealer's book in terms of volatility exposure.

The client, on the other hand, wants to take a short volatility position. One alternative is to be short a straddle. The short straddle position makes a little money with the potential of a large loss. The client earns the premium of the options, but may lose a lot, if one of them ends deep in the money. The box trade allows clients to limit their exposure, while retaining the chance of a big profit.

The dealers were quite happy when they discovered that they could sell the double-barrier boxes and equalize their volatility exposures. The double-barrier options were not too difficult to price either. A Monte Carlo pricing method works fine, and it is very simple to design. Alternatively, many papers have been published on the development of closed-form solutions to the problem.*

DELTA "EXPLODES"

In Figure 12.4, we move the underlying very close to the barrier, we move the time close to the expiration date, and we also reduce volatility.

Consider the dealer who has sold these options. At this moment, the delta-hedge ratio that must be maintained by the dealer is 1,000 percent. Consider that the dealer sold an option with a notional underlying of $10 million. A European option with a delta of 50 percent is hedged with a $5 million notional

---

*For example, see "Barrier Options" by Eric Berger, Chapter 8 in *The Handbook of Exotic Options* (Irwin McGraw-Hill, 1995). Dr. Berger has developed formulas for the pricing of barrier options. These rely on the summation of infinite series. Fortunately, the series converge very fast and only a few terms are needed.

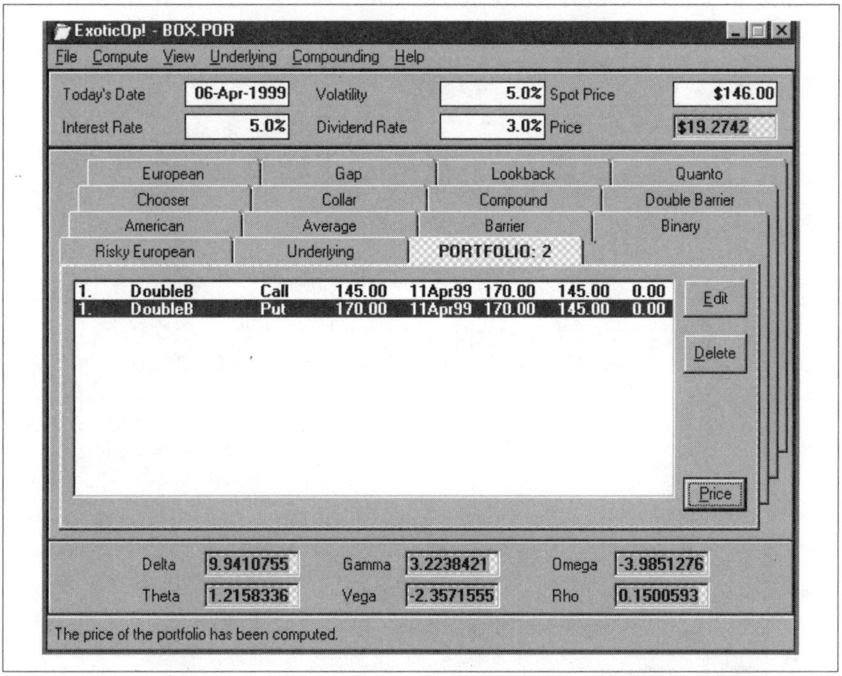

Figure 12.4   A short double-barrier box trade. Note that delta is 1,000 percent!

underlying. The double-barrier box needs to be hedged with $100 million. This is a large amount even in liquid markets.

To make things worse, delta is negative. This means that the dealer must purchase the underlying. But when the dealer purchases the underlying, he is supporting its price. All the dealer wishes for is that the underlying, currently trading at $146, will decline in price below $145 and that the structure will be knocked out. Instead, the dealer finds himself purchasing the underlying and supporting the price. Thus the dealer is "going against himself."

In Figure 12.5 we have the dealer who is short the double-barrier box also long ten units of underlying (or 1,000 percent). Now the dealer is delta-hedged.

Consider what would happen should the underlying decline to below $145. The box trade gets knocked out, and the dealer is left long ten units of underlying "naked." The exotic options book is obviously not equipped to handle a delta of 1,000 percent. The dealer must now sell his entire underlying position in a hurry.

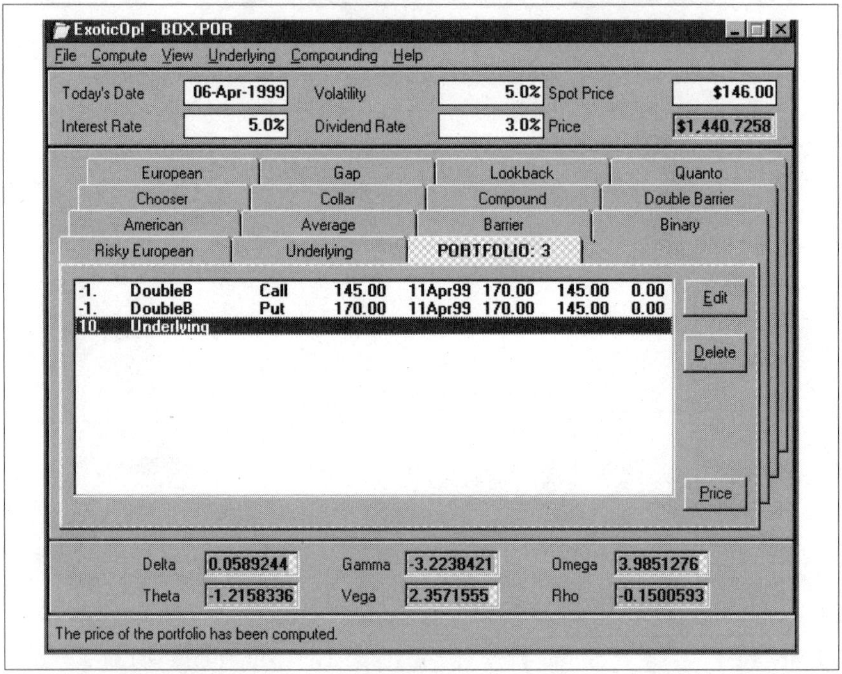

Figure 12.5   A delta-hedged position, short the double-barrier box, long 1,000 percent of the underlying.

The dealer finds himself building up a delta position and then getting rid of it in a hurry.

A POSSIBLE SOLUTION

What can the dealer do to avoid being in this "volatility squeeze" situation? In Figure 12.6 we show the option after volatility has decreased somewhat and the underlying has moved relatively close to the barrier.

The dealer can call the client and inform her that the barrier is at $145 and the underlying is at $147, dangerously close to the barrier. To avoid being knocked out, the dealer proposes to widen the barrier to $140 and $170. This will greatly improve the client's chances of ending in the money. However, the dealer can no longer pay $25 if the client ends in the money, but can pay $7.50 instead. So the client's chances of ending in the money are much improved, but her payout will be lower. This can be an even trade-off since the client will not have to add any more funds. Figure 12.7 shows the double-barrier box proposed by the

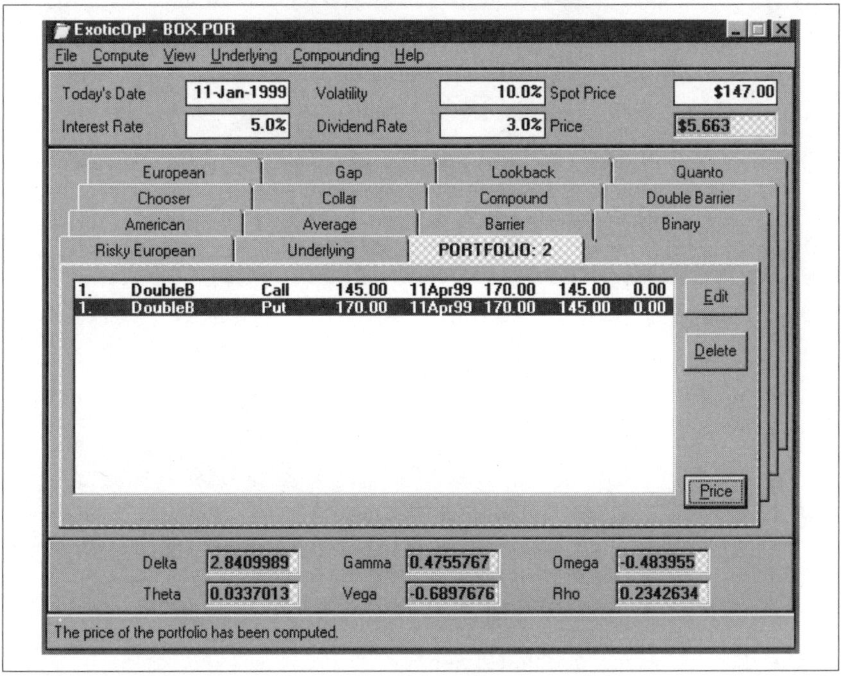

Figure 12.6   The underlying is relatively close to the barrier.

dealer. Its price is $5.13, slightly less than the $5.66 that the previous structure cost.

The call by the dealer has the following effects:

- It saves the relationship since the client is less likely to be knocked out.
- It reduces the chance that the dealer will have to suffer the consequences of the volatility squeeze.
- It makes money for the dealer since the dealer swaps the client from an expensive option to a cheap one.

SUMMARY

Double-barrier box trades are now being transacted on many different asset types. They are done on equities, currencies, commodities, and even credit spreads. Clients find them an excellent vehicle to be short volatility, while dealers find them useful for balancing their volatility exposure.

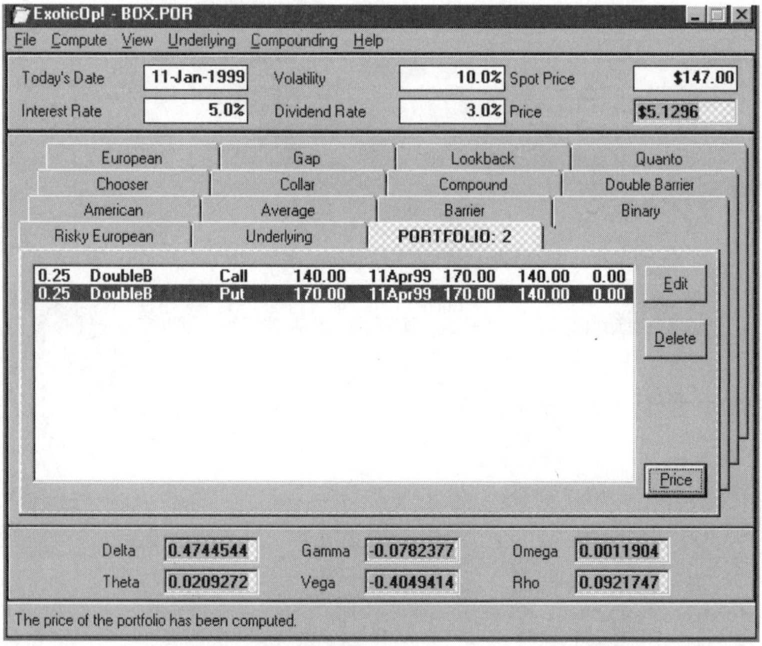

Figure 12.7   A "wider" double-barrier box.

CHAPTER 13

One-Touch Options

INTRODUCTION

In a one-touch option, the investor receives an all-or-nothing payout if the underlying ever touches a barrier.

ONE-TOUCH OPTION AS A BARRIER

Consider a simple barrier knock-out option. If you remove the option, all you have is the barrier with a rebate. Take a call with a barrier at $90 and a rebate of $5, and set the strike of the call option as $9,999. The option itself is worthless since the underlying price is currently at $100. All that really counts is the rebate, because the option is so way out of the money. The rebate pays you $5 if the underlying reaches $90. That is called a one-touch option. You receive a rebate if you touch.

DIFFERENT TYPES OF ONE-TOUCH OPTIONS

One can think of a great variety of one-touch options. In our notation, D is a cash amount, $S(t)$ is the underlying price, and B is the barrier level and $S(t)$ is the price of the underlying at the expiration of the option.

Immediate Payout

- *Up-and-in cash option:*

  Receive D (a fixed cash amount) as soon as $S(t) >= B$

  Payout is made immediately.

- *Up-and-in underlying option:*

  Receive $S(t)$ (the underlying) as soon as $S(t) >= B$

  Payout is made immediately.

- *Down-and-in cash option:*

  Receive D (a fixed cash amount) as soon as $S(t) <= B$

  Payout is made immediately.

- *Down-and-in underlying option:*

  Receive $S(t)$ (the underlying) as soon as $S(t) <= B$

  Payout is made immediately.

In modeling the immediate-payout type of options, we do not have to make a distinction between whether you receive cash or the underlying. Even if you receive the underlying, you will receive it when it is worth exactly B. So you can model this as a cash-paying option with a payout equal to the level of the barrier.

Payout at Expiry

- *Up-and-in cash option:*

  Receive D on the expiration date
  if it ever happened that $S(t) >= B$

- *Up-and-in underlying option:*

  Receive $S(T)$ on the expiration date
  if it ever happened that $S(t) >= B$

- *Down-and-in cash option:*

  Receive D if it ever happened that $S(t) <= B$

- *Down-and-in underlying option:*

  Receive $S(T)$ if it ever happened that $S(t) <= B$

- *Up-and-out cash option:*

  Receive D unless it happened that $S(t) >= B$

- *Up-and-out underlying option:*

  Receive $S(T)$ unless it happened that $S(t) >= B$

- *Down-and-out cash option:*

  Receive D unless it happened that $S(t) <= B$

- *Down-and-out underlying option:*

  Receive $S(T)$ unless it happened that $S(t) <= B$

In modeling the payout-at-expiration type of options, we have to make a distinction between whether you receive cash or the underlying. The underlying that will be received has a value of $S(T)$. This value is probably different from the value of the barrier.

MARKET

Many clients have made money with one-touch options. In 1997, some clients made quick money with dollar-denominated one-touch options at 1.69 Deutsche marks and 120 yen. They had payouts of 6:1 or even 7:1. Sterling–Deutsche mark one-touches at $2.70 were also profitable.

Toward the end of May 1997, some six-month and one-year one-touches were put on to exploit the potential downside of the U.S. dollar against the Canadian below 1.30. These were based on the assumption that the Fed would not raise rates but the Canadian central bank eventually would.

Clients are embedding knock-outs in their one-touch bets. Clients are looking for savings in the 25 to 50 percent range. If a one touch pays 4:1, a one-touch with a knock-out might pay 8:1. For example, the client will receive a $5 payout if the underlying touches $90. But if it touches $110 before that, the client will lose the option and the payout altogether.

APPLICATION

The *conditional premium* option is very popular. A company protects its long currency exposure by buying a plain vanilla put. There is no up-front premium. A premium is paid only if certain triggers are hit.

Suppose, for example, a U.S. corporation expects sterling receivables. It does not want the sterling to weaken. So it buys a conditional premium sterling put with a strike of $1.65 to 1 sterling. The structure has one trigger at $1.70 and another at $1.72.

If sterling declines below $1.65, the company can sell sterling at $1.65 without paying any premium. If sterling ends above $1.65, the company can sell at the spot market without paying any premium for the protection it purchased.

However, if the sterling goes as high as $1.70, part of the premium is due. This is offset by the higher price the company receives for its sterling in the spot market. And if it goes above $1.72, the rest of the premium is due. Again, this is offset by the higher price the company receives for its sterling.

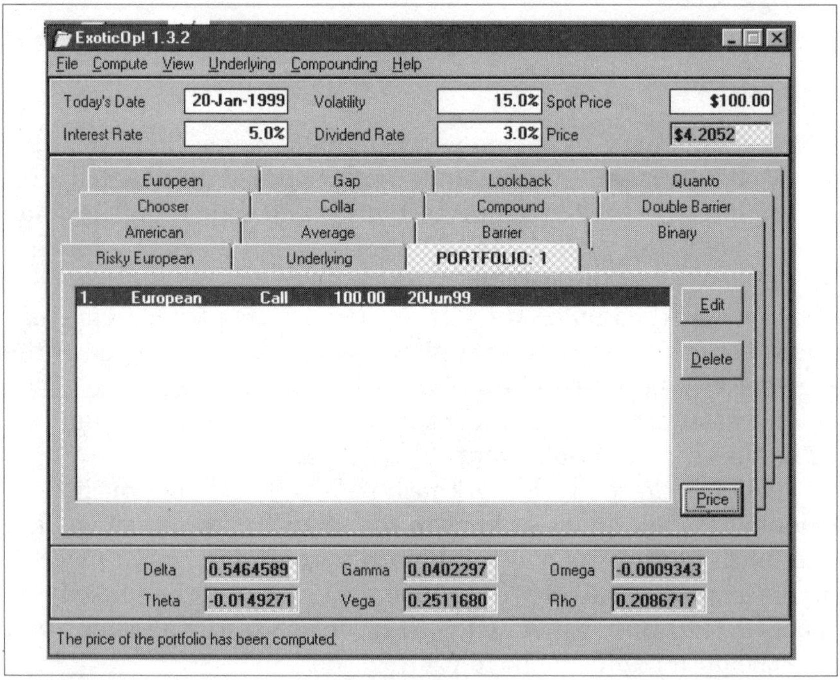

Figure 13.1   A standard European option.

Consider a specific example: Figure 13.1 shows a standard European option. The price of this option is about $4.20.

In Figure 13.2, we have a position in the same European option combined with a short position in one-touch options.

- If the underlying declines and reaches $99, the investor will pay $1.70.
- If the underlying further declines to $98, the investor will pay another $1.70.
- If the underlying further declines to $97, the investor will pay another $1.70.

If the investor is bullish and the underlying just climbs from $100 upward, then she effectively receives a free option that expires in the money. If the investor is wrong and the underlying declines and hits $99, she will have to pay $1.70. The worst case, from the point of view of the investor, is that she will end up paying $1.70 three times, or $5.10.

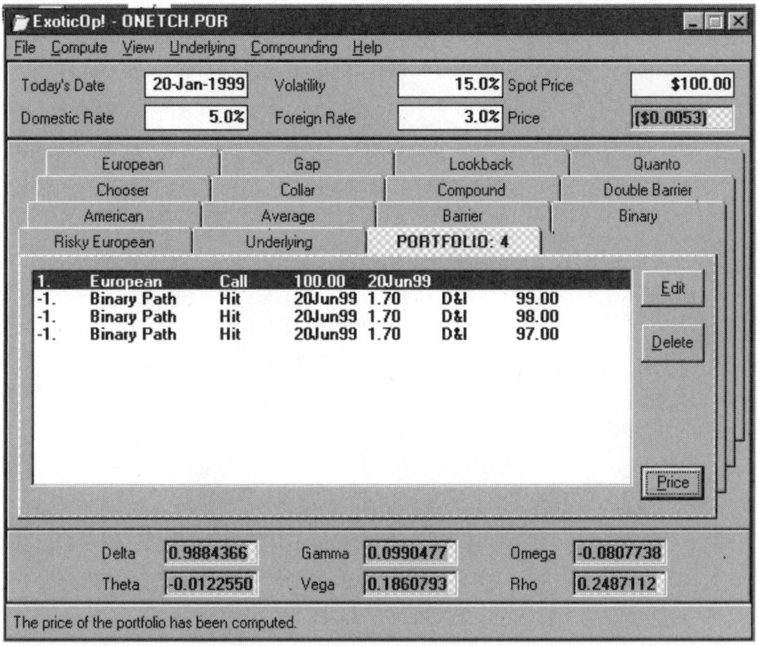

Figure 13.2   A European option combined with one-touch options.

SUMMARY

One-touch options can be thought of as the rebate of barrier options. They can be used to "bet" that an underlying will reach a certain level. They are often combined with other options to create a structure.

CHAPTER 14

Ladder Options

INTRODUCTION

Ladder options are options whose payouts are locked at preordained levels. These options lock in profits when the underlying reaches certain levels.

PAYOFF OF THE LADDER OPTION

The payout for a ladder call can be written as

$$\max \{0, [S(T) - X], \max [L(i) - X]\}$$

where we only consider the ladder levels that were activated by the underlying during the life of the option.

The payoff is the maximal of:

- Zero
- The payoff of a European
- The highest ladder level reached minus the strike

If there are many ladder levels at very close intervals, we obtain a lookback option. That is to say, if the ladder has many rungs, at very close intervals, we obtain a lookback option that catches the absolute maximum level reached by the underlying.

A ONE-RUNG LADDER

A one-rung-ladder call has the payout

$$C = \max [0, S(T) - X, L - X]$$

where L is some predetermined level attained by the underlying. *Question:* Where should you place the rung of the ladder to generate an option whose premium will be maximized? Alternatively stated, if you were to draw a graph of the fair value price of the ladder against the value of the rung, how would the graph look? Is the premium increasing in value? Decreasing?

If L is very close to S, there is a good likelihood that it will be hit—but with a small guaranteed payout. Thus if we place the rung very low, we essentially have a European option (Figure 14.3).

If L is far from S, there is a possibly large guaranteed payout but a very low chance of receiving it. Thus if we place the rung very high, we will, again, have a European option (Figure 14.4).

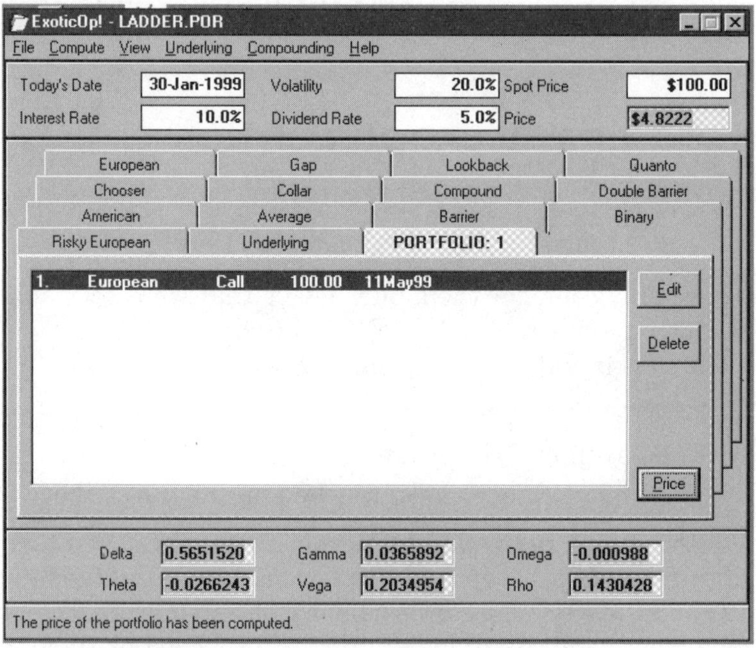

Figure 14.1 A European option.

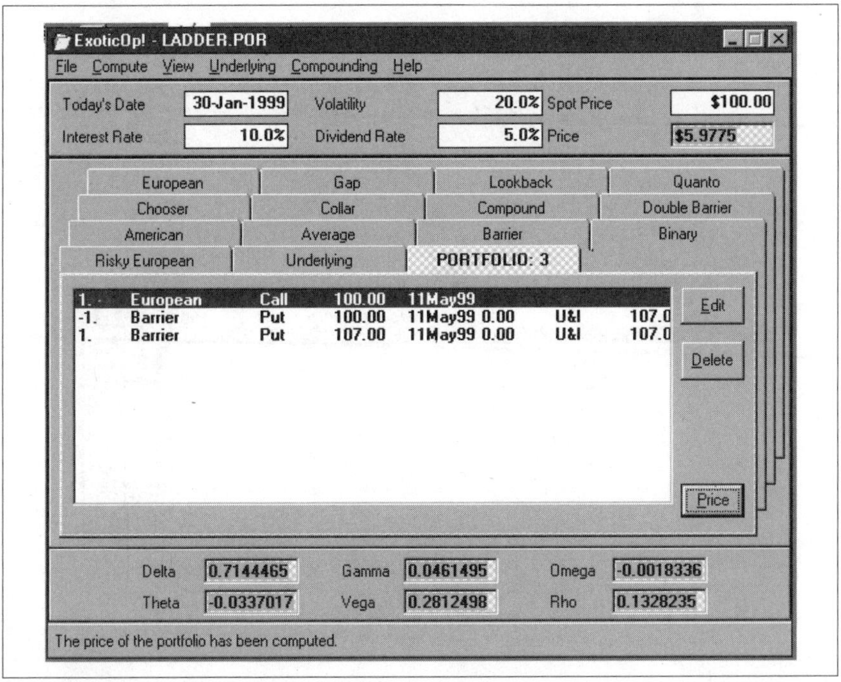

Figure 14.2   A ladder with a rung in the midrange. It is more expensive than a European.

There is an L that maximizes the price of the ladder, as shown in Figures 14.1 to 14.4. We show a ladder with different rung levels. There is a level of the rung which maximizes the value of the ladder.

For the decomposition of a ladder, the strategy is:

1. Long a European call; strike = X.
2. Short a European put; strike = X.
3. Long a knock-out put; strike = X; barrier = L.
4. Long a European put; strike = L.
5. Short a knock-out put; strike = L; barrier = L.

An alternative structure is:

1. Long a European call; strike = X.
2. Short a knock-in put; strike = X; barrier = L.
3. Long a knock-in put; strike = L; barrier = L.

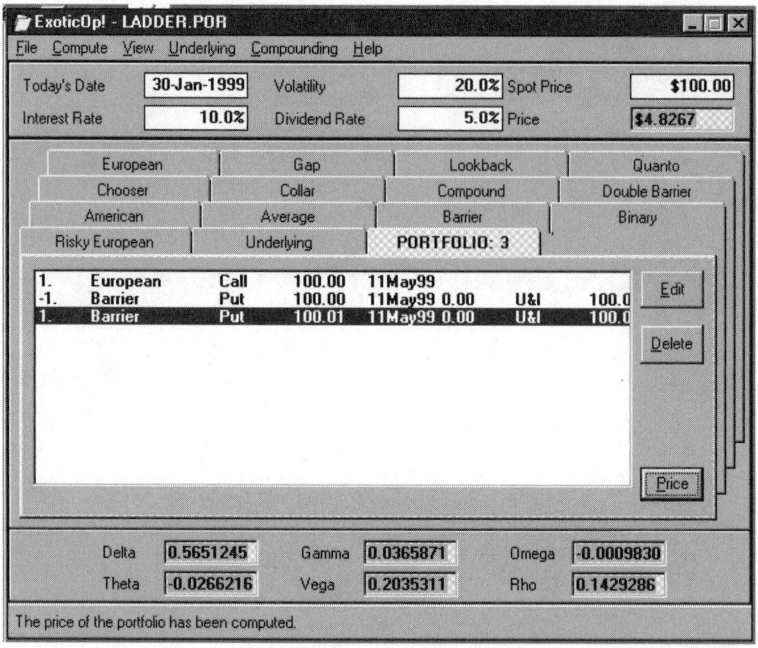

Figure 14.3   A ladder with a very low rung. Essentially, a European option.

Let S = \$100, L = \$105, and X = \$100. Substituting into the decomposition-of-a-ladder equations, we get:

1. Long a European call; strike = \$100.
2. Short a European put; strike = \$100.
3. Long a knock-out put; strike = \$100; barrier = \$105.
4. Long a European put; strike = \$105.
5. Short a knock-out put; strike = \$105; barrier = \$105.

Suppose S never goes above \$105, and say it ends at \$104; the results are:

1. +\$4.00
2. −\$0.00
3. +\$0.00
4. +\$1.00
5. −\$1.00
Sum = \$4.00

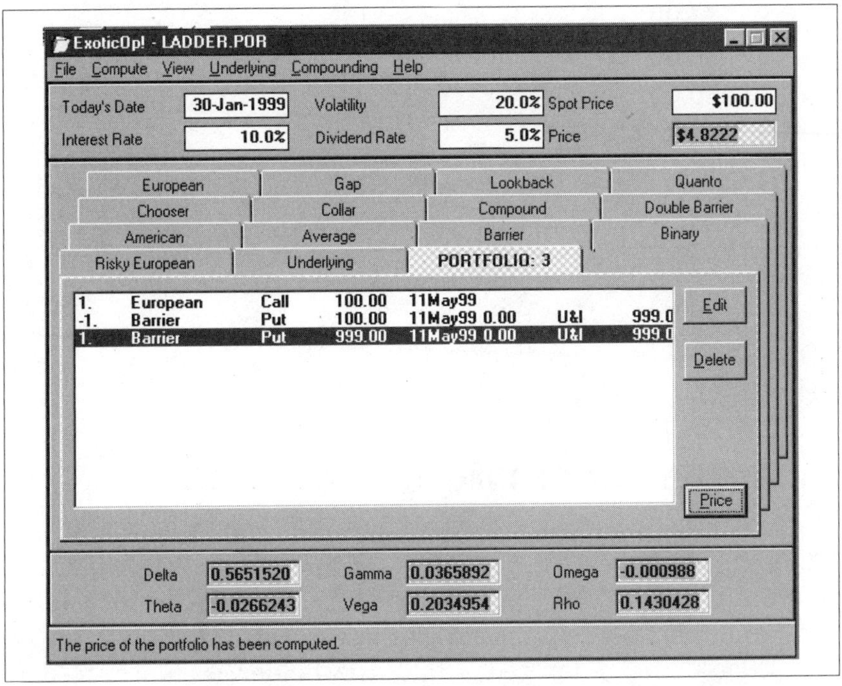

Figure 14.4   A ladder with a very high rung. Also a European option.

Suppose S has climbed past $105 and ended at $104; the results are:

1. +$4.00
2. −$0.00
3. +0.00
4. +$1.00
5. −$0.00
Sum = $5.00

Substituting into the alternative structure equations, we get:

1. Long a European call; strike = $100.
2. Short a knock-in put; strike = $100; barrier = $105.
3. Long a knock-in put; strike = $105; barrier = $105.

Suppose S never goes above $105, and say it ends at $104; the results are:

1. +$4.00
2. −$0.00
3. +$0.00
Sum = $4.00

Suppose S has climbed past $105 and ended at $104; the results are:

1. +$4.00
2. −$0.00
3. +$1.00
Sum = $5.00

A LADDER WITH TWO RUNGS

Assume the underlying index is the S&P 500 and the level is $500. Consider a call option struck at the money ($X = \$500$). The two rungs are at 5 percent and 10 percent, which correspond to $525 and $550. The option expires in six months.

Should the index reach 525, the holder is guaranteed to receive 525 − 500 = 25 points regardless of where the index closed. Should the index reach 550, the holder is guaranteed to receive 550 − 500 = 50 points regardless of where the index closed.

Two-rung ladders may also be created by a combination of barrier options.

For a ladder with more than one rung, it is difficult to find the levels of the rungs that would maximize the price of the ladder. Essentially, we need to do a "brute force" search over all the possible ranges. However, people rarely do that. Usually, rung levels are placed at equal distances.

SUMMARY

Ladder options allow retail investors to capture the upside of an equity market at predefined levels. The holder is protected against a subsequent drop in price levels.

CHAPTER 15

Asian Options

INTRODUCTION

Asian options are particularly suitable for a business that has ongoing expenditures or receivables. Such a business is more concerned with the average price of the underlying items purchased or sold rather than the price on a specific date.

PAYOUT

Consider a regular call option with a payout function of max $(S - X, 0)$, where S is the price and X is the strike.

- An average price call pays max $(A - X, 0)$. The average (A) replaces the price.
- An average strike call pays max $(S - A, 0)$. Here the average replaces the strike in the formula.

This terminology can be confusing because both types of options are termed "call options." To keep them straight, it helps to remember that A is on the left-hand side of the equation of the average *price* call and on the right-hand side of the average *strike* call equation. The same goes for the put option.

EXAMPLE

Consider a company that hedges its monthly cash flows or even its daily cash flows—for example, an airline. It has to refuel its airplanes every day. Let's assume that the airline buys 10,000 barrels of oil every day. What the airline is concerned with is that it show a profit at the end of the year. How much profit does the airline have? It sold so many tickets and received so much money for them. It has also had some expenses, including the purchase of 10,000 barrels of oil every day. That is its profit and loss. Rather than being concerned with the price of oil today and then the price of oil tomorrow, the airline really is concerned with the price of oil over the entire year—the average. That average price will affect its earnings statement. What has it paid on average for this commodity?

An average price call option is suitable to hedge the airline's exposure to oil. The most common type of Asian option is the average price call. It allows the airline to purchase oil at an average price that is capped in advance. By purchasing an Asian option the airline can guarantee itself that the average price it will have to pay for oil will not be greater than $18 a barrel.

Let's look at two strategies from the point of view of the airline:

- One strategy is to buy a strip of European call options, one that expires every day or one that expires every month (see Figure 15.1).
- The other strategy is to buy a single Asian option on the average (see Figure 15.2).

How do the prices compare?

In Figure 15.2, we take the average, starting on January 12, 2000. The averaging ends on June 12, 2000. For the sake of comparison with European options, suppose the company wants to purchase five units of the Asian option. The price for the Asian option is about $17. Now the company is becoming very interested. The company was hedging with a strip of European options and was paying $22. That's a big difference.

There is also another issue, one regarding basis risk. The company buys oil in the spot market every day. Assume that it hedges itself with a strip of Europeans that mature on the twelfth

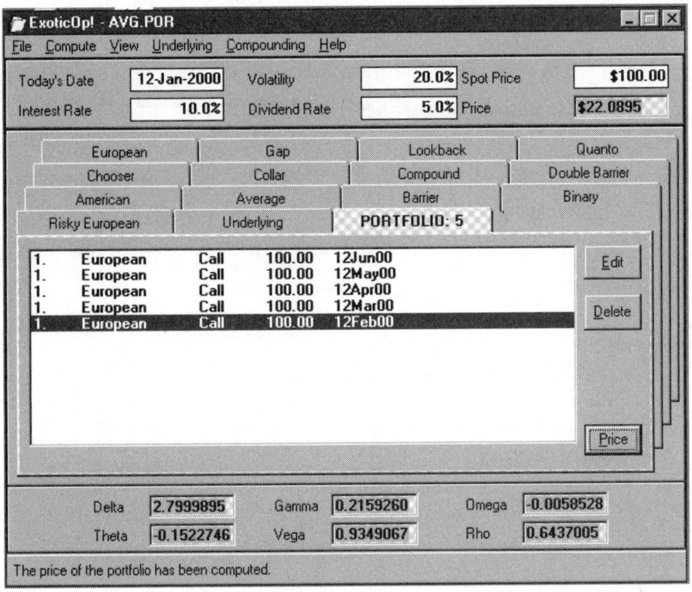

Figure 15.1   A strip of European options, one maturing every month.

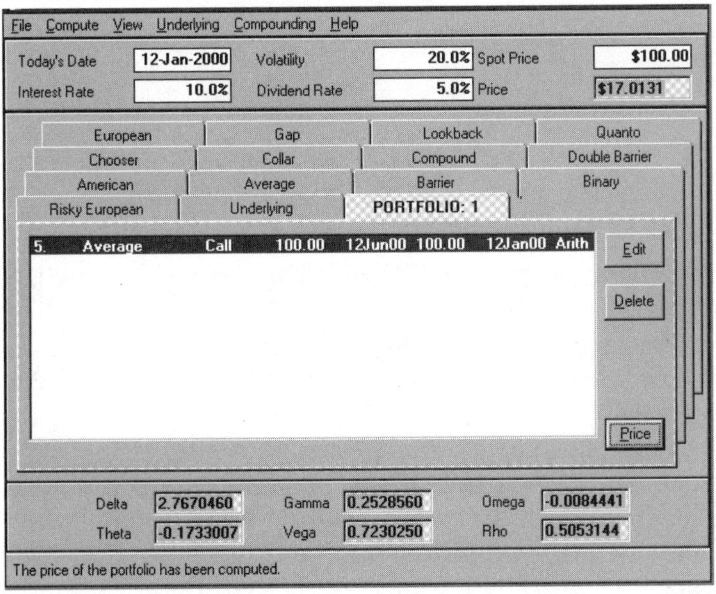

Figure 15.2   An Asian option.

of each month. For some reason (e.g., Saddam Hussein is in a bad mood on the twelfth of every month) the price of oil dips on every twelfth. Thus all the European options expire out of the money, even though the price of oil has been high on other days. So the company still has a basis risk with the strip of European options.

The Asian option matches what the company really wants to hedge, which is the average price. The company is concerned with the daily average, and not with the price of oil on some preselected specific dates.

WHY IS THE ASIAN OPTION CHEAPER?

Let's assume a strike is $18 a barrel. Also assume that the oil prices are as follows:

February 12, $18
March 12, $19
April 12, $17
May 12, $20
June 12, $16

The strip of Europeans will have a payout. The strip will pay out as follows:

February 12, $0
March 12, $1
April 12, $0
May 12, $2
June 12, $0

On months when the oil price is low, the options will expire worthless. But every time the price of oil is high, the European options will pay out. The average of all these prices in this contrived example is $18. So really the airline is quite happy with the price of $18. That's what its target price for oil is, and it doesn't need the extra compensation. The European options had a payout, and this is the reason that the company had to pay more for them initially.

The strip of Europeans paid out $3. The company doesn't mind getting paid out, but the point is that it also paid more premium for these European options. It was overinsurance. This is similar to a person who bought a Chevette, but is insuring it as if it were a Rolls Royce. That person is paying too much insurance.

Consider the Asian option again. A single Asian option is priced at $3.39. A European option with the same strike is priced at $6.03. So we have $3.39 versus $6.03.

Why is the Asian option so much cheaper? It's based on an average. For example, suppose you were asked to guess the height of a person walking on the street. Choose a person at random, that person could be short or could be tall. Who knows? There is a lot of variability in the height of a single person. But instead suppose you were asked to guess the average height of all the people crossing the street on their lunch hour, between 1 and 2 p.m. It is easier to pinpoint that average very accurately because we have sampled a large group of people. The average has less volatility. The same is true of a price series. The average price will vary much less than individual prices. Similarly, we don't know how much a particular person earns, but we know the average family earns so many thousands of dollars, has 2.13 kids, 1.5 goldfish, etc. The average is easier to determine based on many samples rather than one sample. Also, it's variability is less.

ASIAN IS HALF A EUROPEAN

At $3.39 the price of the Asian option is approximately half of that of the European option, which is $6.03. This follows the rule of thumb that the price of an at-the-money Asian option is approximately half that of an at-the-money European. Why half? Assume that today's underlying price is $100. The option's strike is also $100. We price the European option based on the forward curve. Assume that the forward price is $110. So the price of the European has to do with the $110 (the forward price) and the volatility. We price this European option with a distribution around $110. The strike was $100, and so the payout is proportional to $10.

The Asian option, on the other hand, has many distributions around the forward prices every day from now until maturity. The spot price today is $100, and the forward price at maturity is $110. The straight line in Figure 15.3 depicts the

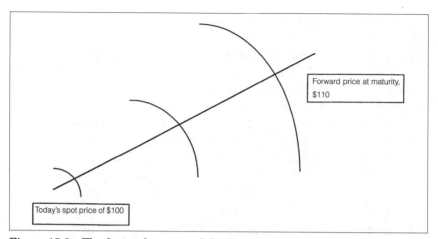

Forward price at maturity, $110

Today's spot price of $100

Figure 15.3 The forward curve and the distribution around it.

forward curve. Close to today, on the left-hand side of the figure, there is an arc that represents the log-normal distribution of possible prices around the forward price. As we move further out in time, the arcs become wider and wider. This illustrates that the price next week is known with some certainty but the price next year has a wider distribution. The Asian option has a payout of max $(A - X, 0)$, where X is $100. The A is taken as the average of all these distributions. Intuitively, A is roughly $105. So the payout of the Asian is proportional to $5. It thus makes sense that an at-the-money Asian option should be priced close to one-half the price of an at-the-money European. Still, that is just a rule of thumb. The precise price depends on the exact forward curve, etc.

TYPES OF ASIAN OPTIONS

An important question in regard to Asian options has to do with the frequency of averaging. Do we take the daily average, the weekly, the monthly, etc.? In this book, for the most part we discuss continuously computed averages. However, other averaging options are available where the average is taken with specific time intervals (e.g., daily closes or weekly prices).

We also note that in the markets it is possible to see the following types of Asian options. Assume that the four successive prices of the underlying are $80, $105, $90, and $110 and that the strike of the Asian is $100.

- *Regular Asian option.* Average of $80, $105, $90, and $110, which is $96.25
- *Floored Asian.* Average of $100, $105, $100, and $110, which is $103.75
- *Super Asian.* Average of $105 and $110 (two numbers), which is $107.50

With a regular Asian option, the payout will be determined by the average of the four prices. The floored Asian replaces any price that is less than the strike with the strike. Thus underlying prices that are less than $100 are replaced by $100 before entering into the average. The super Asian does not consider any underlying prices that are below $100.

The floored and super Asian varieties have evolved because clients wanted positive payouts in scenarios where the underlying price may have been low for a while and then shot up. It is obvious that the floored and super Asian varieties will pay at least as much as the normal Asian options. Of course, the premiums involved will also be higher.

AN APPLICATION

Winterthur Insurance is a Swiss insurance company that has been purchased by Credit Suisse. Winterthur sells life insurance policies in Switzerland in which the policy pays out according to the Swiss Market index (the SMI). The payout of the policy is tied not to the level of the SMI, but to the average price that it has been trading. The old joke mentions the stockbroker who jumps from the roof because the stock market fell. At least his relatives will receive some payout from the insurance company. For Winterthur Insurance, on the other hand, the payout policy is nice because the company can hedge itself by paying $3.39 for an Asian option rather than $6.03 for a European option. And for the client, it's also nice because the client is not exposed to the specific value of the SMI the moment that something happens to him.

ADVANTAGES OF THE ASIAN OPTION

- *Lower option price.* Everybody wants to pay $3.39 rather than $6.03—that's obvious.
- *Matching the exposure.* As we've seen, the Asian matches the actual exposure of the corporation.
- *Decreasing volatility.* The volatility of the average is much lower than the volatility of the underlying price.
- *Resolving settlement uncertainty.* Consider the Asian option depicted in Figure 15.2. The averaging period is from January 12, 2000, until June 12, 2000. Assume that today's date is June 1, 2000. By the beginning of June, we have seen almost all of the prices, and the average is pretty much determined. Even if there is a major crash in the market, the average will not be affected by very much. This is similar to the student who is due to receive a final grade based on the average of all his assignments and exams throughout the semester. If the student receives great marks throughout the entire semester, he can afford not to study for the final exam. Even if the student fails the final exam, his average grade will be well above the passing mark. In our previous example, we had to determine the average height of the people who crossed a particular street on their lunch hour. At 1:55 p.m. we pretty much know the average. Even if a group of tall basketball players comes by, we have already averaged 90 percent of the people that we were going to count. So the basketball players will not impact our average by too much.
- *Low Greeks.* By the beginning of June 2000, the Asian option has a payout that is fairly well determined. Hence, delta is low and so is vega. The client really doesn't care about anything since at this point, the Asian option is really like cash. The client and the dealer almost know what the payout is going to be.

A CURIOUS EXAMPLE

It is an interesting exercise to consider a time line and compare the prices of a European option with those of an Asian option. Initially, when we purchase the option, the averaging period may begin in the future. This is known as a *deferred* averaging option. The price of a deferred averaging option should be very close to the price of a European. Suppose that we are buying the option at the beginning of the year. Its payout will be determined by the average price on the last week of that year. Do we really care that this is an average option as opposed to a European? Not very much. Since the averaging only occurs on the last week of the year and it has not yet begun, it does not affect the price by much.

Consider an Asian option with an averaging period between March 12, 2001, and December 12, 2001. Also consider a European option with an expiration date set to December 12, 2001. As shown in Table 15.1, on September 12, 1999, the price of the Asian is $15.40 and the price of the European is $15.54. There is a very small difference in price between the two.

The fact that the Asian and European are close in price makes sense. You haven't started averaging yet because your averaging period is a long time off. Averaging doesn't really matter when the averaging period is way out in the future. It only matters when you start to move closer to the averaging period.

Now a year has passed, and it is September 12, 2000. The European has a price of $11.28, and the Asian has become cheaper at $8.99.

Once again time passes, and it is now December 12, 2000. The European is $9.95, and that's fine. It decreases in price because of its time value; there's less time. So no surprises so far. And the Asian is $7.04.

Time keeps moving forward, and now it is March 12, 2001— right at the beginning of the averaging period. The European is

TABLE 15.1

Comparison of European and Asian Options

Date	Price of European	Price of Asian
September 12, 1999	$15.54	$15.40
September 12, 2000	$11.28	$ 8.99
December 12, 2000	$ 9.95	$ 7.04
March 12, 2001	$ 8.47	$ 4.72

$8.47 and the Asian is $4.72. Remember the rule of thumb that stated that at the beginning of the averaging period, the Asian should be priced approximately half of the European? So the prices of $8.47 and $4.72 make intuitive sense.

Consider the following trading idea. On September 12, 1999, buy a European option for $15.54 and sell an Asian option for $15.40. How much would you have to spend on this deal? The total cost is 14 cents. Then do not do anything and just wait for March 12, 2001, to come around. On March 12, 2001, simply reverse the trade. Sell the European and buy the Asian. The total received is $3.75. To sum up, this is a trade idea in which you invest $0.14, do nothing, and then recoup $3.75.

We have already seen that the price of the European and the price of the Asian are pretty close if they average a long time into the future. We have also seen that there is a big difference in prices if we start averaging right now. In that case, the price of the Asian is about half of the European. So the numbers in the previous example actually make sense intuitively. Can we really turn $0.14 into $3.75?

Note that we used the very same spot price to price both options. We kept the spot price at $100 all along the way. On March 12, 2001, the assumption that the Asian is one-half of the European only holds true for an at-the-money Asian and an at-the-money European. These options were at the money when we first bought them on September 12, 1999, but they are not likely to remain at the money until March 12, 2001.

For example, if the spot price on March 12, 2001, is $80, then the Asian is priced at $0.06 and the European is priced at $1.06. The difference is only $1.00. The difference we paid on September 12, 1999, of 14 cents, is the present value of the expected value of all these differences which may happen on March 12, 2001. On March 12, 2001, this difference is going to be very large only when both options are at the money. In other circumstances, the difference between the option prices is smaller.

AVERAGE SO FAR

Consider an Asian option in which the averaging has already started. This is known as "in-process" averaging. We are in the midst of the averaging period. A very important question has to do with the *average so far.* Assume that the averaging period is from January 12, 2000, to December 12, 2000. Consider trading the option on September 12, 2000. A lot of the averaging has already been done. That's the point.

In Figure 15.4, we price the Asian option under the assumption that the average so far is $100. The option price is $0.69. In Figure 15.5, we price the same option under the assumption that the average so far is $105. The price is $3.71.

What's really important is not where the spot market is at the moment. It's what the average so far has been. In Figures 15.4 and 15.5, both markets are at $100. The difference is where they have been in the past. This has a dramatic impact on the price of the option. This is obvious because the Asian option in Figure 15.5 is already $5 in the money. Even if the market stays at $100, a lot of time has passed here and the client pretty much will receive a high payout. The Asian option in Figure 15.4 is just at the money. The average so far is equal to the spot price. The

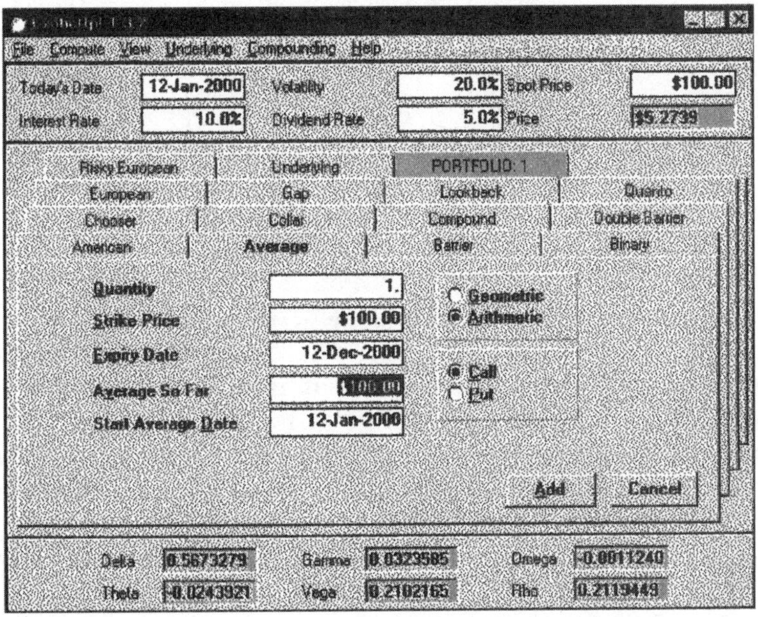

Figure 15.4   An Asian option. Note the average-so-far field that is highlighted.

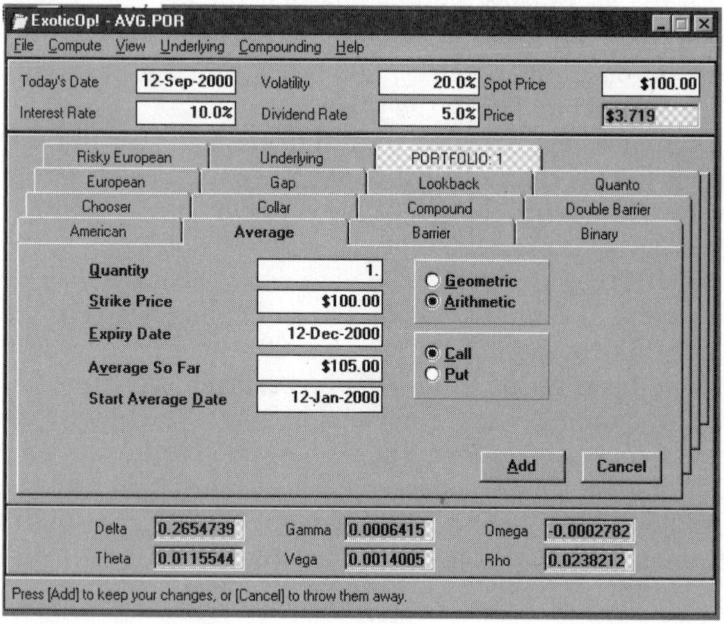

Figure 15.5   The same Asian option. Note the difference between this and Figure 15.4 in the average so far.

option will only pay out if the market begins to climb. Even then, the payout will not be very big. Hence a key component in process-averaging options is what the average is so far.

Dealers in Asian options must capture the average so far and enter it into their systems. In one of the banks in New York where average rate options are traded, there is a clerk who takes an Excel spreadsheet, calculates the average of the relevant underlying instrument, and sticks it into the machine. Every day the clerk updates the average so far. For weekly averaging options, the clerk updates the average once a week, etc. Other dealers may use an automatic system to capture the average so far. Most dealers have a real-time feed that captures the spot price and automatically updates it in their system. They may also have a real-time feed for interest rates, volatility, etc. However, in order to trade Asian options, they have to build a special system to capture the average so far.

AN INTERESTING FEATURE
OF ASIAN OPTIONS

Currency traders who are used to dealing with European options in two currencies know that a currency option may be quoted in either currency. It makes no difference. For example, a USD call/DM put may be quoted either in terms of U.S. dollars or in terms of German marks. In Asian options, one has to be careful of the currency in which the option is quoted.

For the sake of illustration, assume that 1 U.S. dollar is equal to 2 German marks. A German client buys an at-the-money call option on the U.S. dollar. The strike price is 2 German marks per U.S. dollar. The price of the option is 0.2654 German mark. The option gives the client the right to buy a U.S. dollar for 2 German marks on the expiration date. This is illustrated in Figure 15.6.

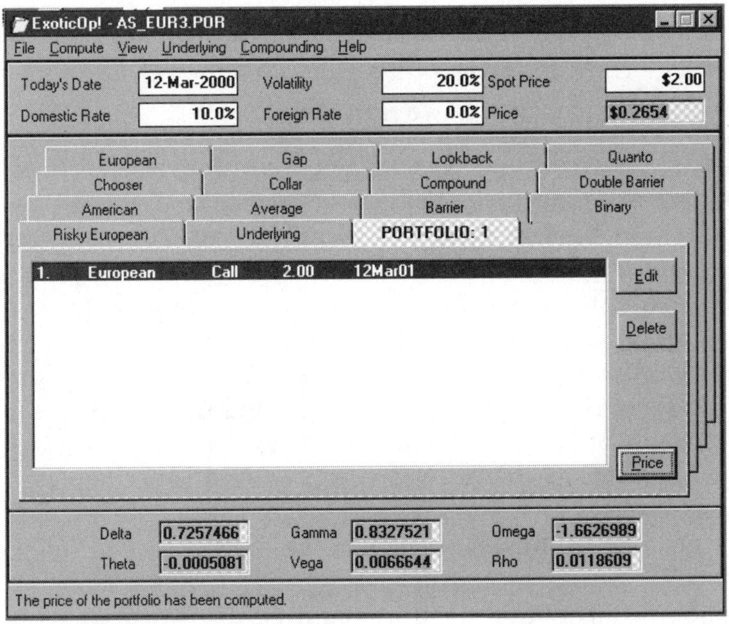

Figure 15.6   A European call option. The client has the right to purchase 1 U.S. dollar for 2 German marks.

A similar option can be purchased in U.S. dollars. This would be a put on the German mark struck at 0.50. The price of this option is 0.0663 U.S. dollar. When pricing the put option, remember to substitute the foreign rate for the domestic rate. So far we have seen that:

- The U.S. dollar call is worth 0.2654 German mark.
- The German mark put is worth 0.0663 U.S. dollar.
- The ratio of these two numbers is 4.00.

We expect the ratio to be 4: First, the U.S. dollar is worth twice the German mark, and so we have to pay double the amount in marks than we would in dollars. Second, the notional of the call option is 1 U.S. dollar; the notional of the put option is 1 German mark. Therefore, there is a 2-to-1 ratio between the notional amounts. Both effects combine so that the ratio of the option prices should be 4 to 1. We have $C(S,X,r,q) = P(1/S, 1/X,q,r)$, adjusted for currency and notional.

We repeat these computations with Asian options and find:

- The U.S. dollar call is worth 0.1413 German mark.
- The German mark put is worth 0.0364 U.S. dollar.
- The ratio of these two numbers is 3.88.

With Asian options it is of paramount importance to specify the currency with which the transactions take place. We observe this effect in the presence of a steep forward curve, where one currency has a high interest rate and the other a very low rate. In the example above, we have one currency with an interest rate of 10 percent and the other with 0 percent.

Unscrupulous option traders have been known to take advantage of this fact. They will call a client and discuss a contract on a U.S. dollar call. The client and dealer have agreed to the price. Then, at the last moment, they call the client and say: "Do you mind if we switch it from a U.S. dollar call to a German mark put? All we have to do is change a few items in the confirmation."

Clients who are used to dealing in European options would not care if the switch was made. In fact, when dealing in Europeans, both options are identical. However, the client should be wary of making such a switch when Asian options are involved. If the dealer wants to switch, a new price should be calculated.

Explanation

Assume a steep forward curve. The European option's price is based on the forward price on the expiration date. We then discount the price at the domestic interest rate. The Asian option's price, on the other hand, is based on an average of prices. One of the numbers that goes into the average is today's spot price. The payout of the option is only received at expiration. We discount the payout at the domestic rate multiplied by the time to expiration. In the Asian option, equidistant points along the forward curve would be computed as

$$S, e^{0.1r*}S, e^{0.2r*}S, e^{0.3r*}S, \ldots, e^{1.0r*}S$$

The payout of the Asian option has to do with the average of all these numbers. We then discount the average by $e^{-1.0r}$.

The payout of the European option is computed based on one forward point:

$$e^{1.0r*}S$$

and then it is discounted at

$$e^{-1.0r}$$

In the case of a European option, the currency in which we quote does not make a difference. In the case of an Asian option, it is of crucial importance. There have been several cases where traders who did not know this were taken advantage of by ones who did.

FACTS

1. Almost all traded average options use equally weighted arithmetic averages.
2. They all use discrete averaging (and not continuous).
3. Average price options are common. The payoff for a call is max $(0, A - X)$.
4. Average strike options are less common.

5. Most are European style.

6. Some are American style, where you can exercise early and receive a payout based on the average so far.

THREE IMPORTANT DATES

We distinguish among three important dates with Asian options:

- *Trade date.* The date at which the trade is contemplated or the option is evaluated.
- *Start average date.* The date at which the averaging begins.
- *Expiration date.* The date on which the payout occurs. Typically the end averaging date is the same as the expiration date.

In deferred averaging options: the start average date is in the future:

---▶

             Start average   Expiration

Today

If the start average date is sufficiently far in the future and the averaging period is small, then the price of the Asian option is similar to the price of the European.

Eventually, the trade date overlaps the start average date and we have

---▶

             Start average   Expiration

             Today

In this situation, an at-the-money Asian costs approximately half the price of an at-the-money European.

Finally, the trade date overtakes the start average date, and we have an in-process average option:

---▶

   Start average   Today   Expiration

As we've seen, once we are in the averaging period, we must consider the average so far.

IN-PROCESS AVERAGES

It is a simple matter to price the in-process average options:

Start average   Today   Expiration

$t1$ $t2$

where $t1$ is the time from the start average to the trade date (today) and $t2$ is the time from today until expiration.

Let

$$a = t1/(t1 + t2) \qquad \text{the fraction of time already past}$$
$$b = t2/(t1 + t2) \qquad \text{the fraction of time in the future}$$

Let the average so far be labeled P (past) and the future average be labeled F (future). Of course, P is known and F is unknown.

The total average will be

$$A = a*P + b*F$$

The average price call option pays out

$$\max (A - X, 0) =$$
$$\max (a*P + b*F - X, 0) =$$
$$\max [b*F - (X - a*P), 0] =$$
$$b*\max [F - (X - a*P)/b, 0]$$

Once the average has started, the Asian is equivalent to b "new" Asian options (whose averaging starts today) with a strike price of $(X - a*P)/b$. Be careful using this formula since a and b are time-dependent. Also, $X > a*P$ is required.

We still have to consider how to price Asian options in which the average has not yet started (deferred averaging) or is about to start today.

PRICING

The pricing of Asian options is extremely challenging since the average of log-normally distributed variables is not log-normal. In addition, the price depends on the entire price path of the underlying. To date, no one has found a "closed-form" solution to Asian options, and, therefore, other methods must be used.

There are many approaches, and a complete survey of the field is beyond the scope of this book. We will just examine a few common approaches:

- Pricing using the $\sqrt{3}$ rule
- Geometric average with adjustments
- Monte Carlo with variance reduction
- Tree-based solutions

The $\sqrt{3}$ Rule

Assume that the underlying has a volatility of σ, and consider the average price option, which pays out max $(A - X, 0)$. At the beginning of the averaging period, the payout has some variability, but as time moves closer to expiration, the payout has less and less variability. When the trade date is close to the expiration date, most of the averaging has been completed and we pretty much know A. Since X is a fixed strike, the payout is almost determined.

The volatility of the payout of an average price option starts positive and, as time passes, dwindles down to zero. On the other hand, consider the average strike option whose payout formula is max $(S - A, 0)$. Close to expiration, A is almost determined, so this is just like a regular European option with the same volatility. But what about before? What is the volatility of an average strike option if the averaging begins today?

Recall that the payout formula is max $(S - A, 0)$, where S stands for S_T, the final price. The variability of the payout of this option is lower than that for a European. If the current spot price of the underlying increases, so will the expected final price. However, the expected average will also increase. These two effects partially cancel each other out. The same cancellation occurs if the spot price decreases. Therefore, the variability of the payout of the average strike option is lower than that of a European. This is illustrated in Figure 15.7.

Phelim Boyle termed the initial volatility of both the average price and the average strike options as the *effective volatility:*

$$\text{Effective volatility} = \sigma/\sqrt{3}$$

Let us divide the averaging period into N subintervals, each with length $= h$.

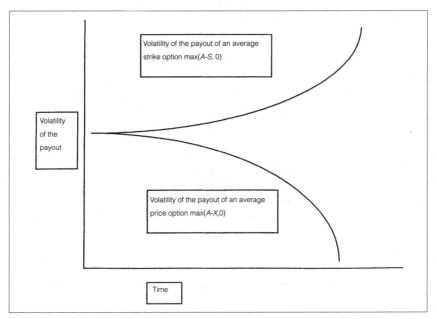

Figure 15.7   The volatility of the payouts of Asian options.

X—X—X—X—X—X—X—X—X—X

There are $N + 1$ prices to be summed up:

$$A(N) = [S(0) + S(1) + S(2) + \ldots + S(N)]/(N + 1)$$

We denote

$$S(k) = S(k - 1) + d(k)$$

We have the following recursion formulas:

$S(0) = S(0)$
$S(1) = S(0) + d(1)$
$S(2) = S(1) + d(2) = S(0) + d(1) + d(2)$
$S(3) = S(2) + d(3) = S(0) + d(1) + d(2) + d(3)$

...

$S(N) = S(0) + d(1) + d(2) + \ldots + d(N)$
$\text{Sum} = S(0) + \ldots + S(N) = (N + 1)*S(0) + N*d(1) + (N - 1)*d(2)$
$\qquad + \ldots + d(N)$

Continue and compute the variance:

var $[A(N)]$ = var $\{1/(N + 1)*[S(0) + \ldots + S(N)]\}$
                                    By definition

$= $ var $\{1/(N + 1)*[(N + 1)*S(0) + N*d(1)$
$+ \ldots + d(N)]\}$
                                    By definition

$= 1/(N + 1)^2 *$var $[(N + 1)*S(0) + N*d(1)$
$+ \ldots + d(N)]$
                          Take $1/(N + 1)$ out of the variance

$= 1/(N + 1)^2 *$var $[N*d(1) + \ldots + d(N)]$
                                    $S(0)$ has no variance

$\approx 1/(N + 1)^2 *[N^2 + (N - 1)^2 + \ldots + 1^2]\ h\ \sigma^2$
                          The variance of each $d(k)$ is $h\ \sigma^2$

$= 1/[N(N + 1)^2]*[N^2 + (N - 1)^2 + \ldots + 1^2]\ T\ \sigma^2$

$\approx 1/(N)^3 *[N^2 + (N - 1)^2 + \ldots + 1^2]\ T\ \sigma^2$

Now,

$$N^2 + (N - 1)^2 + \ldots + 1^2 = N*(N + 1)*(2N + 1)/6 \approx 2N^3/6$$

and so

$$\text{var }[A(N)] \approx 1/(N^3)*2N^3/6*T\ \sigma^2 = T\ \sigma^2/3$$

Therefore, the annualized volatility of the average is $\sigma/\sqrt{3}$.

When the only tool available was the Black-Scholes model, this was the procedure used by the "old-timers" to price Asian options:

- Take the price volatility of the underlying.
- Divide by $\sqrt{3}$.
- Estimate a "spot" price for the average.
- Stick into the Black-Scholes pricing model.

However, we do not recommend the use of this method because:

- It is inaccurate.
- It gives a delta-hedging parameter in terms of A, but the trader needs a delta-hedge ratio in terms of the

underlying. Thus the hedge parameter produced by this method is inappropriate for a delta-hedging strategy.

Geometric Averages

The payout of the Asian option is based on the average price. The average referred to here is the arithmetic average. The arithmetic average of three numbers a_1, a_2, and a_3 is

$$A = (a_1 + a_2 + a_3)/3$$

There is also another kind of average called the geometric average. The geometric average of the same three numbers is defined as

$$G = \sqrt[3]{(a_1 \times a_2 \times a_3)}$$

or as the cube root of their product.

The geometric average does not have very many applications in finance except for investment management. Suppose an investment fund returned 5 percent the first year, 6 percent the second year, and 4 percent the third year. The average return over those three years is computed using the geometric average of these three return numbers. No corporate executive board is going to ask you to hedge its exposure with a geometric average option.

On the other hand, the geometric average of a log-normally distributed variable is log-normally distributed. A hypothetical option designed around the geometric average is very simple to price with a closed-form formula.

Number theory tells us that under all conditions $A \geq G$. The two averages become very close if all the numbers are close to each other.

Many pricing techniques use this fact. The procedure followed is essentially:

- Price an option on the geometric average.

- Modify the option premium to account for the fact that it is an arithmetic average.

For example, when pricing a call option, since $A \geq G$, the price of the arithmetic average call is going to be greater than the price of the geometric average call.

Many papers have been written about exactly how to perform that adjustment. In practice, A and G are quite close to each other if all the numbers within the average are close to each other. Most of the techniques that rely on geometric averages work very well in options where the time to expiration is short and the volatility is low. Under these conditions, the underlying prices that go into the averaging process are going to be close to each other. Hence, A and G are going to be close to each other and the adjustment to the price is going to be small. For long-dated Asian options on highly volatile instruments, these methods tend to lose their accuracy.

Monte Carlo Methods

Monte Carlo methods, so called after the famous casino in Monte Carlo, are based on random number generation and simulation. The Monte Carlo method is the brute force approach to obtaining the "precise" price of the option.

Monte Carlo methods are considered precise because they can simulate a price series and then get the average of that. Then they can simulate another price series and get the average of that. The Monte Carlo method essentially generates a price path, figures out the payout of the option under that price path, and repeats the procedure. By repeating this procedure many thousands of times and averaging over all these results, we can get a precise estimate of the payout of the Asian. Finally, we take the estimated payout and discount it back to the trade date in order to get an option premium.

Monte Carlo methods, pseudo random number generators, and minimal discrepancy sequences like the Sobol and Halton sequences are an area of active research. The main question is how to reduce the required number of simulations and still get an accurate approximation.

One technique that can improve the accuracy of the algorithm is the control variate technique. In this technique, you compute the price of the arithmetic average option using a Monte Carlo simulation. Let A' be the result from your Monte Carlo algorithm. Also, you compute the price of a similar geometric average option with the same strike and the same expiration date, using the same Monte Carlo simulations. This result is called G'. It is important that the geometric average option be priced using the very same Monte Carlo sequences. We also know G is the exact price of the geometric average option via a closed-form formula.

The technique assumes that if the Monte Carlo algorithm made an error in the computation of the arithmetic average, it made a similar error in the price of the geometric average option. Let A be the exact price of the arithmetic average option. We don't know A, and, in fact, that is what we are trying to find out. However, we can say that

$$A - A' \approx G - G'$$

So our best estimate for the price of the Asian option will be

$$A' + (G - G')$$

Intuitively, assume you have some Monte Carlo sequences. But somehow, for some reason, they all happen to drift upward and overestimate the price of the arithmetic average option. In this case, A', the approximation given by these Monte Carlo simulations to the price of the arithmetic average option, is too high. Now we consider the very same Monte Carlo sequences and how they approximate the geometric average option. We label that approximation by G'. But for G' we have a method to test its correctness. We can compute G, the accurate value of the geometric average option. This is done via a closed-form formula that is exact.

Rather than giving out A', the algorithm approximates the price of the option by

$$A' + (G - G')$$

In our case, we can assume that G' is too high. Hence, $G - G'$ is negative, and the approximation A' is adjusted downward.

The control variate technique is also used in conjunction with the computation of the price of an American option. We correct for the price of the American option by using a European option as the control. This technique can be used whenever you have an option that you don't know quite how to price and you have a similar option that you do. In this case, you use the same algorithm for each. Then you correct the price of the option you are not sure how to compute by the correction factor given by the one you are sure of.

Other authors using this technique suggest that

$$(A' - A)/A' \approx (G' - G)/G'$$

which leads to a slightly different adjustment. These authors are using a percentage correction rather than an absolute correction. But in practice, since A and G are close, these formulas are almost the same. Different authors use slightly different variations of the formulas.

With the advent of high-speed computers, the simulation approach is rapidly gaining favor in many applications.

Trees

Let us think about pricing the Asian option with a tree. After building the tree, the algorithm is at a particular node. At that node we know the spot price of the underlying, but we do not know the average so far. Note that there are many paths that lead to this node and each of these paths has a different average so far. So even if you know that the price of the underlying in a particular node is $100, you don't know if the average so far is $95, $100, $105, or any other possibility. Of course, the price of the option depends on the average so far, and each of these possibilities will lead to a different price. So a normal tree is not a very useful method to price Asian options.

If you take N steps on a binary tree, on each step the underlying can go up or down. In general, each of these paths will have a different average so far. So we need to keep track of 2^N averages so far. Consider a tree with only ten levels. Such a tree will result in more than a thousand different averages so far. A tree with twenty levels will result in more than a million possibilities. To add complexity to the problem, the algorithm must update the averages so far on every step.

Hull has described algorithms to price Asian options using trees. In these algorithms, several different averages so far are associated with each node and are updated at every step. The technique works, but the algorithm may be somewhat complicated to implement.

Similar problems of path dependency occur in the evaluation of reset convertible bonds issued in Japan and Taiwan. In the upcoming book on Hybrid Instruments, we describe our algorithm for evaluating these convertibles using an "enhanced tree."

FURTHER RESEARCH

The reason that pricing Asian options is such a challenging problem is that nobody has found a closed-form solution. In fact, Ingersoll and Bergman have shown that you can write down the differential equation for the price of an average rate option. It's just that the equation has not been solved analytically.

On the other hand, there is no proof that it cannot be done. The problem of pricing Asian options is considered to be the "Holy Grail" of finance. Chances are that many new developments will be made in the near future.

SUMMARY

Asian options are very popular with corporations. Such corporations are typically hedging recurring cash flows that occur with regularity. The price of an Asian option is cheaper than a European. It may also depend on the "average so far."

CHAPTER 16

Lookback Options

INTRODUCTION

Lookback options are dream options. Owning a lookback means having no regrets. It is the right to buy at the lowest price or sell at the highest price the underlying has ever achieved.

PAYOUT

The lookback call pays you $S(T) - m$, where $S(T)$ is the final price of the underlying and m is the minimal price attained by that underlying from the initiation date of the option until the expiration date.

To determine the payout of the lookback call, you have to find the lowest price (m) the underlying has achieved. For example, assume that the price of the underlying at expiration is $105. However, its minimal price is $80. The owner of the lookback is compensated by receiving $25. That's the difference between the lowest price the client could have paid for the underlying, $80, and the current price, $105. This way, the client has no regrets that she didn't buy the underlying at the low.

The lookback put is exactly the opposite. What is the highest price it has reached? It's M, and so the lookback put pays you $M - S(T)$.

Note that in the lookback call and the lookback put payout formulas, we do not need the max operator. That is, these options never expire out of the money. Obviously the minimal price cannot be greater than the final price. In rare cases, the minimal price is equal to the final price. This may happen if there is a crash on the expiration day of the option. An option that never expires out of the money, and only rarely expires at the money, is going to be expensive.

EXAMPLE

Figure 16.1 illustrates a lookback call option, and Figure 16.2 illustrates a similar European option. Compare the price of the lookback at $10.76 with the price of the European at $5.94. There is a rule of thumb that states that the price of a lookback is approximately double that of a European option.

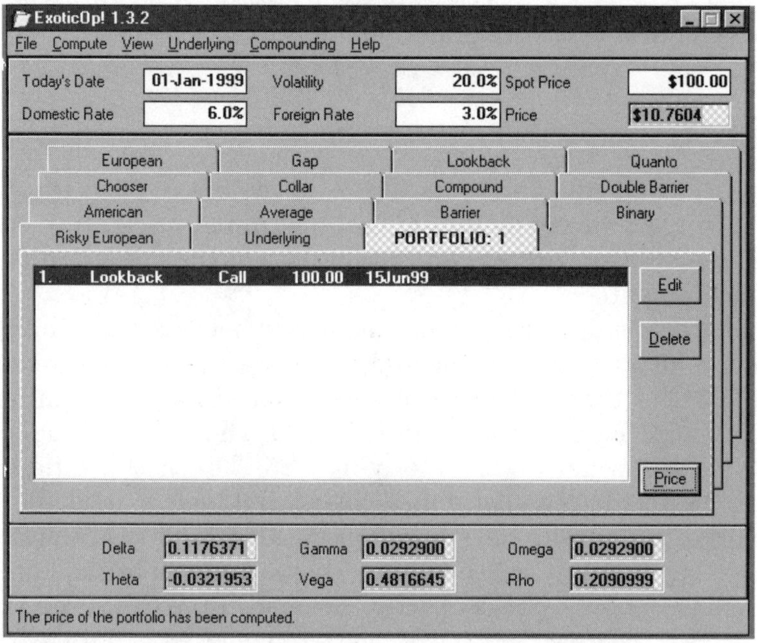

Figure 16.1   A lookback call option.

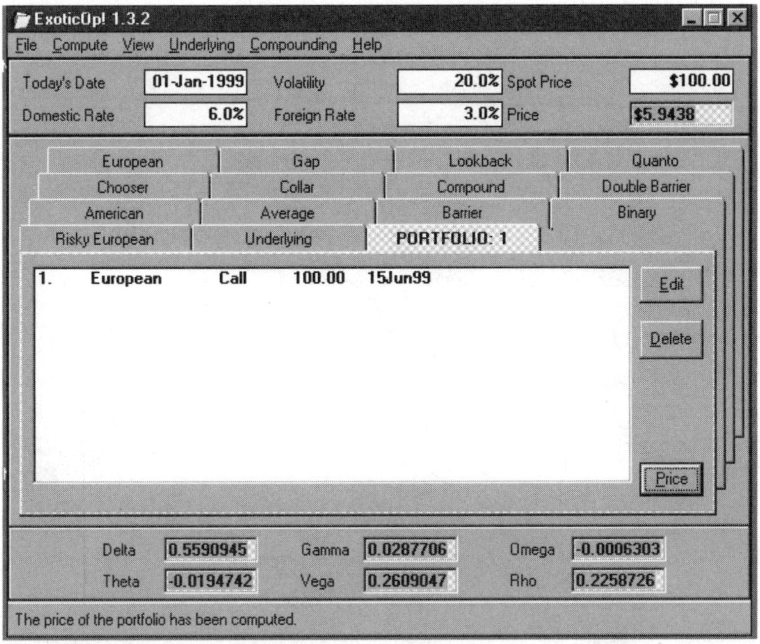

Figure 16.2   A similar European option.

MINIMUM SO FAR

Assume it is now March 15, 1999, and someone is interested in buying the lookback call illustrated in Figure 16.1. Obviously, we are now several months into the life of the option, and we need to consider what is the minimum price that has been achieved so far.

Let's consider two cases. In the first case, the underlying started at $100; began to climb; and now, on March 15, 1999, is worth $120. In the second example, an underlying series started at $100, declined to $80, and now, on March 15, 1999, is $120.

Obviously, we expect to pay more for the option in the second example, as we know that the minimum from which the final payout will be computed cannot be higher than $80. We have no such assurance in the first case.

Figure 16.3 illustrates the first case and Figure 16.4 the second. In the first case, the option is priced at $20.85; and in the second case, it is priced at $40.30. When trading lookback

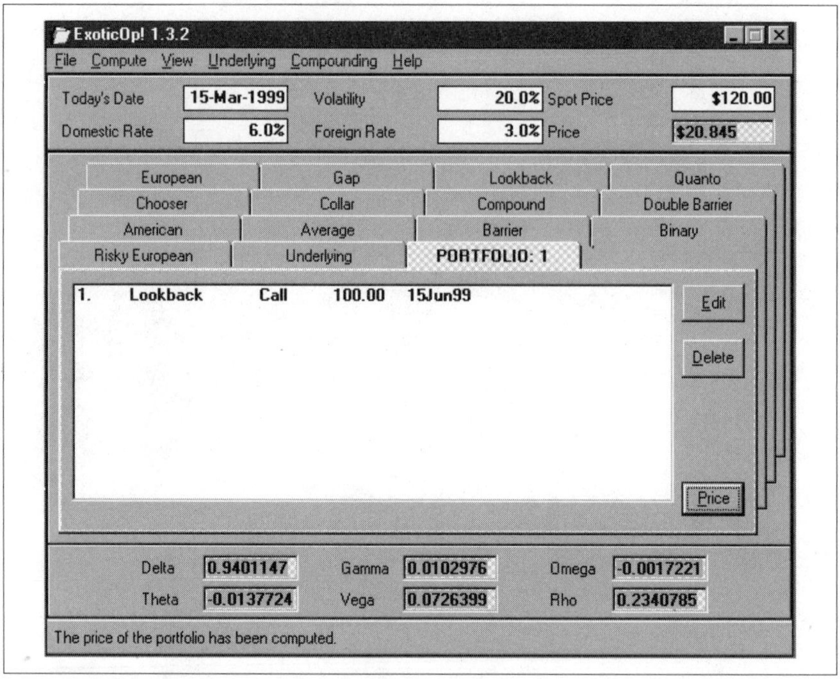

Figure 16.3   A lookback call, minimum so far = $100.

options, it is imperative to consider the *minimum so far* for calls or the *maximum so far* for lookback put options.

A LOOKBACK STRADDLE

A lookback straddle allows you to be the "perfect trader," buy at the low and sell at the high. The payout of the straddle is $M - m$, where M is the maximal value achieved and m is the minimal value.

As illustrated in Figure 16.5, the lookback straddle allows the client to buy at the low and sell at the high for a cost of $21.08. This is a very expensive strategy.

STAGNANT OPTIONS

Many clients have the experience of owning stagnant European options. Perhaps, a client purchased an at-the-money call option. After a while the price of the underlying moves. Suppose that

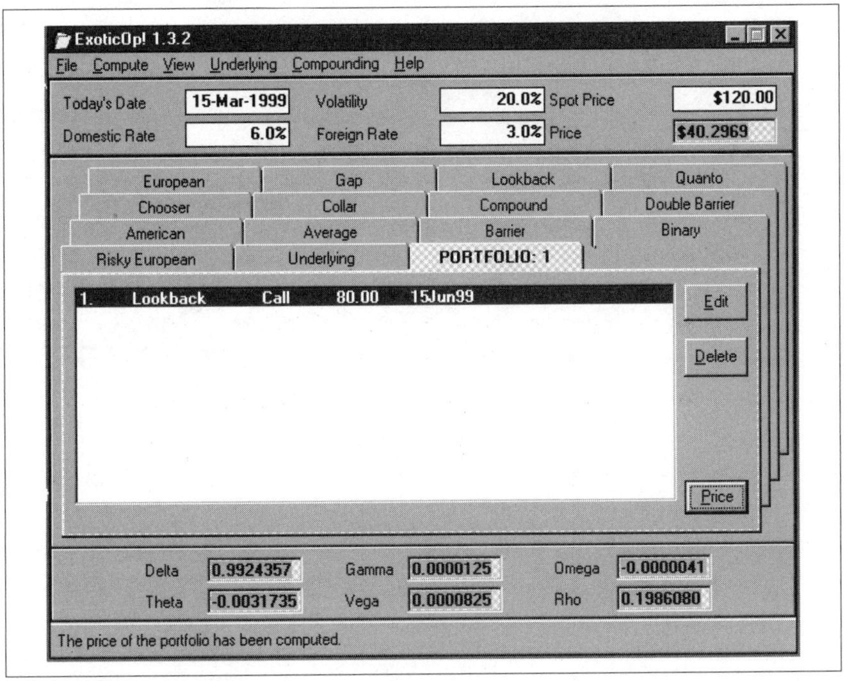

Figure 16.4   A lookback call, minimum so far = $80.

the underlying is an equity and that the stock price moved up. Now the call option is deep in the money, and it behaves like a forward. Alternatively, the underlying may have moved down, and now the call option is out of the money and has zero delta. With a European option it is easy to lose your entire leverage.

The lookback option pays you $S(T) - m$ (the final price minus the minimum). Every time the underlying makes a new low, there is a new m. That is to say, whenever the underlying makes a new low, a new strike is set. So the lookback automatically adjusts the strike price. It never becomes stagnant; it never becomes unexposed to the underlying.

MARKETING LOOKBACKS

An option that is as expensive as a lookback requires some savvy marketing. Here are some marketing pointers for lookback options.

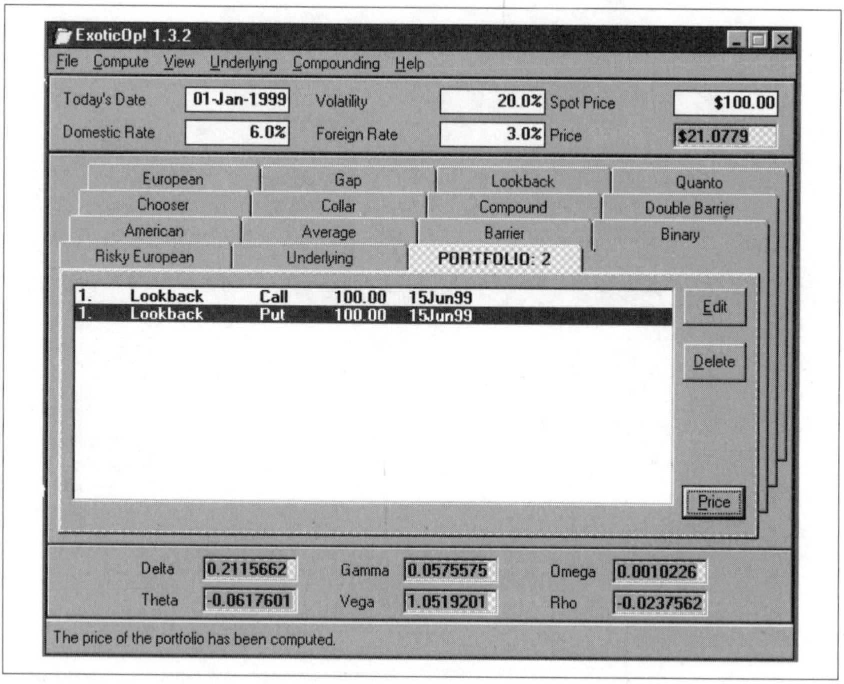

Figure 16.5   A lookback straddle.

- The lookback readjusts the strike, and so it never becomes stagnant.
- A client may have a contractual obligation that gives the client the "best price." A lookback is a natural hedge for such a contract.

FIXED-STRIKE LOOKBACKS

Another variation on a lookback call pays

$$\max (M - X, 0)$$

And the put pays

$$\max (X - m, 0)$$

The fixed-strike lookback call compensates the client for the difference in value between the maximal price and a fixed strike:

$$\max (M - X, 0) = \max [M - S(T) + S(T) - X, 0]$$
$$<= M - S(T) + \max [S(T) - X, 0]$$

Thus the fixed-strike lookback payout is less than or equal to the payout of a standard lookback plus a European option.

If X is chosen to be at the money, for example as $S(0)$ or below $S(T)$, then we can write

$$M - X = M - S(T) + S(T) - X = [M - S(T)] + [S(T) - X]$$

The payout of a fixed-strike lookback is equivalent to the payout of a standard lookback plus a forward deal, struck at X. We will, therefore, limit our discussions to standard-type lookback options.

HEDGING WITH CALLS

How does the dealer hedge the lookback option? The dealer is obliged to pay the holder of the option the final price minus the minimum. Goldman, Sossin, and Gatto have formulated a hedging strategy for the lookback.

Assume that the underlying price series starts at $100. The dealer buys a $100 European call option right away. The price of the underlying starts going up. As long as the underlying goes up, the dealer does not have to do anything. Because the underlying just keeps climbing up, the minimum is equal to the initial price, $100. In this case, the dealer is hedged.

The dealer does have to worry if the underlying starts to go down. Let's say it went down to $95. Now the dealer needs a $95 call to hedge, not a $100 call. The $100 call simply doesn't cover the dealer any more. The dealer should buy a $95 call option and sell the $100 call option.

Assume the price tumbles further to $90. As a result, the dealer needs to buy a new call option struck at $90, and sell the call option struck at $95. Every time the underlying makes a new low, the dealer has to rehedge. Rehedging involves selling an out-of-the-money option and purchasing an at-the-money option, an expensive proposition. If the underlying starts to go back up, the dealer is happy.

To price the lookback call Goldman, Sossin, and Gatto have made use of this strategy. The idea is to price the lookback call as equal to the call at the minimum so far plus some extra money for later on. The extra money is termed the *strike bonus option* (SBO).

The minimum so far is $100. However, we saw that the look-back is priced more than the $100 call option, because the dealer has some money to continue this strategy. If the price tumbles, it's time to sell and buy a new call. It is going cost the dealer more—the SBO.

Therefore, the price of a lookback call is equal to the price of a regular call plus the price of the strike bonus option. In Figure 16.1, we priced a lookback call at $10.76. In Figure 16.6, the underlying has climbed to $105. The lookback call is priced at $12.01.

The $100 call is now worth at least $5 more, but the SBO is worth somewhat less. The SBO is worth less since we only need extra money should the underlying decline below $100. It is currently at $105, and the odds of it declining below $100 are now somewhat reduced. So while the call option is worth more, the SBO is worth less, and the total value of the option did not change by much.

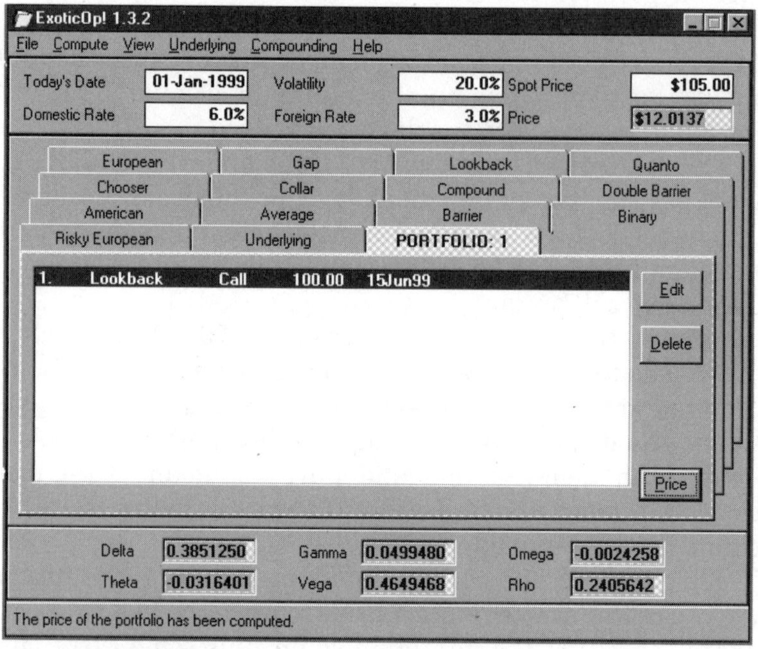

Figure 16.6   A lookback call. The underlying is at $105.

HEDGING WITH STRADDLES

Another hedging method has less variability than hedging with calls. It involves hedging with straddles. Assume the underlying price starts at $100. At $100 the dealer buys a straddle. Then the underlying climbs to $105. At $105 the dealer doesn't do anything. But when the underlying declines and reaches $95, the dealer sells the $100 straddle and simultaneously buys a $95 straddle. Why does the dealer purchase the straddle when she only needs the call to hedge the lookback? The lookback pays $S(T) - m$, and so the dealer only needs to update the hedge when the underlying reaches a new low. When the dealer was hedging with calls, we saw that each rehedge was an expensive proposition, as the dealer sold an out-of-the-money call and purchased an at-the-money call. With straddles, the dealer will sell a $100 straddle and purchase a $95 straddle.

These straddles have approximately the same price because the call is $5 more in the money, but the put that the dealer sells is in the money also. Thus the call is more expensive than the one the dealer is buying, but the put that the dealer is selling is more expensive then the put she is buying. Table 16.1 sums things up. From the point of view of the dealer, she lost some money on the calls and made some on the puts. In total, she almost broke even.

We have seen two hedging techniques for the lookback. At the end you can expect to have the same cost of hedging. When hedging with calls, you spend less money in the beginning but you need extra money (the SBO) to continue the hedge. With the

TABLE 16.1

Dealer-actions as the underlying moves from $100 to $95

The Dealer Sells:	The Dealer Buys:	Result
A 100 call	A 95 call	Dealer loses as the new call is at the money; the old call is out of the money.
A 100 put	A 95 put	Dealer gains as the old put is in the money; the new put is at the money.

straddle strategy, you spend more money at the beginning since you purchase a straddle. But you will spend less money as time progresses.

COMPARISON

The dealer can effectively hedge lookback options with calls or with straddles. The expected values of the cost of these two hedge regimes are equal. The standard deviation of the costs is much lower for the straddle hedging technique. Thus for practical purposes, hedging with straddles is preferred.

In a computational example, we ran the two hedging regimes side by side. We applied these regimes on randomly generated underlying paths. The average hedging costs were almost identical. The standard deviation of the hedge costs with straddles was smaller by a factor of about 12 than the call hedging regime.

HOW OFTEN TO HEDGE?

In real life, hedging involves paying bid-ask spreads. So you have to decide on a hedging strategy. Do you hedge every $5 move, or do you hedge every $1? If you hedge every $5, then you will have less transaction costs but you will have a basis risk. If the underlying ends at $96 and you only hedged at $100 and didn't have a chance to rehedge, you have a $4 basis risk. If the minimum was $96 and then the underlying went up and you didn't hedge at $96, then you have the $4 basis risk. On the other hand, if you start hedging at every little tick, you reduce the basis risk but you increase your transaction costs. To answer the question of how often to hedge, you can look at the liquidity of the underlying instrument. What is the bid-ask spread? If the bid-ask spread is very low, then you want to do more frequent readjustments. If the bid-ask spread is very large, then you want to do infrequent adjustments. You can program this hedging strategy into a Monte Carlo simulation and adjust for bid-ask spreads. For example, every time you do a trade, you subtract two basis points. Then you can design a reasonable hedging strategy.

DELTA OF A LOOKBACK

The delta of a lookback is smaller than the delta of a European. In Figure 16.1 the delta of the lookback is 0.12. In Figure 16.2, the delta of the European option is 0.56.

Why is the delta of the lookback smaller? Right now, the underlying is at $100 and the minimum so far is $100. If the underlying declines, the expected minimum by which the payout will be determined also drops. Note that the final price, $S(T)$, also drops. The payout is $S(T) - m$. The expected value of $S(T)$ drops, and the expected value of m also drops. These effects cancel each other out, and the expected value of the payout remains roughly the same. So we expect the delta of the lookback to be lower than that of a European.

On the other hand, if the price of the underlying increases, the expected value of $S(T)$ rises. However, the expected value of m does not change in the same manner. So the lookback does have some delta. Therefore, the delta of a lookback, while lower than that of a European, is not zero.

DIVERSIFICATION LOST

Suppose a dealer sells some lookback options to a client in January. He also sells some lookback options in February, March, and so on. We can expect that the underlying moves along a forward curve. Assume that the forward curve is upward-sloping and that every month the underlying makes a new high. The dealer sold lookback puts that have to do with the maximum so far. The maximum so far gets adjusted every month. Every time that it makes a new high, the M gets adjusted. The dealer who sold all these options has complete nondiversification. All the strikes (the M values) are exactly the same.

Consider the same scenario, but the dealer sells European options. The options sold in January have a strike of $100, the ones sold in February have a strike of $105, the ones sold in March have a strike of $110, and so on. In this case, the dealer has natural diversification of the strikes.

We saw that the lookback resolved the stagnation problem for the client. This is done at a disadvantage to the dealer. The dealer is nondiversified. Just as we saw that the client's strike keeps getting adjusted, which is good for the client, now we see the opposite side for the dealer.

COMPARATIVE PERFORMANCE

It is interesting to look at a comparative performance analysis of European, Asian, and lookback options. This study was undertaken by James Parsons of LOR Associates. He compared three six-month periods of U.S. dollar–British pound markets. The results are shown in Table 16.2.

Period 1   January 2–June 29, 1989

The dollar-pound exchange rate fell constantly. The maximum rate was obtained early (January 3), and the minimum rate was obtained late (June 14). The European and Asian call option holders lost their entire premium. The lookback did finish in the money since the pound did improve over the last two weeks of the period. The low was $1.5145, and the pound closed at $1.5490. So the lookback did pay out $3.45.

This period was better for the put holder. The lookback put had the maximal payout, but because of its high premium cost, it did not increase as much in percentage terms as the others.

Period 2   June 29–December 29, 1989

This period had a high volatility with no clear trends. The period favored the call holders. The lookback call did not make enough to pay for its premium. The best performer was the Asian option due to its low premium cost.

Period 3   December 29, 1989–June 29, 1990

This was the least volatile period, and it experienced a strong trend. All call buyers had excellent returns. The maximal rate was achieved on the last day, making the lookback put expire worthless.

TABLE 16.2

Comparison of the Performance of European, Asian, and Lookback Options*

Period	January 2– June 29, 1989	June 29– December 29, 1989	December 29, 1989– June 29, 1990
Starting rate	1.8085	1.5490	1.6145
Ending rate	1.5490	1.6145	1.7450
Average rate	1.6870	1.5910	1.6650
Strike rate	1.8085	1.5490	1.6145
Volatility (%)	10.73	12.65	7.82
U.S. interest (%)	9.375	9.0625	8.1875
U.K. interest (%)	13.125	14.1875	14.9375

	European		Lookback		Average Rate	
Period	Calls	Puts	Calls	Puts	Calls	Puts
1. January 2– June 29, 1989						
Option cost ($)	3.85	6.69	8.72	12.04	2.31	3.74
Payout ($)	0.00	25.95	3.45	27.35	0.00	12.15
Net profit (%)	−100	288	−60.4	127.2	−100	225
2. June 29– December 29, 1989						
Option cost ($)	3.72	7.08	8.60	12.54	2.24	3.94
Payout ($)	6.55	0.00	7.70	5.15	4.20	0.00
Net profit (%)	76.2	−100	−10.5	−58.9	87.3	−100
3. December 29, 1989– June 29, 1990						
Option cost ($)	1.55	6.17	4.65	9.50	1.01	3.33
Payout ($)	13.05	0.00	15.05	0.00	5.05	0.00
Net profit (%)	740.1	−100	223.8	−100	399.6	−100

*We assume an underlying of 100 pounds.

Conclusions

It is difficult to draw conclusions from a single study. However, the lookback has difficulties in outperforming because of its high premium costs. Asian options appear attractive in volatile but trendless markets.

APPLICATION

A client wants a 6½-year call option on the index. The strike of the index is going to be the lowest price achieved by the index in the first 6 months. This structure is suitable for a client who predicts a stock market crash followed by a recovery period. The client wants to capture the difference between the price of the index 6½ years from now and its minimal price during the next 6 months.

Assume the index starts out at $100. Then, during the first 6 months, the index drops down to a minimum of $80. After 6 months, the index is at $95; and 6 years after that (when the structure expires), the index is at $150. The client is due to receive $70. How can the dealer hedge this structure?

The hedge is that the dealer buys a 6½-year at-the-money call. The call is struck at $100. This call is not enough, as it is not affected by the minimal price during the first 6 months.

As a result, the dealer also purchases a 6-month lookback call option and sells short the index in a forward deal struck at today's price. The lookback call will pay the difference between the lowest price achieved ($80) and the last price ($95). Thus the lookback call will pay $15. The short forward deal will pay another $5 (the difference between $95 and $100). So the total payout to the dealer from the lookback and the short forward is another $20.

How many lookback options does the dealer need, and how many forward contracts? Remember that the dealer already has a $100 call option. At the end of 6 months, the dealer would like to replace his (now) 6-year $100 call with a 6-year $80 call. How much extra capital will this require? In other words, what is the sensitivity of the price of the option to changes in the strike? This is an unusual question. Normally, we do not consider the sensitivity of the price of an option to changes in the strike price as it is a constant.

Delta is the sensitivity of an option's price to the underlying. It can also be thought of as the sensitivity of the option's price to a change in the strike. Delta here is the delta of an at-the-money 6-year European call option (roughly 0.5).

So the total hedge is

- Long 6½ at-the-money call option
- Long delta units of a 6-month lookback option
- Short delta units of a forward contract with a strike equal to today's price.

SUMMARY

Lookback options by their very nature are appealing to the investor, but they also require a substantial premium. Because of their high initial cost, it is sometimes tough to sell them to clients.

CHAPTER 17

Outperformance Options

INTRODUCTION

Outperformance options have more than one underlying instrument. Consider a U.S. dollar–based investor with a choice between two stocks, stock A and stock B. Currently both stocks cost \$1. The investor would like to purchase the "best" stock, the stock whose price will be highest on a prespecified date. The investor simply purchases stock B and also an outperformance option. The option pays out the difference:

$$\max [A(T) - B(T), 0]$$

At the expiration date, if stock B is higher, the investor already owns the "best" stock. On the other hand, if stock A is higher, the option will make up the difference. The investor owns

$$B(T) + \max [A(T) - B(T), 0] = \max [A(T), B(T)]$$

B-LAND ECONOMICS

Pricing and hedging of outperformance options seem complicated. You have to consider two underlying securities and create a complicated model. However, there is a simplification. Think of an imaginary country called B-land. The currency in B-land is shares of B. All items are priced in terms of shares of B.

Hence, in B-land, the outperformance option is a call option on the shares of A with a strike price of one currency unit, which is the share of B. The volatility of the option is the volatility of shares of A in terms of shares of B.

A U.S.-based investor will look at a series $C = A/B$. Every instant, the investor compares the price of A on that day, $A(t)$, with the price of B on that same day, $B(t)$, and forms the ratio $C(t) = A(t)/B(t)$. $C(t)$ is the price in B-land of one share of A. The volatility we are interested in is the volatility of the series $C(t)$.

Hence, in B-land, the payout of our outperformance option can be written as

$$\max [C(t) - 1,0]$$

We can price this option as an at-the-money option with this new volatility. The option has a spot price of 1 and a strike of 1. We can use a simple Black-Scholes formula for this computation. This will give the price of the option in B-land.

What should we enter as the risk-free rate, and what is the dividend rate? Since we are now in B-land, the risk-free rate is really the dividend rate of B. The dividend rate is simply the dividend rate of A.

After computing the B-land price, we convert the price into U.S. dollars at the current exchange rate, or the spot price of B today. In our example, the price of a share of B at the beginning of the option, in U.S. dollars, is $1. So we multiply the price obtained in B-land by 1.

CHANGE OF NUMERAIRE

We have just changed the *numeraire,* or the basis of our accounting method, from U.S. dollars into shares of B. The Margrabe formula is useful to determine the volatility under the new numeraire. The volatility of A in terms of B is given by

$$\sigma(A)(B) = \sqrt{[\sigma^2(A) + \sigma^2(B) - 2\rho\ \sigma(A)\ \sigma(B)]}$$

where $\sigma(A)$ = the volatility of A
           $\sigma(B)$ =   the volatility of B
           ρ = the correlation between A and B

Estimating the volatility of the series $C(t)$ or using the Margrabe formula should give you identical results.

HEDGING

The dealer who sells an outperformance option first has to hedge it in B-land and then hedge the exchange rate, or the price of B. Basically the dealer needs to hedge with some shares of A and some shares of B.

First the dealer has to hedge his A exposure in B-land. The dealer is short a call. The call has a positive delta, and so the dealer has to be long some shares of A. As a result, now the dealer has no exposures to A in terms of the price of B. That is to say that if the ratio C changes by a little, then the dealer is pretty much hedged. Note that the dealer is not hedged with respect to the price of A or the price of B. The dealer is hedged with respect to the ratio, C, between them.

Consider the ratio $C = A/B$. It starts out at 1. After some time, assume that in U.S. dollars the prices of both shares increased. A is now \$1.20 and B is now \$1.21. The ratio C is approximately 1. Since the dealer hedged with respect to the ratio, he is still hedged.

EXAMPLE

Let us suppose that the dealer sold this outperformance option. Assume that A and B start at U.S. \$1. After some time has passed, A is \$3.00 and B is \$2.00. How do you price the option now? The dealer prices the option using Black-Scholes with a ratio of $C = \$3.00/\$2.00 = \$1.50$. Hence, \$1.50 is the spot price of the option, \$1.00 is the strike, and the volatility used is the volatility of A/B. So the dealer has a price for this option—assume it is 0.70. This price is given in terms of shares of B. The price of the option in U.S. dollars is, therefore,

$$0.70*\$2.00 = \$1.40$$

If this option were to expire today, the payoff would be equal to its intrinsic value, which is U.S. \$1. What is the intrinsic value in terms of the ratio? The strike is 1.00, the spot now is 1.50, and so the intrinsic value is therefore 0.50. If we multiply 0.50 by the share price of *B*, we obtain the intrinsic value in U.S. dollars, 0.50*$2.00 = $1.00. Therefore, the payoff is U.S. $1 by either method.

Keep in mind that the dealer sold the option. Assume that the delta of this position is –0.8. This is a call option that is in the money, and so ordinarily we would expect a positive delta greater than half. In this case, however, the delta is negative because the dealer sold short. Delta is interpreted as the sensitivity of the option price, not to *A* nor to *B*, but to the ratio *C* = *A/B*. What does the dealer do with this 0.8? The dealer has to buy 0.8 share of *A*. Now the dealer is hedged against the ratio *A/B* moving slightly. If both these shares go up or go down together, it is likely that *A/B* will change by only a little bit.

The dealer still has to worry about *B* because the accounting basis is in U.S. dollars. The dealer has to worry about *B* changing with respect to the U.S. dollar. Assume that *B* moves from $2.00 to $3.00 while the ratio of *A* to *B* stays the same. So *A* changes from $3.00 to $4.50. What happens to the intrinsic value of the outperformance option? In *B*-land the intrinsic value is still 1.50 to 1.00, or 0.50. But in the United States, the intrinsic value is, in fact, not $1.00 any more; it's $1.50. The dealer has also protected himself against this increase. From the point of view of the dealer, for every $1 increase in *B* the dealer loses 50 cents, because the dealer will have to pay the client more U.S. dollars. Hence, the dealer has to buy 0.5 share of *B*. This is a local delta hedge.

The dealer hedged with:

- 0.8 share of *A*
- 0.5 share of *B*

The first hedge immunizes the dealer against changes in *A* with respect to *B*, and the second hedge immunizes against small changes in *B* with respect to the U.S. dollar.

EXAMPLE

In 1999, Argentina issued a bond with an embedded option. This option allowed the investor to swap one of two assets *A* or *B* for one of two assets C or D. Naturally, the investor would choose to trade the lowest-priced asset between A and B for the highest-priced asset between C and D. The investor would only do so if there is a positive difference between them. Thus, the investor's payoff from the option could be written as

$$\max\ [\max\ (C,D) - \min\ (A,B),\ 0]$$

SUMMARY

Outperformance options are easy to price and hedge using the Margrabe change-of-numeraire technique. They are useful in situations where the "best" of two assets is desired.

CHAPTER 18

Correlation and Rainbow Options

INTRODUCTION

Once we start thinking about options with two different underlying instruments, we have to consider the correlation between them. In some special cases (e.g., an outperformance option) we don't have to think about the correlation in terms of two underlying variables. Rather, we can just go back and do a change of numeraire and look at it in terms of the ratio of the shares of A to the shares of B.

RAINBOW OPTIONS

The outperformance option is one example within a whole class of options called *rainbow* options. Just as the rainbow has many colors, these options may have many underlying variables. If there are only two underlying variables, the option is a *two-colored rainbow*. For example, you can have a call with a payout that is a function of underlying instruments $S1$ and $S2$. The payout is given by

$$\max [(F(S1,S2) - X, 0]$$

What is the function $F(X1,X2)$? It can be all kinds of things:

Maximum (best of) $F(S1,S2) = \max(S1,S2)$
Minimum (worst of) $F(S1,S2) = \min(S1,S2)$
Weighted sum (basket) $F(S1,S2) = w1{*}S1 + w2{*}S2$

where $w1$ and $w2$ are weights.

APPLICATION

In 1998, we saw many structured notes in Germany which had the following characteristics. At maturity, the holder of the note receives the lowest of:

- 100 Deutsche marks
- Stock A
- Stock B

In this case, the holder of the structured note is short a "worst-of" put option struck at DM 100. On the maturity date of the note, the issuer will sell the lowest-priced stock to the investor and the investor will pay DM 100.

In return for selling this option, the holder of the note is entitled to a premium. Rather than receiving a premium, the holder of the note is compensated by receiving a high coupon.

To value this worst-of put, we need the correlation between A and B. Intuitively, if the correlation between the two shares is high, then the investor is not exposed to a lot of risk by purchasing this structured note. If the correlation is low, the investor is exposed to much more risk and should expect a higher coupon.

Such structures had been marketed in the United Kingdom with much success. But in mid-1998 the U.K. regulator deemed them "inappropriate" for sale to retail investors. The regulator's reasoning was that the retail investor cannot possibly understand the correlation ramifications of these types of trade.

APPLICATION

In 1998 a new retail product was developed. It is one in which the client purchases a zero-coupon bond for $100 and is guaranteed to receive the principal at expiration. Plus, the client will receive a bonus of $20 at expiration if neither the FTSE nor the

S&P 500 has declined. That is, if both indexes end up at levels that are above their current levels, the investor will receive $120. If either the FTSE or the S&P 500 ends below its current level, the client will receive $100.

The structure embeds a variation of a digital worst-of option with an at-the-money strike. This structure is marketed to investors who believe in the equity markets of both the United States and the United Kingdom.

HISTORICAL CORRELATION

Correlation is known to be a very unstable term. Consider the correlation between two indexes or two currencies. Assume you measure the correlation over a three-month period and again over a different three-month period. Very rarely will you get numbers that are the same or even close to each other. Therefore, we can measure historical correlation, but that has even less validity than historical volatility.

What traders actually do is look at a trade and price it over different correlation scenarios. Thus if the historical correlation is 0.5, the traders will evaluate the trade under correlation scenarios of 0.3, 0.4, 0.5, 0.6, and 0.7.

VALUE AT RISK

The RiskMetrics value-at-risk (VAR) model has to do with the matrix of volatility and correlation numbers. One big criticism of this methodology is that you are interested in VAR numbers in the event of an extreme move. That is why you are measuring VAR in the first place. You want to know that 99 out of 100 days you won't lose more than $3 million. But when the market moves a lot, what happens to the correlation numbers? Are they going to stay the same as they were when the market was stable? Probably not. In 1998 there was a crash in the Asian markets. All the historical correlation numbers went flying out the door, and the correlation became almost 1 as all the markets crashed together. Using models based on historical correlation data from stable markets to predict what will happen when the market suddenly shifts is a questionable practice.

IMPLIED CORRELATION

Another approach is to look at option prices that are sensitive to correlation (e.g., crack spread options) and to determine the implied correlation from the price of the option. This technique is difficult to use. In order to determine the price of an option, we need to know the volatility numbers for both underlying instruments. Only if we are absolutely sure of these volatility numbers can we obtain an estimate of the implied correlation. Consider the fact that volatility can only be estimated and we cannot be absolutely precise in the volatility estimates. If we make a small error in our volatility estimates, we will not be able to accurately impute the correlation from the price of the options.

CORRELATION TRADE

Consider a correlation trade. The only place where we can get a good idea of what correlation actually is, is in the currency markets, where we sometimes have a triangle of three independently traded options.

For example, consider the U.S. dollar, Canadian dollar, and Deutsche mark. If we know the volatility of each of those options independently, then we can also get the correlation. Assume we have an implied volatility for the U.S. dollar–Canadian dollar option, we have an implied volatility for the U.S. dollar–Deutsche mark option, and we have an implied volatility for the Canadian dollar–Deutsche mark option. By definition these give us the correlation between the currencies.

In Figure 18.1 we show the volatility numbers for the beginning of 1997. The volatility between the U.S. dollar and the Deutsche mark was 7 percent. The volatility between the Cana-

Triangle Currency Trading		
Sigma1	U.S. dollar–deutsche mark	7%
Sigma2	Canadian dollar–deutsche mark	8%
Correlation	U.S. dollar–Canadian dollar	0.964129
Sigma12	U.S. dollar–Canadian dollar	2.24%

Figure 18.1   A triangle of currency options.

dian dollar and the Deutsche mark was 8 percent. And the volatility on the U.S. dollar–Canadian dollar was 2.24 percent. Then we can also observe the correlation between the U.S. dollar and the Canadian. It is 0.82.

The U.S. dollar is highly correlated to the Canadian dollar, if we look at it from a German investor's point of view. That is, these currencies go up and down together, with a high degree of correlation, as compared with the German mark.

Note: It makes no sense to talk about the correlation of the U.S. dollar to the Canadian dollar. It only makes sense to talk about the correlation of the price series U.S. dollar–Deutsche mark to the price series Canadian dollar–Deutsche mark. In talking about correlation, it's essential to identify the common frame of reference. The correlation of the U.S. dollar and Canadian dollar might look very different from a Japanese investor's point of view than from the German investor's view.

The correlation is not exactly 1 since the U.S. dollar and the Canadian dollar don't always go up and down together; but most of the time they do. The Canadian central bank watches very closely what the Fed does. The United States is Canada's largest trading partner, and the two countries have maintained some relationship in the currency.

Suppose an investor is worried that the correlation is going to break down. What trade should we offer this investor? If the correlation is reduced, what will happen to the U.S. dollar–Canadian dollar volatility? If, in our example above, the correlation goes down to 0.50, then the volatility will go up to 7.55 percent, as illustrated in Figure 18.2.

One idea is for the investor to be long a U.S. dollar–Canadian dollar straddle. If the investor is long a straddle and the

Triangle Currency Trading: Part 1		
Sigma1	U.S. dollar–Deutsche mark	7%
Sigma2	Canadian dollar–Deutsche mark	8%
Correlation	U.S. dollar–Canadian dollar	0.5
Sigma12	U.S. dollar–Canadian dollar	7.55%

Figure 18.2   Triangle currency trade, low correlation.

Triangle Currency Trading: Part 2		
Sigma1	U.S. dollar–Deutsche mark	1%
Sigma2	Canadian dollar–Deutsche mark	2%
Correlation	U.S. dollar–Canadian dollar	0.75 <= Lower correlation; the view was correct
Sigma12	U.S. dollar–Canadian dollar	1.41% <= Lower volatility; straddle was worth less

Figure 18.3   Lower correlation but also lower volatility.

volatility goes up, then the investor makes money. However, this is a little bit dangerous because the straddle is a volatility trade. It is not really a correlation trade.

The investor wants to take a bet on the correlation. She thinks the correlation is going to go from 0.82 to 0.76. Less correlation means higher volatility. If the investor wants to take a view on correlation, why doesn't she just be long a straddle?

In Figure 18.3 we show a rather contrived example. In this example, the correlation between U.S. dollars and Canadian dollars decreased to 0.76 as the investor predicted. But the volatility also decreased, and so the straddle is worth less even though the investor was correct.

A better correlation trade would consist of a:

- Long straddle on the U.S. dollar–Canadian dollar
- Short straddle on the U.S. dollar–Deutsche mark
- Long straddle on the Canadian dollar–Deutsche mark

SUMMARY

Rainbow options are a class of options whose payout formula involves more than a single underlying contract. Some examples of these are the best-of and worst-of options.

CHAPTER 19

Spread Options

INTRODUCTION

One of the only types of exotic options traded on an exchange is the *spread option*—in particular, the *crack spread option* that is trading on the New York Mercantile Exchange (NYMEX). At expiration, these options pay out

$$\max\ [(S1 - S2) - X, 0)]\qquad \text{for a call option}$$

and

$$\max\ [X - (S1 - S2), 0]\qquad \text{for a put option}$$

Here $S1$ is the price of the first underlying and $S2$ is the price of the second.

CRACK SPREAD OPTIONS

We revisit the example from Chapter 1. Consider the business of a refinery. The refinery takes crude oil in, processes it, and produces heating oil. The conversion from crude oil into heating oil is accomplished by a process called *cracking,* and that is the source of the name *crack spread* option.

The refinery computes that it costs $1.50 to perform the cracking process on each barrel. So it wants to make sure that it can sell the difference for $2. That is to say, if it buys the crude oil for $18 a barrel, it wants to be able to sell the heating oil for $20 a barrel. Note that the refinery doesn't necessarily care about the price of the crude oil. What it wants is the right to sell the difference for a certain price. So if crude moves up to $19, the company is indifferent as long as it can sell the oil for $21 a barrel.

The refinery will be unhappy if the difference between crude and heating oil decreases to less than $2 per barrel. But if the difference were to increase, the refinery will make even more money. Why would the difference between crude oil and heating oil change?

Let's suppose that in the near future somebody invents a cheaper way to crack the crude oil into heating oil. The refinery is committed to the old process since it already has all the necessary machines, equipment, etc. On the other hand, a competing refinery may utilize the new techniques and sell heating for only $1 above crude.

Alternatively, suppose the winter is very mild and people don't require as much heating oil as they normally would. However, they still use the crude for everything else. So crude oil doesn't drop in price, but the price of heating oil drops because there is little demand.

How can the refinery hedge itself against a drop in the difference between the price of heating oil and crude? The refinery would like to purchase a crack spread put. The put option payout is

$$\max \; [\$2 - (H - C), 0]$$

On expiration date, we examine the price of heating oil, H, and the price of crude oil, C. If the difference between them is less than $2, the option will make up the difference.

OTHER EXAMPLES

Other examples of crack spread options may include:

- Heating oil versus crude oil
- Gas oil versus crude oil
- Jet oil versus crude oil
- White sugar versus raw sugar

For example, an airline is exposed to the price of jet oil. The airline has already sold tickets in advance. If the price of jet oil increases, the airline's profits will diminish. It is relatively simple for the airline to hedge itself on the price of crude oil. There is active trading in oil futures and options. However, the airline is still exposed to significant basis risk between the price of crude and the price of jet oil. The airline might use a crack spread call to hedge itself against increases in the spread.

PRICING

There are several ways to price options on spread. In Chapter 17 we saw an outperformance option. The outperformance option is a special case of the crack spread where the strike is zero. There is no cash involved. Since there isn't any strike, we are able to do the change of numeraire. In the general case, however, some cash is involved, so we need other ways to model the spread options. There are several approaches we can use.

SPREAD IS LOG-NORMAL

In the first approach, you can think of the spread as log-normal. You then price the options with a Black-Scholes formula. However, it is well known that the spread is not normally distributed. The difference (or the sum) of two log-normal variables is not log-normal. For example, in the general case, the difference between two underlying instruments could become negative. But a log-normal distribution for the spread would not allow that. In the refinery case the spread cannot become negative. You will never see heating oil cheaper than crude oil. In a case that involves stocks A and B, however, you have the right to sell the difference between A and B for X. The difference between A and B can become negative, which means it is not log-normal.

SPREAD IS NORMAL

Other market participants model a spread as a variable with a normal distribution. The normal distribution allows the spread to become negative.

The above approaches have the following difficulty. Once you price the option, you obtain a delta with respect to the spread. As the spread itself is a nonfungible variable and cannot be traded directly, these approaches are not useful for computing hedge parameters. The dealer can hedge with stock A and can hedge with stock B, but the dealer cannot hedge on the difference between them. What the dealer requires is a model that gives a delta ratio with respect to A and another delta with respect to B.

TWO-FACTOR MODELS

In order to model a spread option, we need a two-factor model. This can be implemented in a quadranary tree or a pyramid.

As inputs, the two-factor model requires:

- Two underlying asset prices
- The drift rates μ_1 and μ_2
- Their individual volatility numbers σ_1 and σ_2
- The correlation between them, ρ

For example, we can implement a two-factor model using a quadranary tree. Each node has four descendants. We build the tree going forward in time. At each node we have two state variables, $S1$ and $S2$.

In addition, each node has four descendants:

- $S1(U1), S2(U2)$
- $S1(U1), S2(D2)$
- $S1(D1), S2(U2)$
- $S1(D1), S2(D2)$

$U1$, $D1$, $U2$, and $D2$ are the up and down moves of $S1$ and $S2$ respectively.

With each of these events we associate, respectively, a probability:

- *puu* (the probability that both underlying instruments went up)
- *pud* (the first went up, the second went down)
- *pdu* (the first went down, the second went up)
- *pdd* (both went down)

The node values and probabilities are imputed so that the tree is arbitrage-free and matches the drift rates, volatility numbers, and correlation coefficient. Note that each node has four descendants. A complication arises since we want the tree to be recombining. Assume that we are in a particular node. Its descendants are A, B, C, and D. A is the price of the option when both underlying instruments increase. B, C, and D are the values in the other cases.

In any case, we build the tree going forward in time. After the tree is built, we can price options via this tree as usual. The price of the option at an expiration node is the payout of the option. Then go backward in time. The value of an option at an internal node is given by

$$e\ (-r\Delta t)\ *\ (puu\ *A + pud\ *B + pdu\ *c + pdd\ *D)$$

Continue in this fashion until the initial node. The value in the initial node represents the price of the option. The tree can accommodate an American option with an early exercise.

COMPUTATIONAL EXAMPLE

Consider a European call option on the spread. Let us see what the price is under various correlation numbers. Figure 19.1 shows the price of the spread option under various correlation assumptions. A negative correlation means that crude oil and heating oil will probably diverge from each other. We have the right to purchase the difference. The difference can become more valuable, and the payout of the option can become quite large.

Heating Oil/Crude Oil Correlation	Spread Option Price
1	$1.24
0.5	$2.866
0	$3.807
−0.5	$4.531
−1	$5.117

Figure 19.1   Effects of correlation on option price.

SUMMARY

Spread options are very useful to sellers and buyers of the spread. These options have been successfully implemented at the NYMEX. When trading spread options, the most important piece of the puzzle is the correlation. As evident from Figure 19.1, such options are very sensitive to correlation.

CHAPTER 20

Quanto Options

INTRODUCTION

The *quanto* option is a member of the family of equity-linked foreign exchange options. These types of options are rapidly growing in popularity and demand. One of the most important recent trends in the world market is the globalization of finance, and these options allow investors to participate in the economic growth of other regions. Another trend is the dissolution of the separation between the various desks within the dealing room. By their very nature, these options combine equity plays with foreign currency and so both desks must get involved.

EXAMPLE

Consider a Nikkei put option purchased by a U.S.-based investor. The Nikkei is a Japanese index traded in Japanese yen. The investor may wish to make a pure equity play without exposing himself to foreign currency risk.

The exchange rate is 1 U.S. dollar equals Q Japanese yen. At the initial time when the investor purchases the option, 1 U.S. dollar = 100 yen, and so $Q(0) = 100$. Of course, at expiration, the final exchange rate might be different. We can label the final exchange rate by $Q(T)$. The situation is illustrated in Figure 20.1.

X--X

Initial time   Expiration
$Q(0) = 100$ $Q(T) = ?$

Figure 20.1 Progression of the exchange rate.

Let $S(0)$ be the current level of the Nikkei. At the initiation of the trade the Nikkei is at 18,000, and so $S(0) = 18,000$. Of course, at expiration the final level of the Nikkei, $S(T)$, may be different. This is illustrated in Figure 20.2.

Assume the investor buys an at-the-money put with a strike of 18,000. We now consider several types of options.

A NORMAL OPTION

The normal put option pays out

$$\max\,[18,000 - S(T),0]\qquad \text{in Japanese yen}$$

The client bears all the currency risk.

The Nikkei can drop by a lot, which will cause the option to expire in the money. The client will receive a large amount of Japanese yen. But now assume that the Japanese yen tumbled in comparison with the U.S. dollar so that the payout in U.S. dollars will be small. For example, on expiration, $S(T) = 16,000$. The client will receive 2,000 Japanese yen. If we assume that $Q(T) = 150$, the client will only receive 13.33 U.S. dollars as opposed to the 20 U.S. dollars that the investor would have received had he not been exposed to the currency risk.

Alternatively, the Nikkei can drop by a little, which will cause the option to expire somewhat in the money. However, the

X--X

Initial time   Expiration
$S(0) = 18,000$ $S(T) = ?$

Figure 20.2 Progression of the level of the Nikkei.

Japanese yen may climb so high that the payout translated into U.S. dollars will be very high. For example, on expiration, $S(T)$ = 17,000. The client will receive 1,000 Japanese yen. If we assume that $Q(T)$ = 50, the client will now receive a whopping 20 U.S. dollars as opposed to the 10 U.S. dollars he would have received had he not been exposed to the currency risk.

THE FLEXO OPTION

The flexo option pays out

$$\max [\$180*Q(T) - S(T),0] \qquad \text{in Japanese yen}$$

Therefore, the currency risks are shared by the client as well as by the dealer.

Assume that the U.S. dollar climbs and closes at $Q(T)$ = 150. Also assume that the Nikkei doesn't change, and it closes at 18,000. Even if $S(T)$ = 18,000, the client is going to receive some money on the expiration date. The payout to the client will be

$$180*150 - 18,000 = 9,000 \text{ Japanese yen} \qquad \text{or 60 U.S. dollars}$$

In the flexo option, the dealer has some exchange rate risk.

As well, the client has some exchange rate risk. Assume that the Nikkei goes down but also the U.S. dollar declines. In this case, the client, who was supposed to receive something, may receive nothing. For example, suppose the Nikkei declines to a level of $S(T)$ = 17,000 and the U.S. dollar declines to $Q(T)$ = 90 Japanese yen. The client's payout will be zero:

$$\max (180 * 90 - 18,000, 0) = 0$$

THE QUANTO OPTION

The quanto option payout is

$$1/Q(0) * \max [18,000 - S(T), 0] \qquad \text{in U.S. dollars}$$

The currency risk is borne by the dealer.

In the quanto, for every point that the Nikkei falls below 18,000, the investor will receive a payment of 0.01 U.S. dollar. For every 100 points the Nikkei falls, the investor gets 1 U.S.

dollar. Note that it doesn't matter where the Japanese yen exchange rate is at expiration. In the quanto option, the currency risk is all borne by the dealer. The quanto lets the client really focus on the position in the equity markets and not care about the currency because there is no currency risk for the client.

PRICING AND HEDGING

We next turn our attention to the pricing and hedging of these different types of options.

The Normal Option

The normal put option is very simple. On the initiation of the trade the dealer follows these steps:

- The dealer sells the client an option on Japanese equity.
- The dealer prices the option in Japanese yen.
- The dealer converts the price into U.S. dollars at the exchange rate $Q(0)$.
- The dealer receives a premium in U.S. dollars and translates them back into Japanese yen at the then current exchange rate $Q(0)$.
- The dealer hedges the option in the usual manner, as a normal put option on the Nikkei.

On expiration date, the dealer:

- Converts the payout from Japanese yen to U.S. dollars at the exchange rate in effect on that date, $Q(T)$
- Sends the client a check in U.S. dollars for the payout amount

Nothing special was done here.

The Flexo Option

We can think of the flexo option in terms of either the Japanese yen or the U.S. dollar.

Japanese Yen

In Japanese yen the option payoff is

$$\max [180^*Q(T) - S(T), 0]$$

We can use the Margrabe change-of-numeraire formula for an option to exchange one asset for another. The option allows us to exchange $180^*Q(T)$ for $S(T)$. Thus we need to compute a new volatility. It is the volatility of $180^*Q(T)$ as compared with $S(T)$.

U.S. Dollar

If we think of the flexo option as a U.S. dollar option, the payout is given by

$$\max [180 - S(T)/Q(T), 0]$$

There are two alternatives.

1. *Form a synthetic ADR.* Form a price series of the Nikkei in U.S. dollars. This would be how the Nikkei would trade in the U.S. markets. Consider the level of the Nikkei $S(t)$ and the exchange rate $Q(t)$ for a time period. For example, we can form a daily price series. Then we compute a new series that is the ratio $C(t) = S(t)/Q(t)$. $C(t)$ is the daily price, in U.S. dollars, of the Nikkei. Then, compute the volatility of this series.

2. *Alternatively, use the Margrabe change-of-numeraire formula to convert the Nikkei volatility to U.S. dollar terms.* The formula takes into account the volatility of the U.S. dollar as well as the correlation between the U.S. dollar and the Nikkei.

All three approaches are identical.

The Quanto

The quanto option has a payout that is defined by

$1/Q(0) * \max [18,000 - S(T), 0]$ in U.S. dollars

$= Q(T)/Q(0) * \max [18,000 - S(T), 0]$ in Japanese yen

$= 1/Q(0) * \max [Q(T) * 18,000 - Q(T) * S(T), 0]$ in Japanese yen

$= 1/Q(0) * \max [Q(T) * 18,000 - M(T), 0]$ in Japanese yen where $M(T) = Q(T) * S(T)$. This can be evaluated by Margrabe's change-of-numeraire formula using $M(T)$.

There are closed-form formulas for the quanto and flexo options.

QUANTO INTO A HIGH INTEREST RATE CURRENCY

A result of this analysis is that if the correlation is zero, a quanto call option with a high interest rate currency is cheaper than a standard option. Assume that one purchases a call option on an equity traded in a country with a low domestic interest rate. The quanto call option itself is denominated in a currency with a high interest rate.

Assume we use a quanto call option on a Japanese yen stock and pay the proceeds in U.S. dollars. The Japanese yen forward curve is determined by the Japanese interest rate. So the stock has a small drift rate. The drift of a stock denominated in Japanese yen is much lower than that of a stock denominated in U.S. dollars.

The situation is illustrated in Figure 20.3. The stock is expected to grow at a low drift rate, but then we discount the forward value of the stock at a high interest rate. In a normal Nikkei option, the drift rate is about 50 basis points and we discount back at about 50 basis points. With an S&P option the drift rate is about 5 percent, and we discount back at about 5 percent. With a quanto option, we take the Nikkei, which grows at 50

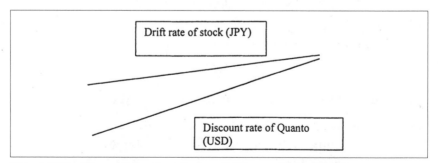

Figure 20.3   The combination of a low drift rate and high interest rate makes for a cheap option.

basis points, and discount back at the 5 percent, because the option is a U.S. dollar instrument. As illustrated in Figure 20.3, the stock grows at 50 basis points, but then we discount back at 5 percent. So the main lesson here is that quanto into high interest rate currency makes for a lower-priced call option. Of course, the reverse is true for a put option.

EXAMPLE

Consider a six-month quanto option. The equity has a 20 percent volatility, currency has 10 percent volatility, and the correlation is zero. We assume no dividends are being paid. Assume an interest rate of 5 percent for the United States and 50 basis points for Japan. As illustrated in Table 20.1, the quanto call option costs less than the normal European call option and the quanto put costs more than the European put. As discussed above, these costs match our expectations.

HEDGING

How does the dealer hedge the quanto option? To replicate the quanto, the dealer needs the underlying and also currency 1 versus currency 2. The dealer obtains two delta-hedge ratios. One hedge ratio is in respect to the stock and the other in respect to the currency. Then, the dealer can continually adjust her exposure to both underlying instruments: the equity and the currency.

In Table 20.2, we price the quanto call option under various equity prices and foreign exchange rate scenarios. The rows across the top show various Nikkei levels, and the left-hand column shows different exchange rates. As evident from Table 20.2,

TABLE 20.1

Quanto and European Options

	Normal Option	Quanto Option
Call	$12.33	$10.12
Put	$7.93	$9.69

TABLE 20.2

The Price of a Quanto Call under Various Scenarios

	Nikkei Levels		
Exchange Rates	17,900	18,000	18,100
99		$10.22	
100	$9.609	$10.125	$10.625
101		$10.025	

if the Nikkei changes by 100 points, the value of the option changes by roughly $0.52. Therefore, the dealer must establish a long position of 0.52 share for each call option sold. We also note that the option decreases in value as the U.S. dollar strengthens. For every 1-point change in the exchange rate, the option loses about $0.10 in price. Therefore, the dealer who sold the option should be long roughly 1,000 Japanese yen against the U.S. dollar for every option sold. The value of 1,000 Japanese yen will also change by roughly $0.10 with every 1-point change in the exchange rate.

To summarize, the dealer must hold positions in both the equity and the currency. These positions are designed to offset the effects of these two underlying instruments on the price of the option. Note that this is a dynamic hedging strategy.

An alternative way of hedging the quanto is one in which the dealer holds a position in a standard Nikkei option denominated in Japanese yen and a position in the exchange rate.

SUMMARY

Quanto options are quite popular with investors who wish to take a position in a foreign equity market without taking on extra currency risk.

CHAPTER 21

Basket Options

INTRODUCTION

A basket option is an option that has a lot of underlying securities. The underlying of a basket is an index created by merging all these underlying securities via a predetermined weighted-average formula. This is not too different from a simple call or put option on the SP100 index (OEX options).

The main difference between an OEX option and a basket option is that the basket does not have to be defined as a separate security. The OEX index exists separately from the options. A basket option can be constructed, for example, on the weighted average of several currencies. Each of these currencies exists on its own, but the specific weighted average that is tied to the basket is not in itself a financial instrument.

PAYOFF FORMULA

The payoff formula for a basket call option would be

$$\max (B - X, 0)$$

Similarly, for the put, the payoff formula is

$$\max (X - B, 0)$$

where X is the strike and B is the price of the basket, which is defined as

$$B = w_1 S_1 + w_2 S_2 + \ldots + W_n S_n$$

The S_i's represent the various instruments in the basket, and the w_i's represent their respective weightings, for $i = 1$ to n.

APPLICATIONS

Consider an investor who is bullish on the technology sector in Holland. That investor would like to have an option on the dozen largest technology companies in the country. The investor is not interested in a specific company but in the sector as a whole. A basket option is the ideal instrument for such an investor.

Consider a major international corporation such as Gillette. Gillette has manufacturing facilities in many countries and sells razor blades in even more countries. And it receives payments in many different currencies. Such a company is exposed to the basket of the underlying currencies that are received in all the many different countries in which the company conducts its business. Gillette does not want to hedge each currency exposure separately. Rather, it prefers to hedge all of them together in its domestic currency, the U.S. dollar.

Of course, for successful basket hedging, Gillette must have an estimate of the various weightings involved. It must know its estimated monthly cash flows in each of the currencies. Note that this is nothing new. It would have also had to estimate its monthly cash flows in each currency in order to hedge its exposure with standard European options.

A question may arise. Since Gillette receives income in so many currencies, it is diversified anyway. So why should it hedge its currency risk at all? As we shall see, the fact that Gillette is diversified in so many currencies will reduce the price of the option it needs to hedge its exposure. But even though it is partially hedged by diversification, Gillette would still like to hedge its exposure to foreign currencies.

A BASKET OPTION VERSUS
A BASKET OF OPTIONS

An investor who is exposed to a basket could obviously purchase a basket of European options. A separate European option is required for each of the underlying instruments. The notional amounts of these options are determined by the size of the exposure to each of the currencies.

This is very similar to the situation in Asian options. An investor who is exposed to the average price over time can purchase a basket of European options with maturity dates in every month. Alternatively, the investor may purchase a single Asian option.

An investor who is exposed to the average price of several underlying instruments can purchase a series of European options. An option is purchased on each of the underlying instruments. Alternatively, the investor may purchase a single basket option on the entire basket of underlying instruments. The basket option is obviously cheaper if these instruments are well diversified.

CORRELATION

We've already mentioned that the basket option is cheaper than a series of European options. But by how much? This depends on the correlation between the underlying instruments in the basket.

If the correlation between all these underlying instruments is low, the savings are substantial. On the other hand, if the underlying instruments are highly correlated, the basket option will be just as expensive as a series of European options. Consider a German investor who trades in Deutsche marks. The investor buys a basket option on the rates of the U.S. dollar and Canadian dollar against the mark. If the correlation between the U.S. dollar–Deutsche mark rate and the Canadian dollar–Deutsche mark rate is 0.95, the investor probably won't save that much money. On the other hand, consider a U.S. investor who buys a U.S. dollar option on the deutsche mark–U.S. dollar rate and the Japanese yen–U.S. dollar rate. These rates have very low correlation numbers. In this case, the basket option is much cheaper and the investor saves on premium costs. The investor saves since if one exchange rate goes up and the other one goes down, the average stays the same and we get a cancellation of profits.

The main formula used by basket option traders is

$$V = \sqrt{(\sum_{}^{n} w_i^2 \, \sigma_i^2 + \sum_{i=1}^{n} \sum_{j=1}^{n} w_i \, w_j \, \rho_{ij} \, \sigma_i \, \sigma_j)}$$

where V = the volatility of the basket
w_i = the weight of asset i
ρ_{ij} = the correlation coefficient between assets i and j
σ_i = the standard deviation of asset i

In this formula, the w_i's represent the weights or the dollar proportion that you put into asset i. A weight of 0.5 means half of your portfolio in face value is invested in this asset.

Consider a cautious investor. The investor has his portfolio invested in an asset with a volatility of 15 percent. This is what the investor is comfortable with. The portfolio manager calls up the investor and suggests to him that he invest half his money in a highly volatile asset, one with a volatility of 25 percent.

The investor is not too pleased with this advice. His main goal is to reduce the volatility of his portfolio. However, assume that the correlation between the two assets is zero. The two investments are totally independent of each other. In this case, the volatility of the portfolio is roughly 14.58 percent. Note that the volatility of the portfolio is lower than the volatility of each of the assets that were used to construct the portfolio. This is due to the benefits of diversification. In this example, the inclusion of a highly volatile asset actually reduces the volatility of the portfolio. Of course, if the correlation between the two assets would have been negative, the volatility of the basket would have been lower still.

PRICING BASKET OPTIONS

For baskets that consist of two assets, we can use a two-factor model implemented as a pyramid or a quadranary tree. These have been described in my book *Option Embedded Bonds*, Irwin, 1996.

As the number of assets in the basket is increased, the pyramid (or multifactor tree) model becomes more and more complicated. For a five-item basket, we would need a tree where each node has thirty-two descendants. After a while this becomes computationally intractable.

Consider a basket option on the geometric average. As discussed in the chapter on Asian options, the geometric average of log-normal variables is log-normal. Hence, we can find a closed-form solution for a basket on the geometric average. Similar to the case of the Asian option, the price of the geometric basket option is then adjusted to account for the fact that the option trades on an arithmetic average rather than on a geometric one.

As we include more and more securities in the index, the index itself can be thought to have a log-normal distribution. For example, no one considers decomposing the OEX index into its 100 component stocks and estimating the pair-wise correlation coefficients between all these stocks. Instead, we consider the index to have a log-normal distribution.

This is due to the *law of large numbers*. As we incorporate more and more underlying securities into the index, it begins to have a distribution that resembles log-normal. The more underlying securities we place into the index, the more it looks log-normal.

For typical equities and currencies, the law of large numbers kicks in at about six to eight underlying securities. Once there are more than eight underlying securities in the index, its distribution begins to resemble log-normal.

So if you have just two underlying variables, you can't use a log-normal distribution. On the other hand, if you have 100 stocks, you do use a log-normal distribution. An option on two underlying securities cannot be evaluated with a Black-Scholes formula, but options on 100 securities are evaluated using Black-Scholes.

For most practical purposes and most underlying securities, the crossover point is in the area of six to eight underlying securities.

HEDGING OF BASKET OPTIONS

Hedging of basket options presents a very real problem. When a dealer hedges a basket, there is the following typical scenario:

The dealer sells to an investor a basket option that contains, say, thirty-five shares. The dealer prices the option using Black-Scholes, and now he has to delta-hedge it. To properly hedge the basket option, the dealer must purchase the thirty-five stocks in the basket. Every time the delta-hedge ratio changes and the option requires rehedging, the dealer will have to simultaneously buy or sell the thirty-five stocks that constitute the basket. That will lead to high transaction costs. Each adjustment of the hedge is actually thirty-five independent trades.

Another alternative is to create a subbasket of shares and delta-hedge using the subbasket. For example, the dealer may choose four of the thirty-five stocks and delta-hedge using just the four. Of course, the index of the thirty-five stocks may appreciate in price, while the index of the four stocks drops in price. This is known as *basis risk*. The subindex did not adequately track the index. This technique is similar to one in which an option trader sells a U.S. dollar–Swiss franc option and hedges with the U.S. dollar–German mark since it is a much more liquid currency. That is to say, even if the dealer hedges with the correct delta-hedge ratio, he may still not be able to cover his exposure. The basis risk is similar to situations where the broad index outperformed the large-cap index. So if one is hedging a basket option on the broad index with the large-cap stocks, he is subject to basis risk.

To summarize, we have two conflicting requirements:

1. On the one hand, to choose a large subbasket that will track the basket reasonably well
2. On the other hand, to reduce the transaction costs choose a small subbasket

In order to track well, the dealer decides to add more and more instruments into his subbasket. After all, if he put all the securities into the subbasket, the subbasket would track the basket perfectly. On the other hand, he also wants low transaction costs. Low transaction costs push him to reduce the number of instruments in the subbasket. At the extreme, the dealer can reduce the subbasket all the way and end up with just one single share. Now transaction costs are low, but the subbasket doesn't track the basket well. Obviously, there is some compromise in there.

Here are some of the techniques used by traders:

1. Hedge the basket with the most liquid stocks within the basket. This has the effect of reducing transaction costs.
2. If the basket is not equally weighted, hedge the basket with the instruments to which it has the largest exposure. For example, in Hong Kong the Heng Seng index is composed of more than thirty stocks weighted by their market capitalization. A subindex of the five largest stocks tracks the index with extreme accuracy.
3. In baskets involving currencies, if the basket includes the Greek drachma, so does the replicating portfolio. The Greek currency has shown time and again that it does not correlate well with any other currencies. If you have a special uncorrelated asset, it should go into the subindex.
4. Another technique involves initially hedging with the entire basket. However, when a dynamically changing delta forces the dealer to rehedge, then he rehedges with a subbasket. Once in a while (e.g., once a quarter) the dealer rebalances to cover the entire basket. This technique is a compromise. However, day to day, the dealer transacts with a subindex, thereby saving on transaction costs.

In general, how does one create the subindex? As this is a problem with two opposing requirements, there is no perfect solution. However, one can use an optimizer to find an optimal solution. Working with an optimizer entails taking a historical data set and dividing it into two parts:

1. The *training set,* or the *in-sample* data set
2. The *test set,* or the *out-of-sample* data set

Assume you've decided to use four shares to track the index

of thirty-five shares. But you don't know which four shares you want and what percentage of each of those shares you should hold. Take the training set and let the optimizer find the best four shares and also the proportion to invest in each of those four shares. These four shares seem to track the index pretty well. Now you need to ask yourself, have you found a stable relationship or a random one? Have you simply fitted the data, or did you find something that is meaningful? To answer these questions, turn off the optimizer and simply compare the tracking error of the four shares against the index of thirty-five shares on the test data. Since the test data were not shown to the optimizer and were kept out of the sample, then if the four shares of the index track well on the test data, it is reasonable to believe that the relationship is stable.

For example, suppose you used ten years of data from the 1980s as the training set and the data from the 1990s (until today) as the test set. The idea here is to pretend that you would have done this entire project at the end of December 1989. Then your boss would have given you permission to go live with this tracking as of January 1, 1990. How would it have done? The test set is an additional data set that you do not show to the optimizer. If the tracking also works well in the test set, it gives you more confidence that this subindex works well. It did not track just by some fluke chance. This tracking actually works because of some fundamental reason.

Tracking based on historical data is quite dangerous. In our historical data set there is a big bull market, a small drop, and then another big bull market. So now we can just assume that the subbasket works in generally uprising markets. But what happens if there is a crash? Will the tracking hold or not? We cannot be sure since a crash scenario may not have been included in our data set.

Purists like to split the data even further and also consider a validation set. This is used as a "double-blind" study. With the use of the training set and the test set, we can create and test many possible subindexes. We then choose the best-performing subindex in terms of both tracking error and transaction costs. Finally, we use the validation set to check the one model that we have selected.

THE DEARTH OF DATA

Consider the problem of predicting the number of sunspots on the sun. This is actually an important problem since the sunspots may interfere with electronic equipment such as cellular phones. Several hundred years' worth of data are available relating to sunspots, collected by scientists in the eighteenth and nineteenth centuries. Scientists today can use those data because the sun has not changed much since the eighteenth century. Financial markets, on the other hand, have changed quite a bit.

1. First, many instruments that exist today did not even exist 20 years ago. And for those that did exist, their historical prices were probably not kept in readable electronic format.

2. Even if a perfect record of historical prices was kept, does one really want to use those data? Financial markets were very different 20 years ago.

Whatever you do, in finance there is never enough data.

Another approach is to simulate the movements of the instruments underlying the basket. You can use Monte Carlo algorithms to simulate the future stock prices of the 35 stocks within the index and the four stocks within our subbasket.

A simulation of many different underlying securities requires some correlation coefficients. Which coefficients should you use? Do you use the historical correlation that existed in the past and assume that the future will mirror the past? Do you use some extreme correlation coefficients? Do you use the historical correlation coefficients augmented by scenario analysis; the scenarios are that the correlation coefficients have changed. There are no good answers to all these questions. In practice this is a real problem that dealers face when they sell these basket options.

MAJOR RISKS IN WRITING BASKET OPTIONS

The writer of the basket option faces several risks:

The correlation risk. For example, a dealer sells a basket option with an assumed correlation of 0.5. Therefore, the dealer charges the client a low price. However, the correlation rapidly changes to 0.8.

The tracking error. The dealer hedges with the delta-hedge ratio. The dealer is faithful to this delta, but then at expiration there is a big tracking error between the dealer's subbasket and the index on which the option is actually based.

Rebalancing costs. Of course, these costs are increased because we are dealing with many instruments—not one stock, but a lot of them. Maybe some of these stocks are not that liquid.

EXAMPLE

A corporation has the following positions in foreign currencies. These positions are in U.S. dollars. Note that the amounts were chosen to make this a roughly equally distributed portfolio.

Country	Position	Spot Rate	Three-Months Forward Rate
Germany	DM 50 million	1.6900	1.7045
Japan	¥ 3 billion	101.00	100.92
France	FFR 120 million	5.9500	6.0194
Switzerland	SFR 45 million	1.5000	1.5053
United Kingdom	£ 25 million	US $1.49	US $1.4805
Italy	L 48 trillion	1,600	1,624.54
Netherlands	NLG 60 million	1.9000	1.9154
Australia	A $30 million	US $0.6775	US $0.6728

Converting this portfolio at the forward rates produces a value of US $226.91 million. A basket option to protect this value would cost 1.94 percent, or US $4.402 million. If, at the end of three months, the spot value of the portfolio is less than $226.91 million, the option would make up the difference.

A series of eight European options, all struck at the three months forward, would cost US $5.574 million or about 26 percent more.

All currencies have three-month volatility numbers between 11.8 and 13.1 percent (the Australian dollar is 10.6 percent). However, the volatility of the entire portfolio is only 9.84 percent due to low correlation coefficients between some of the currencies.

A series of individual options may pay more at expiration. If the Japanese yen increases in value, the European option on it would pay out. However, the basket might dampen out the increase in the yen. This is called *cancellation of profits*.

We can take out the uncorrelated currencies and leave a highly correlated basket. The price difference between the basket and the individual options would diminish as well as the probability of cancellation of profits.

If we remove the Australian dollar from the basket and increase all other currencies proportionally, the price of the basket option rises to 2.1 percent, or $4.765 million. The volatility of the portfolio rises to 10.63 percent since we remove the Australian dollar position.

A basket of seven options to hedge the individual currencies would cost 2.49 percent, or US $5.65 million. The difference between the strategies is now only about 18.57 percent.

If, further, we remove the yen from the basket and rebalance proportionally, then:

- A basket option would cost 2.22 percent, or US $4.992 million.
- A series of six options would cost 2.479 percent, or US $5.625 million.
- The savings are only 12.68 percent (of the basket option).

SUMMARY

Many corporations are offlaying their entire foreign currency risk by purchasing one basket option. These options are also used to track specific stock indexes. Hedging a basket option is quite challenging.

CHAPTER 22

Interest Rate Options

INTRODUCTION

In this chapter, we will consider the special problems relating to interest rate options, such as swaptions, call and put options on bonds, caps and floors, and captions and floortions.

SWAPS

Consider an interest rate swap. In an interest rate swap one counterparty pays a fixed rate of interest and the other counterparty pays a floating rate, e.g., Libor. The party (the bank in our illustration below) that receives the fixed rate is called the swap seller. The party (the company in the illustration below) that pays the fixed rate is called the swap buyer.

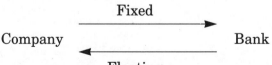

Fixed

Company   Bank

Floating

The swap has a final maturity date and is settled periodically (e.g., every three months). Determining the fixed rate is not too difficult if the forwards Libor rates are known. These are available, as there is a liquid market on Libor futures for many maturity dates. All one has to do is to figure out a fixed rate so that the present value of the cash flows received will be equal to the present value of the cash flows paid. In an upward-sloping yield curve, the fixed-rate payer may expect to pay some sums at the beginning of the swap and recoup sums toward the end of the swap. This is illustrated in Figure 22.1.

SWAPTIONS

A *swaption,* or a swap option, represents the right to initiate a swap for a certain price at a later time. It is an option to start a swap. Consider a firm that has 500,000 Irish pounds and wants to protect the return on these funds for three years. People are uncertain what interest rates will be in the future. Some people think rates will be higher; others feel they will be lower. In the past the company may have used interest rate swaps. The company realizes that if it uses an interest rate swap now, it may give up the possible benefit of higher interest rates. The company may be tempted to use a swaption. The swaption gives the company the chance to use an interest rate swap at a certain fixed rate in the future, but the company does not have to do so. In this way the swaption protects the company against falling interest rates while giving it the freedom to enjoy any increase in rates. If the company enters into a swaption, it will need to pay the bank a premium.

The swaption gives the company a period of time when it can use a certain fixed return on its funds. It might do this if this guaranteed rate is a better rate than would be available in the market.

date	# days	forward libor	spread bps		cash flow from fixed payer	PVCF		
28-Mar-98	92	3 months 5.50%	0			$0.00		act/365
28-Jun-98	92	3x6 5.70%	0	33	$830.33	$0.00	notional	$1,000,000
28-Sep-98	91	6x9 5.75%	0	13	$326.22	($842.26)	fixed rate	
28-Dec-98	90	9x6 5.80%	0	8	$198.02	($1,185.24)	5.83%	
28-Mar-99	92	3x12 5.85%	0	3	$72.56	($1,403.04)		
28-Jun-99	92	5.90%	0	-2	($51.86)	($1,497.36)	Pv of the amount that the fixed rate payer have to pay	
28-Sep-99	91	5.95%	0	-7	($177.89)	($1,487.00)	$0.00	
28-Dec-99	91	6.02%	0	-12	($300.61)	($1,308.23)		
28-Mar-00	92	6.05%	0	-19	($475.13)	($1,022.75)		
28-Jun-00				-22	($555.97)	($555.97)		

Figure 22.1   Finding a fixed rate so that the present value of the swap is zero.

Consider the two examples:

- In three months' time the interest rate swap rate for 2¾ years is at 7.5 percent. The company uses its swaption and asks the bank to provide it with an interest rate swap for this period at the agreed rate of 8 percent. The bank does this, and so the 8 percent return for the time that is left is protected. (Alternatively the company could ask the bank to pay it compensation equal to a margin of 0.5 percent for the same period.)
- In three months' time the interest rate swap rate for 2¾ years is at 8.4 percent. The company does not want to use its swaption and instead deposits its funds at the market rate of 8.4 percent.

In these circumstances the swaption protects the company against falling interest rates and also allows it to take advantage of the rise in rates.

The swaption is basically an option. The underlying of the option is not stock, nor equities, nor commodities—it is interest rates. The buyer of the swaption wants to be protected if interest rates go down, but free to gain if interest rates go up. As we've seen, the swaption gives the company the chance to use an interest rate swap at a certain fixed rate, but the company doesn't have to do so. If interest rates are very low, the company will give that low interest rate to the seller of the swaption and the seller will give the company a high interest rate, which is fixed in advance. All rates are multiplied by a notional amount. But if interest rates are high, the swap will not be activated. So if interest rates are very low, the buyer of the swaption will activate the swap and get high rates, thus protecting its return. Of course, a premium is associated with the swaption, because it's a right, not an obligation.

We look at swaptions from the point of view of the fixed-rate side. Hence:

- A *payer's swaption* is the right to be a fixed-rate payer.
- A *receiver's swaption* is the right to be a fixed-rate receiver.

The company in the example above purchased a receiver's swaption.

PRICING OF SWAPTIONS

Consider a two-year swap in which the bank pays you a fixed rate (e.g., 6 percent) and you pay the bank a floating rate. If interest rates go down, you will want to activate this swap. If interest rates go up, you just forget about this whole thing.

Then, on top of that, you have a swaption that allows you one year from now to activate the swap for two years. Now, the swap itself is a two-year instrument. One year from now, at exercise time, what will you do? You will exercise the swap if it makes sense to do so. To determine that, you are going to check the value of a 6 percent two-year swap. That value obviously has to do with the interest rates. Now, and here is where it gets a little bit complicated, the value of this swap does not have to do with just the spot Libor rate. The value will be determined by the entire Libor forward curve. To determine the value of the swap, you will need to examine the entire term structure of interest rates up until the expiration of the swap. For example, it could be that today's spot Libor rate is very low, but it's a very upward-sloping yield curve. So in two years the expected rate might be very high. In this case you may not want to activate your 6 percent swap, and you will let your option expire worthless. For instance, assume that today's interest rates are 5.90 percent. If you just activate the 6 percent swap, you are going to pay the bank 5.90 percent and it is going to pay you 6.00 percent. You are happy.

But assume that the forward Libor curve is very steep. So for the next two years, Libor rates are expected to climb all the way up to 7.00 percent. That's the expected three-month rate two years from today. In this case, you may not want to activate this swap because it will lock you in.

The price of these interest rate options is not based on one number, which is the spot Libor rate, but, instead, it is based on the entire yield curve. That's why the pricing models are somewhat more complicated.

REPRESENTING THE YIELD CURVE

Up to now, we have been modeling one spot price of one underlying. Now we have to model the entire yield curve.

The first question is, how do we put this curve into the computer? That is, how do we represent a bunch of interest rates in the machine? There are many alternative methods. In this section we consider some of these.

One idea used, for example, by Bloomberg LP, is to take the U.S. government key benchmark bonds. These include the three-month Treasury bill, the six-month T-bill, the one-year note, the five-year bond, the ten-year bond, etc. These are specific bonds that are very liquid. Many of these bonds are outstanding, and they are heavily traded with relatively low bid-ask spreads. The system takes these certain key benchmark bonds and connects them with straight lines. This procedure is known as *linear interpolation*. So if we know the rate for both a five-year bond and a ten-year bond, and we have a seven-year bond, the rate on the seven is an interpolation of the rates of the five- and the ten-year bonds.

To compute the price of a long-term cash flow, the machine will take the key benchmark rates and interpolate them with straight lines. This is the so-called par curve. Then it will extract the zero-coupon curve, the *spot curve,* from the par curve. The cash flow will be determined by that twenty-year zero-coupon rate that was extracted from the par curve.

The other approach says that these specific benchmark bonds are not indicative of the entire yield curve. In this approach we consider all U.S. Treasury bonds. We graph the yield to maturity of each bond against its maturity date. We graph all of the U.S. Treasury bonds—several hundred of them. Even if bonds have very similar maturity, they might have slightly different yields. One bond may have a low coupon and the other a high coupon. One bond is very liquid; the other bond less so. Some bonds are more convex than others. Some bonds have prices below par and some above par, making them attractive or unattractive to certain investor classes who worry about capital gains taxes.

A graph of bond yields versus the time to maturity will look like a series of points scattered about. Intuitively, they are all close to some curved line that is our concept of the yield curve. To find that curved line, we can construct a nice curve using the techniques of *cubic splines,* or *exponential* cubic splines. Numerical analysis has many techniques to make a very smooth curve that will be as close as possible to as many points as possible.

Maybe we should not take all the bonds. Some of the bonds are not that liquid and may not have traded in several days, and so their prices are "stale." So before constructing the curve, we may want to remove the illiquid bonds. Different models define *liquidity* in different ways.

So even before designing an interest rate model, we already have difficulties in representing today's yield curve. Most academics focus on the choice of the model. While this is an important question, we also need to consider the precise representation technique.

There are a lot of problems to resolve before we consider the question of how to model a yield curve, or how to build an interest model. The representation problem, just how to put this yield curve into the machine, is difficult. There are many alternative methodologies of doing so: cubic splines, exponential cubic splines, quadratic curves, etc.

It turns out that carmakers in Detroit face the very same problems. The carmakers want to build you a nice car that will be very smooth with an aerodynamically shaped windshield, etc. With computer simulation of wind resistance, the carmakers use very similar techniques to represent the windshield on the computer. They use splines and other mathematical tools to design the windshield. That's why the windshield today looks smoother than that of a Model T Ford.

The representation problems are illustrated by the following case study.

MODEL RISKS: A CASE STUDY

One incident that is relevant here has to do with the use of a model to determine the relative richness or cheapness of bonds. Several years ago our team entered all the government of Canada (GoC) bonds into a theoretical pricing system. At the time there were some seventy-five outstanding bonds. The system had a tool that theoretically priced all these bonds, and compared the theoretical prices with prices obtained from the market. If the market price is below the theoretical price, the bond is considered cheap, and if it is above, the bond is considered expensive. The system would examine one bond after another and sort them according to the theoretical model into ones that are cheap and ones that are expensive. We programmed the system to print this report every morning at 5 a.m.

The sales team found this to be an interesting tool. The sales team members used it to call on their clients with the list and recommend trades. If the client owned a bond that the system considered expensive, the sales team would recommend that the client substitute the expensive bond for a cheap bond. At least they had some basis of conversation. This worked for several months. Every morning the report was printed and distributed to all the salespeople. In addition, the report was faxed to several of the firm's branches and offices so that the salespeople in the other offices would also have trades to recommend to their clients.

One morning, the members of the sales team were all very upset. It turns out that while the market had hardly moved, the list changed drastically. The salespeople had been recommending some bonds as cheap and others as expensive for several weeks and now the list showed them in reverse—what was expensive was now cheap and vice versa.

The salespeople were perplexed. The market moved just several basis points. If the yield curve had shifted by a lot, they would have expected the list to change. But from yesterday to today, almost nothing happened in the market.

But something did happen to the system. One of the programmers of the system had decided that night that in the case of the Canadian yield curve the seven-year bond was not really a benchmark issue. Hence, while the yield curve yesterday was constructed out of the five-, seven-, and ten-year bonds, the new yield curve was constructed out of the five- and ten-year bonds. These are connected via linear interpolation. As the interpolated point is quite close to the seven-year bond yield in terms of pricing, it doesn't make much difference. A specific bond may change its price by a few basis points. So rather than being priced at $101.98, say, it will be priced at $101.96. The change did not affect the price by much. But when you attempt to sort the bonds via an expensive-cheap system, this tiny change makes a big difference in the ordering of the list.

MODELING THE POTENTIAL FUTURE VALUES OF THE CURVE

We have seen several techniques for representing the yield curve. In fact, we've just represented today's curve. However, we also have to consider the potential future values of this curve. Intuitively, we can think of a binary stock price tree, where at each node the stock went either up or down. We can think along the same lines for the yield curve. In this binary tree, one node represents today, and it contains the yield curve today. In the next periods the nodes will represent some yield curves in the future. The main difference between the binary stock tree and this one is that for this one each node contains an entire yield curve rather than just one stock price. The problem is that this is very difficult to do. How do we know where the yield curve can go? What are the potential future values of the entire curve? Rather than just moving up or down, the yield curve can flatten, can become steep, can develop more or less curvature, etc. In addition to potential future values of the entire yield curve, we have to assign probabilities to these potential curves.

Note that we are not trying to determine the forward rates. We know what they are. What we are trying to determine is the potential shapes of the par curve some time in the future and the probabilities of those scenarios.

From today's par curve we can extract the forward rates. We don't need a tree. We can just calculate them exactly. Assume that we are trying to price a swaption. Whether or not the client will exercise her swaption depends on the price of the swap on the expiration date of the swaption, a date that is in the future. Since the price of the swap depends on the entire yield curve, we have to consider the possible yield curve one year from today. Well, we know the yield curve today, but we do not know the yield curve one year from now. Suppose, though, we have some scenarios for what the yield curve will be one year from now and the probabilities associated with those scenarios. Then, we could price the swap under each of those scenarios. We would multiply the price of the swap under each scenario with the probability of getting to that specific scenario. We then discount back to today and find the value that one should pay for the swaption. This is analogous to what we would do with a regular option. So we are not concerned with the forward values. We are concerned with the possible future term structures of interest rates.

The above is an intuitive explanation. Realistically, however, we don't know where the term structure of interest rates will change in the future. With the stock price all we had to do was model one number. At each period, the stock price could move either up or down. At each period, the yield curve, on the other hand, may shift up or down in parallel, may flatten or become steep, may develop curvature, or may do a combination of all these things. We also have to take volatility into account. The higher the volatility, the more the curve in the future may deviate from what is expected by the forward curve.

In practice, to model the swaption, we will have to convert from the U.S. Treasury par bond curve to the swap curve, which will involve adding on a credit spread (e.g., the so-called Ted spread, the spread between the U.S. T-bill and the Libor rate).

We can also consider the modeling of a callable bond—a call option on a bond. Now we need an interest rate tree that is based on the par curve of an issuer with the same credit rating as the bond. In the previous section we discussed a swaption as one example of an interest rate option. But even if one models the swap rates, the same questions remain. Do you take some benchmark swap rates and do linear interpolation, or do you take the entire swap rate curve and do some kind of exponential cubic spline technique?

At the end of the day, we have to design an interest rate model. We have to price the swaption.

THE REQUIREMENTS OF AN INTEREST RATE MODEL

Before designing the model, consider the requirements we need to meet:

- *Put-call parity.* One of the first things the trader is going to check is whether the model being developed satisfies the put-call parity. If simple put-call parity doesn't work, she is going to throw it out the window.
- *Consistency.* We also have to be consistent with the observed term structure of interest rates. What does that

mean? After building this model, if one were to price the ten-year benchmark bond, it better give the price that the ten-year benchmark bond is trading at. This is obvious. This is equivalent to somebody building an option pricing model that can't even price an at-the-money three-month call option correctly. If it can't price a simple option, how will it deal with a complex chooser? In order to price complex swaptions, the model has to at least price regular bonds correctly. Since the trader knows the market price for the benchmark bonds, the model better price them correctly.

- *Speed.* Bond traders are known to be very impatient. If they press *enter,* activate a software program, and it keeps them waiting for more than a few seconds, they are going to lose interest. The traders want results very fast. In real life, the trader will need to evaluate a lot of options. Each option must be evaluated many times in order to compute various sensitivity parameters, to compute the value at risk and create three-dimensional graphical representations of the results. Since each option may be evaluated many times, the trader doesn't want a slow model.

- *Ease of calibration.* How many unobservable parameters does one have to enter into the model? One of the reasons that the Black-Scholes model has become so popular is that the traders just have to put in the volatility to get an option price. That's only one parameter they have to estimate. All the other parameters are determined exactly. For interest rate options, a trader might have to estimate a dozen or more different parameters. Each of those parameters is a guess, or a "guesstimate." Obviously, the more unobservable variables, the less sure we are of our prices. So we want to reduce the number of observable variables the model requires.

- *Complexity and intuition.* Maybe the trader does not follow the stochastic calculus proof required to understand the Black-Scholes theory. But almost all traders can understand the principle of the payout times the probability of receiving that payout—at least it makes intuitive sense. If we can demonstrate that the model comes to the same number, the traders will develop some trust in the formula. Alternatively, the traders may understand the Monte Carlo method. It is quite intuitive to simulate many possible price paths in the future and find the expected payout of an option. The traders do not have to learn three years of calculus and understand all the mathematical formulas. But it is essential that they have some intuition about the theory behind these formulas.

- *Versatility and coherence.* We also want a model that will be able to handle a lot of instruments within the same framework. The interest rate option book may contain a combination of interest rate swaptions, caps, and floors, as well as other options. Since the trader manages an entire interest rate book, she has to price them all.

MODELING THE SHORT RATE

One of the main ideas in regard to interest rate modeling is that you don't really need to model the entire yield curve. Instead, it is sufficient to model the behavior of the *short rate*. If you know the short rate today and how it will evolve in the future, then an entire yield curve could be constructed.

In theory, model a theoretical rate called the *continuously compounded instantaneous rate*. What is the rate that would be charged on a loan for one millisecond? Alternatively, you can think of it as modeling the overnight rate, a very short term interest rate.

Since many of the interest rate options are Bermudian in nature, the standard method is to build a tree. In each node of the tree, rather than having the entire yield curve, you just have the short rate. The entire yield curve is actually made up of the short rate today and its values in the future.

Some authors like to use binary trees, where each node has two descendants; and other authors prefer trinomial trees, where each node has three descendants. Whatever tree you decide to build, it has to be calibrated to the entire yield curve of today.

This is to comply with the requirement that the model price the benchmark bonds correctly.

DEMONSTRATION

To demonstrate the principles involved in model creation, we consider a binary interest rate tree. The first thing to do is to choose a time step. For ease of presentation, we will choose a one-year time step. Assume that the par bonds pay annually. Also assume that the current par bond yield curve is given by the following table:

Term	1 year	2 years	3 years	4 years
Yield	3.00%	3.50%	4.00%	5.00%

We also assume an interest rate volatility of 30 percent. We will be building an equal probability tree.

At the base of the tree we have the one-year rate today, which is equal to 3.00 percent.

3.00%	$103.00
$100.00	

This one-node tree prices the one-year benchmark bond correctly.

We want to continue building this tree. We have the following setup:

now	one year
	5.208% $103.50
	98.37638
3.00%	
$100.00	
	2.858% $103.50
	100.6239

The two-year bond pays a sum of $103.50 upon maturity. We have to find the interest rates after one year. In an equal probability tree, if the low interest rate is r_1, then the high interest rate must be

$$r_1 {}^* e^{2\sigma\sqrt{\Delta t}}$$

In our example, the time step $\Delta t = 1$ and the volatility $\sigma = 0.30$.

If we are at a node that is one period before final maturity, we discount the cash flow to be received at maturity by the interest rate at that node. Thus, the price of a bond paying $103.50 in one year, given that the interest rate is 2.858 percent, is

$$\$103.50/(1 + 2.858\%) = \$100.6239$$

Similarly, if the interest rate at a terminal node is 5.208 percent, the price of the bond at that node is

$$\$103.50/(1 + 5.208\%) = \$98.376$$

So our problem is to find the interest rate r, so that the two-year bond yielding a coupon of 3.50 percent will be priced at par. This problem can be solved by a numerical method known as *goal-seek*. The only interest rate r_1 that prices the bond at $100 is 2.858 percent.

The formula for the price of a bond at an internal node is as follows. We examine the two descendants of that node. Suppose that the price of the bond in one descendant is A and the price in the other is B. Then the price of the bond at the internal node is

$$(0.5*A + 0.5*B + \text{coupon})/(1 + \text{interest rate at that node})$$

In our case, $A = \$100.6239$, $B = \$98.376$, the coupon is $3.50, and the interest rate at the internal node is 3.00 percent.

$$(0.5*\$100.6239 + \$0.5*98.376 + \$3.50)/(1 + 3\%) = \$100$$

Of course, had we assumed a different r_1, the price of the bond would have been different. Setting r_1 to 2.858 percent was the only way in which we could force the price of the two-year bond to be $100.

The next step involves finding the potential rates two years in the future. Again, we use the same arguments. If the low interest rate two years from today is r_2, then the other two interest rates are given by

$$r_2 * e^{2\sigma\sqrt{\Delta t} r_2}$$

and

$$r_2 * e^{4\sigma\sqrt{\Delta t} r_2}$$

We can again solve for r_2 using a goal-seek numerical method.

now	one year	two years	
		8.56%	$104.00
		95.80082	
	5.208%		
	96.53957		
3.00%		4.70%	$104.00
$100.00		99.33423	
	2.858%		
	101.4603		
		2.58%	$104.00
		101.3865	

Finally, we repeat the procedure for the four-year bond. This bond pays a coupon of 4.50 percent, and so our complete interest rate tree is

now	one year	two years	three years	
			13.66%	$104.50
			91.93987	
		8.56%		
		91.2648		
	5.208%		7.50%	$104.50
	94.5372		97.21161	
3.00%		4.70%		
$100.00		98.6569		
	2.858%		4.11%	$104.50
	102.4612		100.3701	
		2.58%		
		103.1229		
			2.26%	$104.50
			102.1923	

PRICING A VANILLA BOND

Once the interest rate tree is built, we can price bonds using that tree. For example, we can price a bond with a coupon of 4.75 percent. This involves keeping the same interest rates as were computed before, and assigning different cash flows and different coupons. We now work backward in time:

coupon now	4.75% one year	two years	final price three years	$100.91
			13.66% 92.15983	$104.75
		8.56% 91.7035		
	5.208% 95.2041		7.50% 97.44417	$104.75
3.00% $100.9065		4.70% 99.1214		
	2.858% 103.1634		4.11% 100.6102	$104.75
		2.58% 103.6028		
			2.26% 102.4368	$104.75

Note that in order to price a vanilla bond, one without any options, we do not need a tree. We could have just stripped the bond into its component cash flows and priced each of them using the zero-coupon yield implied by the par curve. In fact, the price of this bond is independent of the volatility used. We change the volatility from 30 to 3 percent and observe the new tree:

coupon now	4.75% one year	two years	final price three years	$100.91
			6.74% 98.13431	$104.75
		5.38% 97.8024		
	4.141% 98.7761		6.35% 98.49657	$104.75
3.00% $100.9081		5.07% 98.4301		
	3.900% 99.5946		5.98% 98.8402	$104.75
		4.77% 99.0268		
			5.63% 99.16601	$104.75

Note that the bond is priced literally the same under both interest rate volatility numbers. As we moved volatility from 30 to 3 percent, the bond price moved from $100.9065 to $100.9081. This small difference is due to round-off errors.

However, note the large differences in the values of the interest rates at the corresponding nodes. The top interest rate at the 30 percent volatility was 13.66 percent. The corresponding figure under 3 percent volatility is 6.74 percent.

PRICING A CALLABLE BOND

The pricing of a callable bond proceeds in much the same way as we priced a noncallable bond, except that at each node we impose a question. Is the company that issued the bond going to call the bond? The company will call the bond for $100 when:

1. It is allowed to do so.
2. It is profitable to do so.

Condition 2 simply states that if the expected price of the bond if it is not called is greater than $100, then the company will call the bond. Alternatively, if the expected price is lower than $100, then the company will refrain from calling it.

If, in a specific node, the company will call the bond, then the price of the bond must be reset to the call price. The price of the call option is the difference in price between the callable bond and the noncallable vanilla bond. This is illustrated below. We consider the same 4.75 percent bond with a call feature in years 2 and 3. In the call schedule, we enter a very high call price (e.g., $1000) year 1 to deactivate the call. For years 2 and 3 we enter a call price of $100 to allow the company to call at par. Nodes in which the company will call the bond are those in which the price of the bond is highlighted. (See table on the next page.)

Of course, when the company issues a callable bond, the company receives a smaller price than it would for a noncallable bond. The difference is the call price, in this case $0.987. The company can sell the bonds for $99.921 rather than for $100.907 for a noncallable bond.

coupon	4.75%		final price $99.921	
call schedule	1,000	100	100	call price
now	one year	two years	three years	$0.987
			13.66%	$104.75
			92.1627	
			92.1627	
		8.56%		
		91.7050		
		91.7050		
	5.208%		7.50%	$104.75
	95.0662		97.4460	
	95.0662		97.4460	
3.00%		4.70%		
99.921		98.8305		
		98.8305		
	2.858%		4.11%	$104.75
	101.2704		100.6112	
	101.2704		100.0000	
		2.58%		
		102.1174		
		100.0000		
			2.26%	$104.75
			102.4374	
			100.0000	

PRICING OTHER INSTRUMENTS

Other interest rate instruments could be priced in a similar fashion: bonds with embedded put options, swaptions, caps and floors, and so on.

OPTION-ADJUSTED SPREAD

Option-adjusted spread (OAS) methodology is an attempt to answer the question of relative value between bonds.

Example: Suppose we are offered two bonds:

1. A 4.75 percent four-year noncallable bond at a price of $100.45

2. A 4.75 percent four-year bond, callable for par at years 2 and 3 at a price of $99.50

How can we compare the value between the two bonds? A yield-to-maturity comparison is not very relevant, as we are not sure of the maturity of the second bond. It could mature in year 2, 3, or 4.

The concept of OAS involves comparing the market price of the bond with that of the model. Consider the noncallable bond. The model's price for that bond is $100.907. The idea of OAS is to shift all interest rates in the internal tree computed by the model in parallel. The interest rate tree is shifted until the price computed by the model matches the price observed in the market.

coupon call schedule now	4.75% 1,000 one year	1,000 two years	OAS 12.7026 1,000 three years	call price $0.00
			13.78% 92.05983 92.05983	$104.75
		8.69% 91.4976 91.4976		
	5.34% 94.8809 94.8809		7.62% 97.33094 97.33094	$104.75
3.1270% $100.450		4.82% 98.8889 98.8889		
	2.99% 102.8021 102.8021		4.24% 100.4886 100.4886	$104.75
		2.71% 103.3537 103.3537		
			2.38% 102.3103 102.3103	$104.75

NOTE   The call prices are set to $1000 to deactivate the call feature.

Using a goal-seek method, we moved all interest rates up and down in parallel to match the model price with the given market price of $100.45. The bond's OAS can be said to be 12.70 basis points. Note how all interest rates have moved upward by 12.70 basis points. For example, the initial rate, which was 3.00 percent, is now 3.1270 percent.

We repeat the computation for the callable bond:

coupon call schedule now	4.75% 1,000 one year	100 two years	OAS 14.51719 100 three years	call price $0.885
			13.80% 92.04515 92.04515	$104.75
		8.70% 91.4680 91.4680		
	5.35% 94.7280 94.7280		7.64% 97.31453 97.31453	$104.75
3.1452% $99.500		4.84% 98.6309 98.6309		
	3.00% 101.0309 101.0309		4.26% 100.4712 100	$104.75
		2.72% 101.9731 100.0000		
			2.40% 102.2922 100	$104.75

We find that the OAS of the callable bond is 14.51 basis points. This shows that the callable bond is a slightly better bargain than the noncallable.

Even this simple demonstration has an important point to it: The OAS score is model-dependent. The OAS measures how the market price of a bond differs from the model's price. The basis of comparison is the internal model. The same two bonds may have received different OAS scores if we had used a different model. Perhaps, we would have arrived at an opposite conclusion.

THE JAPANESE CASE

In Japan, interest rates are very low and interest rate volatility is very high. We assume the following benchmark yields:

Term	1	2	3	4
Yield	0.15%	0.30%	0.50%	0.80%
Volatility		100%		

As you can see from above, we also assume a volatility of 100 percent.

Consider the interest rate tree that arises out of this model:

	now	one year	two years	three years	
				10.07%	$100.80
				91.58096	
			2.86%		
			93.6394		
		0.796%		1.36%	$100.80
		97.0678		99.4452	
	0.15%		0.39%		
	$100.00		100.4417		
		0.108%		0.18%	$100.80
		101.6322		100.6145	
			0.05%		
			101.4416		
				0.02%	$100.80
				100.7749	

The model says that in three years we may expect an interest rate of 10.07 percent. In fact, if the model were to be extended to 20 years in the future, we might see rates as high as 2,000 percent. Such examples have prompted the development of alternative models.

OTHER MODELS OF INTEREST RATES

There is a whole literature on interest rate models. It is a big area of research; a lot of it is very academic. Every bank tends to build or buy its own favorite model. There are several dozens of interest rate models, and quite a few different models are actually used in practice.

Some of the models are more applicable, and others are not so applicable. Some of them are nice and analytic and you can get some nice formulas, but they are very hard to calibrate.

The different models assume that the short-term interest rate will develop differently through time.

GEOMETRIC RANDOM WALK

As an example of the geometric random walk, consider the Rendelman and Barter model. The defining differential equation is

$$dr = \mu r\, dt + \sigma r\, dz$$

Here dr is the instantaneous change to interest rates, μ is the drift rate of interest rates, r is the interest rate, σ is the volatility, dt is an instantaneous change in time, and dz is a normalized Weiner process. We can rewrite this as a difference equation:

$$\Delta r = \mu r\, \Delta t + \sigma r\, z\, \sqrt{\Delta t}$$

Here Δr is the change in the short rate from one period to another, Δt is the time step through which interest rates are modeled, and z is a normally distributed random variable with a mean of zero and a standard deviation of 1.

In this model, the short rate is assumed to be log-normal (similar to a stock). Essentially, we have been using this model in our previous examples.

SIMPLE GAUSSIAN

The simple Gaussian model is an example of a *mean-reverting* model. The defining equation is

$$dr = a^*(b - r)\, dt + \sigma\, dz$$

Note the parameters a and b. The parameter b is the long-term mean of interest rates. The parameter a is the *speed of mean reversion*. If the value of r is below b, then dr will tend to be positive. That means that interest rates will rise. On the other hand, if r is larger than b, then dr will tend to be negative, which will push interest rates down.

Of course, a and b are unobservable parameters. They cannot be determined directly from the market. This means that the user of the model will have to go through a process of calibration. This process will be described below.

In this model, volatility is independent of rates. The Vasicek and Merton models are examples of the Gaussian approach. Since the volatility is independent of rates, negative interest rates are possible.

SQUARED GAUSSIAN

In the squared Gaussian model, the volatility parameter is multiplied by the square root of the interest rate. The defining equation is

$$dr = a*(b - r)\, dt + \sigma \sqrt{r\, dz}$$

Since volatility behaves like the square root of the rates, higher rates lead to higher volatility, and rates cannot become negative. The Cox-Ingersoll-Ross model is an example of this approach.

BLACK-DERMAN-TOY

The defining equation of the Black-Derman-Toy model is

$$dr = [ar + br \ln (r)]\, dt + \sigma(t)\, r\, dz$$

This model has a term structure of volatility. Thus the volatility of the short rate may be different from the volatility of the long rate. In fact, the model complies with an entire term structure of volatility.

In a typical market we observe that the short-term interest rates will move more than the long-term interest rates. So the volatility of the short rate is higher than the volatility of the long rate.

OTHER MODELS

There are many other models of interest rates, including:

- Dothan

$$dr = \sigma\, r\, dz$$

- Brennan-Schwartz

$$dr = (a - br)\, dt + \sigma\, r\, dz$$

- Constantinides-Ingersoll

$$dr = (\sigma\, r)^{**}1.5\, dz$$

Most single-factor models have the same general formula:

$$dr = (a - br)\, dt + \sigma\, r^c\, dz$$

where a and b may be parameters that will be set by calibration and c is usually a predefined constant.

THE BRACE, GATAREK, AND MUSIELA MODELS

The Brace, Gatarek, and Musiela (BGM) models developed an entire complex mathematics to model the Libor rate directly. Rather than focusing on the continuously compounded instantaneous short rate, they use the specific Libor rate as the underlying. This allows these models to avoid many of the problems related to calibration (see below). The difficulty with these models is that a trader will not be able to run a combined book of interest rate swaps on the three-month Libor and the six-month Libor. Under these BGM "market models," there are two different underlying instruments, and the two books must be treated separately.

MULTIFACTOR MODELS

The general formulation of multifactor models is via a differential matrix equation:

$$dX = \mu(t,X)\, dt + \sigma(t,X)\, dz$$

Here, X is a vector of factors. For example, they could be the yields at several specified maturity dates. Typically, one component of X is the continuously compounded short rate r. In most multifactor models, the volatility is modeled as a random variable with its own process.

Duffie and Kan

The Duffie and Kan model is a relatively simple multifactor model in which the parameters are stationary and do not change with time.

$$dX = \mu(X)\, dt + \sigma(X)\, dz$$

Other Examples

Other examples of multifactor models are:

- Brennan-Schwartz
  $X1$. Spot rate
  $X2$. Rate on a perpetual
- Schaefer-Schwartz
  $X1$. Spot rate
  $X2$. Long-term spot rate
- Longstaff-Schwartz
  $X1$. Short rate
  $X2$. Volatility of the short rate

In this model both the volatility and the rates are mean-reverting.

The HJM Model

The Heath-Jarrow-Morton (HJM) model is a multifactor model that is implemented as a nonrecombining tree. The computational requirements of this model tend to be expensive. Recent work has focused on reducing the computational requirements of this model.

NO UNIFIED THEORY YET

In the equity, currency, and commodity world, everybody in the industry follows the Black-Scholes model in one way or another. Most dealers will tend to use the Black-Scholes model or extensions of Black-Scholes, or Black-Scholes with some modifications; but everybody agrees on the basic Black-Scholes.

For options on interest rates, there are a whole variety of models.* Although there are different models and different approaches to modeling interest rates, so far there is no unified theory on the process that underlies the behavior of interest rates.

CALIBRATION

If different traders use different models, an interesting question is how can they come to agree on a price? Certainly, if we actually compute the price of the same option using different models and assuming the same parameters, we will get differing results. Some experiments have shown that in some cases the results differ by as much as 100 percent. For liquid caps and floor options, different dealers will give quotes that are within 0.1 basis points of each other.

Yet, obviously, in the market there is a price. The reason is that all traders who use models actually perform a step known as *calibration*. The calibration of a model is a very important step in this whole procedure. Model calibration is further complicated by the fact that as the models become more and more complex, they tend to have more and more unobservable factors. These factors must be calibrated to the market.

Traders are going to calibrate their models to the same market. After calibration, the internal parameters of the model may be quite different. Hence trader A may have a mean reversion rate that is completely unrelated to the mean reversion rate used by trader B. The numbers are not going to be the same because each model has a different dynamic.

If a trader gives the model the details of an interest rate cap, the model is going to price that cap. The model can find a price only after the trader has determined all the parameters that control the model. Model calibration is the process used to find the unobservable parameters.

The process of calibration proceeds by assuming that we know the price of caps. Since at least some of the caps are liquid

---

*In one of my previous books, *Option Embedded Bonds,* an entire chapter is devoted to a mathematical review of interest rate models.

and tradable, we can observe these caps and their prices in the market. We also know the price of several floors, swaptions, bonds, callable bonds, noncallable bonds, etc. In essence we have an entire collection of financial instruments whose prices are known.

Given values for the unobservable parameters, the model will determine a value for these instruments. The calibration process requires us to find the values of the internal parameters of the model so that the model will compute prices that match the prices observed in the market. The observed market prices of all the instruments in our collection will be matched by the model.

For example, one of these market instruments is a two-year, 6 percent cap. We know how much such a cap costs. Say, in this case, it costs 53 basis points. That's what it is traded for in the market. If the trader puts this two-year, 6 percent cap in her model, she would like it to be priced at 53 basis points. The trader would also like the model to give a price of 53 basis points.

The goal is to find the internal parameters used by the model (a, b, c, σ, and others) so that the model will price the cap at 53 basis points. In addition, we have a whole collection of instruments whose market prices must be matched by the model. The trader may know the prices of a two-year cap, a two-year floor, a three-year cap, a three-year floor, etc.—an entire collection of instruments. Each of those instruments has a market price. Now the trader wants to find the internal parameters of the model that will give prices that are consistent with the observed market prices of liquid instruments.

In a previous section, we built our term-structure model. We built a little interest rate tree. That tree was calibrated to match the prices on the one-year, two-year, three-year, and four-year benchmark bonds. Obviously, a more sophisticated model will require calibration to more instruments. We have 6 percent caps, floors, swaps, swaptions, bonds, etc. However, the process of calibration is essentially the same. This final interest rate model will have a lot more parameters. It at least should match the observed market prices.

Now, maybe it can't match all the observed prices exactly, but we could require the model to match the market prices as closely as possible. While the cap may not be priced at 53 basis points, at least it should be priced close to that figure.

Theoretically what the dealers want to do is come in every morning and calibrate before they start trading. They take all the observed market prices from yesterday's close. Then they find the parameters of the model so that the model will give them the correct market prices. The model is now calibrated to the market.

The question is why do they need to do this? If they already have the market prices and the model is simply going to give the same prices as the market, why do they need a model?

The model is useful for several reasons:

1. The client may want a 2½-year, 7 percent cap that is not tradable in the market. For those off-market instruments, the trader cannot obtain market prices, and so she has to rely on her model to price it. The model prices the off-market instrument based on the interest rate model that was created and calibrated to the market.

2. Even more important than pricing off-market instruments, the trader needs the model for hedging. The trader must determine her hedge ratios. While prices are observable in the market, hedging parameters are not. For purposes of hedging, the trader needs to answer the question of what happens to an option when interest rates move up and down. Or what happens when volatility moves? What's the vega? The trader can't see vega in the market because the observed price of 53 basis points is under 30 percent volatility. The trader also needs to determine the price of a cap under 25 percent and 35 percent volatility.

3. In a similar way, the model can be used for risk management. The bank needs to be able to reevaluate the portfolio under many market scenarios and determine that the portfolio produces the required profit without too much unbearable risk.

Thus the importance of the model is for pricing of new off-market instruments and also for hedging and risk management.

CALIBRATION IS UNSTABLE

The calibration described above is done by solving a high-dimension, highly nonlinear minimization problem. The trader has a model, and she calibrates it. There are many cases in which the market moves by very slight amounts, but the model responds by a massive change of internal parameters. Thus while the market instruments have shifted in price by a few basis points, the internal parameters of the model may have moved by a lot.

What happens if these parameters move by a lot? Chances are that the trader will feel the brunt of it. Suppose a trader is in the midst of pricing a new deal and gave the client a price yesterday of 74 basis points. However, because of the instability of the model, the computed price today is 254 basis points. This is not acceptable to the trader.

AD HOC SOLUTION

What dealers actually do in practice is as follows. Since they cannot guarantee the stability of the high-dimensional, nonlinear minimization problem, they use an ad hoc solution. They decide to calibrate most of the parameters in the model only once a week. On the other hand, they will calibrate some of the parameters once a day, and they may adjust volatility several times a day. They have taken a staggered approach to calibration.

THE NATWEST EXPERIENCE

In 1996, it emerged that NatWest Markets did not calibrate its models at all. The models the company used were quite sophisticated. They allowed the usage of an entire surface of volatility (the so-called volatility smile). The NatWest models allowed for different volatility parameters for every strike and for every term to maturity.

However, rather than using a surface, NatWest used a single constant-volatility parameter. Since the company did not calibrate, other market participants purchased cheap options from NatWest and sold NatWest expensive options. This mistake resulted in a loss of tens of millions of pounds.

DIFFERENT MARKETS EXHIBIT
DIFFERENT BEHAVIORS

The problem of calibration becomes even more important when we realize that different markets exhibit different behaviors. Several years ago, my coworkers and I did a study which compared the short rate with the long rate. The Fed may manipulate the short rate, increasing or decreasing as it sees fit. Markets price long-term rates in expectation of the Fed's actions. The Fed may raise or lower the short-term rate. Then the market determines what the long rate is going to be. The market goes through an auction process for the thirty-year bond. We compared the short rate with the long rate in several countries. We found that when the Bundesbank (BUBA), the central bank in Germany, raised the short rate, the long rate dropped. In the United States when the Fed raised the short rate, the long rate actually increased. Our team was quite confused by this result. We went back and checked to make sure our database was correct; we verified that the program was correct, etc.

In searching for answers, we consulted an economist, who explained that this result makes a lot of sense. The economist said that in Germany when the BUBA raises short rates, it is fighting inflation and the market believes that it will succeed. So the long rates drop. In the United States when the Fed raises short rates, the market believes that the Fed is doing too little, too late, and inflation is going to run amok. Therefore, long-term rates also rise.

This example shows that if you were pricing interest rate options in the United States instead of in Germany, you would have to calibrate your model totally differently. In addition, the mean reversion rate of the United States and the mean reversion rate of Germany are different. The correlation between short rates and long rates in the United States will be quite different from the correlation in Germany. In the United States the correlation is positive because both rates tend to move up together. In Germany, on the other hand, the correlation is negative.

A RECOMMENDATION

It is very hard to come up with a general conclusion because these instruments are traded over a wide variety of markets. Even if you do a limited study in one country, you can't really apply the results somewhere else.

THE JAPANESE ZERO-STRIKE FLOORS

In 1996 dealers were trading zero-strike floors on the Japanese Libor. A zero-strike floor is a floor that pays out only if interest rates are negative. Imagine a Japanese investor going to the bank, giving the bank 100 yen, and receiving 90 yen three months later. To U.S.-based investors the possibility of negative interest rates seems crazy. Why would somebody pay for an option that can never be in the money? Can you ever have negative interest rates? Negative rates existed in Switzerland in the 1950s. The Swiss banks had negative rates for foreign investors who were hiding their money from tax authorities. But there has never been an example of a country that has negative domestic interest rates for its own people.

Yet these zero-strike floors were traded. At the time, there were big discussions about the possibility of negative rates. Some academics believed that negative rates are impossible. We can assume that the Japanese investor would rather sleep with his yen under his mattress than invest them with a negative rate. On the other hand, the Mitsubishi Corporation has billions and billions of yen in cash. The Mitsubishi Corporation is not going to put its yen under a mattress. So who knows, maybe there is some probability of negative interest rates.

The point is that a model of Japanese Libor may have to assume the possibility of negative rates. Almost all models of U.S. Libor assume positive interest rates.

CONCENTRATE ON THE IMPORTANT

Litterman and Scheinkman found that three factors affect yields on fixed-income securities. After performing a principal component analysis, they found that the three factors and their contributions to the returns are:

l Level of rates (85 percent)

s Steepness (10 percent)

c Curvature (2–3 percent)

Consider a portfolio manager in the investment management business who manages a portfolio of bonds. Where does the return on the funds come from? It turns out that 85 percent of the return comes from the level of rates. So if rates move up or down, that determines the return. That's obvious. Another 10 percent comes from the steepness of the yield curve, and so the portfolio manager can do some "steepening trades"—long the short bond and short the long bond. When the yield curve steepens, that trade could be successful. A tiny portion of the return comes from the curvature. The portfolio manager could engage in some barbell strategies—long both the short and the long bond while shorting the midrange bond.

WHICH MODEL DO YOU NEED?

A one-factor model is pretty good at determining upward and downward shifts in the general level of the yield curve. The one-factor model already gives you about 85 percent of the return, what you need to know. Consider a typical fixed-income portfolio manager—maybe a one-factor model is all the manager needs. For example, the one-factor model will compute an adequate figure for the duration of a bond.

On the other hand, a specialist in complex swaptions may need more sophisticated models. An arbitrage specialist who is doing butterfly spread trades with zero duration, playing on the curvature of the yield curve, may need a more sophisticated multifactor model.

SUMMARY

Interest rate models are an active area of research. Rather than study all the many models available, we discussed some examples and offered some insights into the main issues regarding these instruments.

CHAPTER 23

Final Words

The process of innovation if the financial markets continues. There are several trends:

1. Rather than produce exotic options on simple underlying instruments, the trend is to create simple options on exotic underlying instruments.

   The market has created a plethora of new derivative instruments. These include:
   - Credit derivatives (see my book entitled *Implementing Credit Derivatives*, McGraw-Hill, 1999).
   - Weather derivatives
   - Catastrophe bonds

   The payout functions of these options are very simple to understand. However, it is the underlying instruments of these that make them very difficult to hedge.

2. The convergence between the insurance markets and the derivative markets.

   On the one hand, insurance companies are offering annuities with embedded equity derivatives; see the discussion on *Equity Linked Insurance* in Chapter 7. On the other hand, derivative dealers are offering credit derivatives. Some of the credit derivative products are similar to credit guarantees which traditionally have been offered by mono-line insurers.

3. The growing sophistication in the field.

In the old days, traders relied on "gut instinct" and market knowledge and understanding. There is no question that the usage of models has increased in all sides of the business. Models are routinely used to price instruments and to perform risk management functions. The number and expertise of quantitative analysts ("quants") continues to grow.

Clients are also becoming more sophisticated. Many large firms have dealing rooms which rival the banks.

4. Education

Many universities now offer advanced degrees in financial mathematics or related disciplines. For example, the mathematics department at the University of Chicago offers a graduate level program in financial mathematics. I am a lecturer in that program.

As a consequence of these programs, the number of traders who are familiar with mathematics, modeling, and computer software continues to grow.

5. Computers and Internet

The Internet has given investors access to a lot of information, data, and quantitative models. In addition, the prices of computers have come down while their power has increased. Today, the average investor has more information and computer power at their fingertips than the large brokerage houses had several years ago.

6. Competition

International trading barriers are being removed all

over the world. For example, Europe is being united into a single market. Businesses must stay competitive to survive, not only in their own countries but worldwide.

It is obvious that these trends will only escalate in the future. Therefore, it is imperative for every participant in the financial markets to keep on upgrading their skills.

INDEX

303

About the Author

Israel Nelken, Ph.D. is president of Super Computer Consulting, Inc., which specializes in software development, exotic options, convertible bonds, fixed income mathematics, and statistical analysis. Dr. Nelken is a lecturer in the University of Chicago Master of Science in Financial Mathematics program. His sold-out seminars in New York and London cover topics ranging from exotic options and financial engineering to credit derivatives, energy derivatives, and convertible bonds. His previous books include *The Handbook of Exotic Options, Implementing Credit Derivatives,* and *Option Embedded Bonds.*